Faith and Work

Christian Perspectives, Research, and Insights Into the Movement

A Volume in Advances in Workplace Spirituality:
Theory, Research and Application

Series Editor:
Louis W. (Jody) Fry, *Texas A&M University Central Texas*

Advances in Workplace Spirituality: Theory, Research, and Application

Louis W. (Jody) Fry, Series Editor

Faith and Work

Christian Perspectives, Research, and Insights Into the Movement

Edited by

Timothy Ewest
Houston Baptist University and
Visiting Research Collaborator
Princeton University

Information Age Publishing, Inc.
Charlotte, North Carolina • www.infoagepub.com

Library of Congress Cataloging-in-Publication Data

CIP data for this book can be found on the Library of Congress website:
http://www.loc.gov/index.html

Paperback: 978-1-64113-063-9
Hardcover: 978-1-64113-064-6
E-Book: 978-1-64113-065-3

Printed in the United States of America

Dedication

This book is dedicated to Christians who rise each day to join with the rest of humanity in the common rhythm of work. These individuals engage in work because it enables them to express and form their Christian identity, and thus work provides them a deep meaning and purpose for their lives. The action of these Christians is an uncontestable fact which is often over-looked by researchers, governments, and communities, but is predicated within these chapters.

CONTENTS

BOOK SERIES INTRODUCTION

Louis W. (Jody) Fry
Series Editor

A major change is taking place in the personal and professional lives of many organizational leaders and their employees as they aspire to integrate their spirituality and religion with their work. Many argue that the reason behind this change is that society is seeking spiritual solutions to better respond to tumultuous social, business, geopolitical changes. The result has been a remarkable explosion of scholarship that provides the opportunity for more specialized interest areas, including the role of spirituality and religion in shaping organizations: structures, decision making, management style, mission and strategy, organizational culture, human resource management, finance and accounting, marketing and sales—in short—all aspects of leading, managing, and organizing resources and people. As evidenced by the growing influence of the *Journal of Management, Spirituality and Religion* and the success of the Management, Spirituality, and Religion Interest Group of the Academy of Management, a field with a broad focus on workplace spirituality is gathering momentum.

This book series, *Advances in Workplace Spirituality: Theory, Research, and Application*, focuses on the study of the relationship and relevance of spirituality and/or religion to organizational life. Its vision is to draw from a diverse range of scholarly areas to become a pivotal source for integrative theory, research, and application on workplace spirituality. The purpose of the series is to (1) provide scholars with a meaningful collection of books in key areas and create a forum for the field, (2) support a growing

Faith and Work: Christian Perspectives, Research, and Insights Into the Movement
pp. ix–x

trend toward paradigm integration and assimilation through the interdisciplinary nature of this series, and (3) draw from a wide variety of disciplines for integrative thinking on workplace spirituality with the broad goal of adding to the value of workplace spirituality theory, research, and its application. The series aims to serve as a meeting forum and help cross-fertilization in these communities. Our sole criterion is academic rigor and scientific merit.

The latest edited book of this series, *Faith and Work: Christian Perspectives, Research, and Insights Into the Movement*, is truly groundbreaking. Spirituality-based models have dominated management, spirituality, and religion theory, research, and practice. However, today there is an emerging consensus that new religion-based theories and models are needed, not only for organizations that employ workers from different spiritual and religious traditions, but also for public and private organizations whose cultures and employees embrace diverse religious beliefs and practices as central to their work. This is especially true for the Christian tradition since Christianity in all its forms and manifestations comprise almost a third of the world's population.

This book helps fill this need by providing a language and framework for practitioners and scholars alike to think about ways that Christian thought might shape and inform organizational life. In doing so, Volume Editor Timothy Ewest draws on a talented and diverse group of interdisciplinary and international scholars to contribute fresh thinking about Christian perspectives, practices, and insights into the faith at work movement at the individual, organizational, and societal levels. Whether you are a believer or not, a Christian or not, or simply interested in big ideas, I trust you will find this book informative, thought provoking and, for some, a call to action.

FOREWORD

David W. Miller
Director, Princeton University Faith & Work Initiative,
President, the Avodah Institute

New York City is seldom the first city that comes to mind when writing about the Buckle of the Bible belt. Cities like Nashville or Abilene usually vie for that bragging right. Yet there I was, on Wall Street attending a secular corporate leadership event for senior executives in the financial services sector, talking about God.

Over cocktails, one executive squinted at my name tag which read, "David W. Miller, PhD, Princeton University Faith & Work Initiative." Eschewing any attempt at courtesy, he asked me, "what on earth is a 'Faith & Work Initiative' and why are you attending this event?" I responded, "I'm in the God business." I waited to see whether he would make a quick excuse about needing to refresh his drink and run in the opposite direction, or whether he might pause and say something like, "I waited to see whether he would make a quick excuse about needing to refresh his drink and run in the opposite direction, or whether he might pause and say something like, 'tell me more.'" Whenever I am feeling mischievous and do this at corporate events, I never cease to be amazed that four out of five people are curious and want to know more.

The growing body of evidence and scholarly literature from a variety of disciplines seems to validate this vignette. People of all faith traditions and backgrounds, including atheists and agnostics, are increasingly curious about the phenomena of "integrating faith and work." Somewhat ironically, even those active in a worship community express disappoint-

Faith and Work: Christian Perspectives, Research, and Insights Into the Movement
pp. xi–xiii

ment at how little guidance or encouragement they get from their clergy person during the Sabbath sermon.

Professor Timothy Ewest, my friend, colleague, frequent collaborator, and editor of this timely and important book has organized this text along three different but related planes. As I observed in my 2007 book, *God at Work: The History and Promise of the Faith at Work Movement* (Oxford University Press), people and organizations involved in the movement tend operate on three levels. Many focus on the micro or individual level, trying to draw on and integrate their faith teachings as part of their personal understanding of their day-to-day work activities and conduct. Others focus on the mezzo or organizational level, focusing on how their faith tradition and teachings might impact companywide decisions, products, and services. And yet others focus on the macro or wider stakeholder impact of their work on society. And of course, many seek to understand how their faith should function on all three levels.

Ewest has drawn on a talented and diverse group of interdisciplinary and international scholars to contribute fresh thinking about Christian perspectives, research, and insights into the faith at work movement. The book is structured to lead the reader through the individual, organizational, and societal aspects of faith at work. The contributing scholars raise important content questions, including: finding meaning and purpose in one's work; caring for creation; embracing diversity while sustaining Christian values; responding to those who feel their faith is marginalized by society; and identifying the constructive role that Christian faith might play in shaping and informing ideas and actions amidst these contemporary questions.

As the title of this book declares, it is written out of a distinctly Christian worldview. And yet, there is no such thing as a single "Christian worldview," just as there is no such thing as a single Jewish or Muslim worldview. Yet Ewest has gathered scholars from various Christian traditions, geographies, and accents. My personal hope is that this book might be a template to prompt edited volumes from other religious traditions, following suit with similar self-reflections and perspectives on faith and work at the personal, organizational, and societal levels. I suspect we will undoubtedly notice different accents within and between the traditions, even as we will find a vast amount of resonances and shared teachings.

As for Christianity and its three major branches (Orthodox, Roman Catholic, and Protestant), each have varying theological accents, doctrinal foci, and practical teachings, even as they are all united under foundational beliefs about Jesus Christ as the risen Messiah. Christianity as a whole is very interested in what it means to be a human being, created an image of God, and what it means for humanity to cultivate and tend the garden, that is, to work. This book helps us explore these profoundly important questions.

In recent decades, the church and the theological Academy have largely ignored these two questions. Despite some notable exceptions over the past few years, most seminaries have abdicated constructive engagement with or equipping of laity involved in the workplace and the wider economic sphere. This book helps bridge that gap by providing a language and framework for practitioners and scholars alike to think afresh about ways that Christian thought might shape and inform their individual, organizational, and social engagement in the marketplace.

Whether you are in the God business or not, a Christian or not, or simply interested in big ideas, I trust you will find this book of existential and practical value.

CHAPTER 1

THE REASON OF FAITH

Macro-, Mezzo-, and Microemergences of Faith in the Workplace

Timothy Ewest
*Houston Baptist University and
Visiting Research Collaborator Princeton University*

Although the expanding literature regarding the impact of spirituality on organizational life is creating recognition within the Academy of Management and organizations regarding the importance of this topic, the importance of religious faith, or faith and work within organizational life (Miller, 2007), while identified as foundational (Benefiel, Fry, & Geigle, 2014) is still formative and at times lackadaisical. This aimlessness leaves organizations unprepared to engage with people of faith and may be demonstrated in American life in part by the persistent rise in Equal Employment Opportunity Commission claims in the United States pertaining to religious discrimination (Greenwald, 2012). The nascent development of faith and work research may be surprising when one considers that the Pew Forum on Religion & Public Life (2008, 2013) determined that 92% of the American population said they believe in God, and 83% of Americans self-identified with a religious group. Globally, the changes within religious growth, adherence, or decline are specific to geographic

Faith and Work: Christian Perspectives, Research, and Insights Into the Movement
pp. 1–11

regions, culture, and politics (Ashforth & Vaidyanath, 2002), yet, research indicates that world religious adherence is currently at 80%, and by 2050 it is predicted to rise to 85% (Johnson, 2010). Today, Christianity in its various manifestations and sects comprises nearly 2.18 billion adherents worldwide, almost a third of the world's population (Christianity, 2011). Finally, the assertion by theories such as the secularization theory, positing that societies are collectively secularizing, has been refuted, creating permission to move forward with research that considers the impacts of the sacred on society (Casanova, 2011).

Yet even with the projected global growth of faith communities, the way forward for people of faith to bring their whole selves, including their faith, into the workplace is opaque and resources to support them are scant (Miller & Ewest, 2014). Challenges concerning integration of faith into the workplace abound, even from within the Academy of Management whose values are committed to "embracing the full diversity of members backgrounds and experiences" (www.aom.org). Consider Mitroff (2003) whose research was considered seminal in the emergence of the field of spirituality in the workplace, who states, "I still believe that formal, organized religion has very little, if any, role to play in the workplace" (p. 378). Nolan (2006) concurs, suggesting businesses have always regarded religion as an issue to be left outside the organization. The sentiment is replete within scholarship, which has emphasized spirituality and ignored religion as not worthy of scientific study (Tracy, Phillips, & Lounsbury, 2004) or homogenized religion amending it to spirituality (Day, 2005), because spirituality is perceived by some as the best chance of attaining the humanistic ideal of a more humane workplace (Garcia-Zamor, 2003). Moreover, religion is also seen as pejorative by many in organizations (Mitroff & Denton, 1999). But the reality is, while degrees of religiosity vary within individuals and groups, religious faith acts as a means to form and inform personal identity (Emmons, 2003), and while its expression is moderated by the workplace, it none the less is present within organizational roles, and these functions impact society (Miller, 2007).

This chapter acts as both an introduction to the book, including the scope and aims found within these chapters and also as a means to provide an orientation to the subject. Within the multiple theoretical and research dimensions of management, religion and spirituality, this book explores theoretical, conceptual, and strategic theories and research which consider how individuals and organizations integrate their Christian faith in the workplace, and how these groups attempt to change society as a whole. Each chapter presents a critical insight from the individual, organizational, or societal perspective into the various aspects of how Christians live out their faith in the workplace, and in doing so provides illumination of experiences, inspiration for further research and confirmation of research discoveries already made.

Those who adhere to a faith tradition are longing for theories and insights into how they can be true to their faith within the workplace (Miller, 2007) and yet be sensitive and respectful to others of varying faith commitments and beliefs and levels of religiosity (Hicks, 2003). Yet for Christians, respect of other faith traditions is complicated since Christianity is the historically dominate religion in most of the Occidental world, which has resulted in the secularizing and institutionalizing of Christianity within the workplace as represented in holidays and days off (Alexis, 2012). The direct challenge for a Christian desiring to be tolerant toward those outside their faith is that religious perspectives are suggested to have preface judgment, guidance and ethical decision making associated with them; thus instinctively being evaluative of the world around them is a natural disposition for Christians, or any religious individual with high religiosity (Fernando & Jackson, 2006; Graafland, Kaptein, & Mazerereeuw, 2007).

But then, Christianity itself is not monolithic. Within Christianity there is divergence and thus a need for respect and sensitivity in how Christians are to regard and embrace other Christians. For example, when the three largest and longest historically established traditions within Christianity: Catholicism, Protestantism, and Orthodoxy regard the five ancient creeds and the hundreds of modern Christian creeds, these three great traditions only officially agree fully on one church creed, the Nicene Creed. This is ironic since the creeds were a means to codify central beliefs and preserve orthodoxy (correct belief), thus the affirmation of only one creed is an attestation to various belief differences within Christianity. So, while from the outside Christianity may appear as a great monolith in actuality, Hicks (2003) proposition of respectful pluralism has double entendre for Christians. Alternatively, there have been collective ecumenism movements throughout history and in modern times between all three great Christian traditions endeavoring to reconcile disparateness (Fitzgerald, 2004). This book seeks to foster an ecumenical perspective by capturing research and perspectives from authors who personally adhere to these traditions or presenting research from one of the three traditions: Protestant, Catholic, and Orthodox—in some cases both.

While at varying levels of religiosity, Christians do bring their faith to work and their work is informed, formed, transformed, or malformed by their faith. This movement is historical and characterized by a desire for people to live a holistic life which integrates their Christian faith into the workplace, also deemed *faith at work* (Miller, 2007). Historically, Christian's faith integration is manifested individually or collectively and is demonstrated in the ways it shapes and informs the values systems, ethics, characterization and attitudes toward work (Benefiel et al., 2014; Miller,

2007; Miller & Ewest, 2014). And, any suggestion that religious faith is not existent and more specifically, is not used or able to function or have a role within the American workplace should be regarded as a personal opinion, a proscriptive statement, or a bias, and not a fact-based statement based on research, since it contends with credible research depicting individual faith and workplace integration strategies (e.g., Miller, 2007; Thompson, 2015). Moreover, it contends with research which delineates organizations that are presently driven by and actively embrace faith traditions (e.g., Tyson Foods, Tom's of Maine). The chapters in this book describe the role or roles religion can or does play within the individual's life, organizational life, and faith's interconnections to society.

This edited volume uses three organizing themes based on the historical movements of the faith and work movement as traced by Miller (2007) in the book, *God at Work: The History and Promise of the Faith at Work Movement*. These organizing themes, while not congruent to the historical epochs, do capture the ways in which people of faith have historically attempted to integrate their faith into the workplace. These themes include: Individual integration strategies, organizational integration strategies, and societal integration. The book is correspondingly broken into these three parts, based on each contributing author(s) placement of where their research fits best within this schema, although many if not most of the research projects have implications for all three areas of the schema, suggesting a high degree of concurrence exists.

Concurrence, and more importantly dialectic between the individual, organizations, and societies was an observation made early on by Weber (1904–05/1958), who noted that there was an interchange between ideas, institutions and individual behaviors, which he labeled *elective affinities*. The dialectic he noticed is best recognized as the Protestant Work Ethic, and has experienced expansive research (Creed, Dejordy, & Lok, 2010; Geren, 2011) pertaining not only to Protestants but also to other religions (Zhang, Liu, & Liu, & 2012; Zulfikar, 2012). Therefore, the divisions or themes that are used in this book are simply lenses or academic distinctions used to better understand what is occurring regarding the interaction of faith in the workplace. Even within the academic disciplines it is historically the case that the psychologist focus research on individuals (e.g. Emmons, 1999) and the sociologist focus research on groups (e.g., Wuthnow, 2007), but even so, there are applications of research that become intersubjective (e.g., Anthony Giddens).

PART I: INDIVIDUAL

The first section of the book considers theories, strategies or research pertaining to personal strategies for individuals who wish to integrate their

Christian faith into the workplace. These chapters include attempts of Christian individuals to find individual purpose, or meaning in work, the integration of faith into ethics, character, or organizational practices (e.g., finance). It may also include attempts of individuals to bring needed personal transformation to others.

In Chapter 2, "Ancient Spirituality at Work," Elden Wiebe of King's University and Cathy Driscoll of Saint Mary's University begin the discussion arguing that researchers have sought one operationalized definition of spirituality, but have avoided using grand narratives from faith and wisdom traditions. Drawing on Brueggemann (1978) whose work describes a prophetic imagination, wherein the individual uses symbols from their deepest memories which provide hope and a life giving order both for the present and the future. They suggest that a grand narrative, or meta-narrative is inscribed within a Christian's identity and this Christian identity is expressed in the workplace, but rooted in faith beliefs and traditions. Their research finds that Christian business leaders actuate their Christian identity within the workplace, and do so expressing their adherence to the ancient Christian themes.

In Chapter 3, "The Impact of College Type and Occupational Category on Faith Integration in the College Workplace," Sharlene Buszka, of Daemen College and myself identify how college-type or occupational-type roles affect employees' work-related faith integration in higher education. These determinations are made using Miller's (2007) Integration Box, later with Miller and Ewest (2014) to be revised as The Integration Profile instrument. Miller's four manifestations or expressions of faith integration in the workplace allow for research and analysis of the Faith at Work movement. The Integration Profile consists of a framework that describes workplace faith integration in four distinct ways; enrichment, ethics, expression, or experience (Miller, 2007). The findings from this chapter indicate a difference between occupational category and college type regarding their levels of faith integration.

Chapter 4, "Work as Worship: Bringing Meaning to Work Through an Integrated Faith," features research conducted by Simone Meskelis and J. Lee Whittington, both from the University of Dallas. They argue that an organizations primary purpose is to improve the well-being of all stakeholders, and that employee well-being can be achieved through engaging in meaningful work. They contend that research connecting spirituality or a person's inner life is associated with numerous positive workplace outcomes, but their efforts make a crucial departure from similar research by examining the impact of an integrated faith on the experience of meaningfulness at work. Their research reports the results of field studies that were conducted to examine the relationships among integrated faith, meaningfulness, and engagement. According to their conceptual model, the integrated faith of the individual is the antecedent to the experience of meaningful work. And, meaningfulness in turn is proposed to have a direct impact on the level of employee engagement.

Peter McGhee of Auckland University of Technology and Myk Habets of Carey Graduate School, use Chapter 5, "Priests of Creation, Mediators of Order: Taking God to Work," to build on the notion that individuals want to integrate their Christian faith into their work. To demonstrate this, they employee the work of Scottish theologian Thomas Torrance, in particular, his view of human beings as "priests of creation" and "mediators of order." The chapter begins with an explanation of what the roles of priests of creation and mediators of order entail, the relevance these roles have regarding an individual's labor, and how individuals might enact these callings in and through their work. From these ideas McGhee and Habets formulated a methodological framework which provides the basis for a deductive analysis of Christians enacting their spirituality in several large New Zealand based service organizations.

To close out Part I of the book, Chapter 6, "As the Birds to Flying, So Is Man Born Unto Work': Martin Luther's Notion of Work as an Individual Source for Meaning," contributed by Peter Seele, Università della Svizzera italiana, and Lucas Zapf, University of Basel, considered the reformatory notion of work as put forward by Martin Luther. This reformatory notion is used by them as a source for producing meaning for the individual and also for the individual within their organizational work environment(s). They suggest that theoretical positions such as Luther's regarding the importance and centricity of meaningful work, allows individuals to frame contributions from work as a higher level order, that is to input meaning into work that is beyond the work itself. This chapter resolves by offering the reader a model which describes of economic impact of religion.

PART II: ORGANIZATIONAL

Part II of the book considers theories, strategies or research pertaining to strategies of organizations which attempt to aid in their employee's integration of faith into the workplace, or theories which help the individual find their collective Christian identity. While the individual has an agentic role within organizations and society, here the emphasis is on collective identity and larger structures. This may include seeing the organization as a vehicle of transformation (e.g., corporate chaplaincy programs, pedagogy, human resource policies). It may also include attempts of organizations to bring needed personal transformation to others, a family, group or a community.

The Catholic tradition has a longstanding developed theology, Catholic social teaching, addressing the integration of faith in the workplace. Chapter 7, "Decent Work, Meaningful Work, and Developmental Work: Three Key Ethical Perspectives From Catholic Social Teaching," written by Domènec Melé, emeritus professor of business ethics, IESE Business School, develops a detailed analysis of Catholic social teachings on the ethics of work. In this chapter three concepts are presented which summarize most of these teachings: those of decent work, meaningful work, and developmental work. The chapter resolves with an invitation to rethink organizational topics such as job design, incentive systems, control and trust, participation, initiative, and empowerment.

Chapter 8, "Caring for Employees: Corporate Chaplains as a Manifestation of Faith and Work," finds David Miller and Dennis LoRusso at Princeton University along with Faith Ngunjiri of Concordia University, explaining a new strategy used by organizations to incorporate faith and work: corporate chaplaincy. Specifically they discuss their research into workplace chaplaincy which indicated that executive leadership typically implemented corporate chaplaincy programs to extend holistic care to their employees. These programs bring many workplace benefits. Their chapter also explores the history of workplace chaplaincy, but with specific consideration of the ways Christian leaders envisage chaplaincy program as manifestations for integrating their own faith into the workplace, and what this reveals about the faith of the leader. Their findings are based on interviews with executive leadership and categorized within Miller's (2007) four manifestations of faith, also used in Chapter 3.

Allan Discua Cruz at Lancaster University Management School, considers family business as an ideal place for the organizational (albeit familial) integration of faith in the workplace, in Chapter 9, "Faith, Family and Work: A Christian Perspective on Family Businesses." To accomplish this Cruz begins with a discussion of the early relationship between Christianity and the family. He then considers contemporary conceptualizations and typologies of family businesses, before moving on to theoretical perspectives. Finally, he presents a Christian perspective on succession.

Closing out this section of the book, Chapter 10, "Innovative Work and Worship Contexts and Their Associations With Regulatory Focus Mindsets and Nascent Hybrid Entrepreneurship," contributed by Mitch Neubert and Kevin Dougherty from Baylor University. This chapter describes the influence of two prevalent organizational contexts, where people work and where they worship, on a specific type of entrepreneurial behavior, nascent hybrid entrepreneurship. Their research contributes both to the understanding of nascent entrepreneurs and also contributes to how these entrepreneurial mindsets are shaped by their place of worship. The findings of their research indicate that organizational contexts do matter in shaping the mindsets or ways of thinking that contribute to nascent entrepreneurial behavior. Their research found that workplace innovativeness and congregation innovativeness are associated with a promotion-focus mindset, and, in turn, a promotion-focus mindset is positively related to nascent entrepreneurship.

PART III: SOCIETY

The final section of the book considers theories, strategies or research pertaining to larger movements, or collective actions, of groups and individuals who seek to change and transform society through their faith activities in the marketplace (e.g., social entrepreneurship). This section seeks to explore the nature of the aforementioned collective individual actions and organizational movements, seeking to understand the directions, intent, and effect.

Chapter 11, "Ethiopian Orthodox Christianity: History, Teachings, and Workplace Implications for the Diaspora," contributed by Tamarat Gashaw of Wartburg College and myself, describes the beliefs and practices of the Ethiopian Orthodox Tewahedo Church (EOTC), including its origins. The chapter then considers the implications of the followers of the EOTC for the ongoing diaspora to the United States, considering immigration patters of EOTC Christians. The chapter resolves by giving special attention to issues regarding Equal Employment Opportunity Commission claims, offering some possible organizational considerations. Specifically to stress the importance of religious accommodation in the American workplace by providing the EOTC as a counter narrative to the widely accepted narrative of an American "Christian" workplace. The governing and accepted narrative describes an American workplace where it has secularized Christianity and must accommodate other religious faith traditions (Alexis, 2015), and where Christians may tend to feel they deserve a special status (Hicks, 2003).

Chapter 12, "The Holistic Motivation of Social Entrepreneurs," contributed by Julia R. Marra and Kent W. Seibert of Gordon College, complement the work of Mitch Neubert and Kevin Dougherty in Chapter 10, but consider societal implications. Their research considers what drives an entrepreneur to pursue the calling of simultaneously pursuing business profit and societal problem solving, whether the focus be social problems or environmental ones. This chapter begins to consider the question by reporting the results of an exploratory study of what motivates people to become social entrepreneurs. Their results demonstrate a preliminary conceptual model of social entrepreneurial motivation, among these motivational drivers discovered is religious belief.

The final chapter of this section is Chapter 13, "Heading for the Multi-faith Workplace," submitted by Stuart Allen of Robert Morris University and Peter Williams of Abilene Christian University. Their chapter explores how the Christian community can play a role in the largely secularized chain of preparation from higher education to the workplace, as a means to support a common Christian mission. They discuss the context, changes, and challenges Christian workers face, and emphasize the opportunities inherent in the adjustment to a more pluralistic society and workplace. The chapter resolves by proposing ways the Christian community can support current and future workers, adding to the flow of conversation on faith in the workplace.

SUMMARY

Jesus of Nazareth was regarded by his initial, mostly Jewish followers, as a Jewish rabbi or teacher. But, during his life he was also regarded as the incarnate Son of God from heaven, who as cocreator with the Father, ushered in an earthy kingdom, and through his suffering and atoning death and ensuing resurrection offered forgiveness of sins and the restoration of a fallen creation, as well as its ultimate judgment.[1] The reality of the life and work of Jesus of Nazareth as lived out and expressed in his followers is continued within the chapters that follow.

Yet, if one cannot accept as fact that Jesus of Nazareth was a rabbi, teacher or the incarnate son of God, the fact which cannot be argued, is Jesus's followers, albeit open to interpretation, and levels of saliency, must be regarded as a historical social force (Eliade, 2013; Durkheim, 1994).

NOTE

1.   An abridgment of the Nicene Creed.

REFERENCES

Alexis, Y. G. (2012). Not Christian, but nonetheless qualified: The secular workplace—Whose hardship? *Journal of Religion and Business Ethics, 3*(1), 1–24.

Ashforth, B., & Vaidyanath, D. (2002). Work organizations as secular religions. *Journal of Management Inquiry, 11*(4), 359–370.

Benefiel, M., Fry, L. W., & Geigle, D. (2014). Spirituality and religion in the workplace: History, theory, and research. *Psychology of Religion and Spirituality, 6*(3), 175–185.

Brueggemann, W. (1978). *Theology of the Old Testament: Testimony, dispute, advocacy.* Minneapolis, MN: Fortress Press.

Casanova, J. (2011). *Public religions in the modern world.* Chicago, IL: University of Chicago Press.

Creed, W., Dejordy J, R., & Lok, J. (2010). Being the change resolving institutional contradiction through identity work. *The Academy of Management Journal, 53*(6), 1336–1364.

Cunningham, L. S., & Reich, J. J. (2009). *Culture and values: A survey of the humanities.* Boston, MA: Cengage Learning.

Day, D. (2005). Religion in the workplace: Correlates and Consequences of individual behavior. *Journal of Management, Spirituality and Religion, 2*(1), 104–135.

Durkheim, É. (1994). *Durkheim on religion* (W. S. F. Pickering, Ed.). Atlanta, GA: Scholars Press.

Eliade, M. (2013). *The quest: History and meaning in religion.* Chicago, IL: University of Chicago Press.

Emmons, R. A. (1999). *The psychology of ultimate concerns: Motivation and spirituality in personality.* New York, NY: Guilford Press.

Emmons, R. (2003). *The psychology of ultimate concerns: Motivation and spirituality in personality.* New York, NY: Guilford Press.

Fernando, M., & Jackson, B. (2006). The influence of religion-based workplace spirituality on business leaders' decision-making: An inter-faith study. *Journal of Management & Organization, 12*(1), 23–39.

Fitzgerald, T. E. (2004). *The ecumenical movement: An introductory history* (No. 72). Santa Barbara, CA: Greenwood.

Garcia-Zamor, J. (2003). Workplace spirituality and organizational performance. *Public Administration Review, 63*(3), 355–363.

Geren, B. (2011). The work ethic: Is it universal? *Journal of International Business & Cultural Studies, 5*(1), 51–58.

Greenwald, J. (2012). Religious discrimination claims rising. *Business Insurance, 46*(7), 3–18.

Graafland, J., Kaptein, M., & Mazereeuw-van der Duijn Schouten, C. (2007). Conceptions of god, normative convictions, and socially responsible business conduct: an explorative study among executives. *Business & Society, 46*(3), 331–368.

Hackett, C., Grim, B. J., Skirbekk, V., Stonawski, M., & Goujon, A. (2011, December). Global Christianity: A report on the size and distribution of the world's Christian population. Washington, DC: Pew Research Center's Forum on Religion & Public Life.

Hicks, D. A. (2003). *Religion and the workplace: Pluralism, spirituality, leadership.* Cambridge, England: Cambridge University Press. doi:10.1017/CBO9780511615474

Johnson, T. (2010). A statistical approach to the world's religions adherents, 2000–2015 CE. In J. G. Melton & M. Bauman (Eds.), *Religions of the world: A Comprehensive encyclopedia of beliefs and practices* (Vol. 1, pp. lv–lix), Santa Barbara, CA: ABC-CLIO.

Miller, D. W. (2007). *God at work: The history and promise of the faith at work movement.* New York, NY: Oxford University Press.

Miller, D., & Ewest, T. (2014). The present state of workplace spirituality: A literature review considering context, theory, and measurement/assessment. *Journal of Religious & Theological Information, 12*(2), 29–54.

Mitroff, I. (2003). Do not promote religion under the guise of spirituality. *Organization, 10*(2), 375–382.

Mitroff, I., & Denton, E. A. (1999). *A spiritual audit of corporate America: A hard look at spirituality, religion, and values in the workplace.* San Francisco, CA: Jossey-Bass.

Nolan, J. (2006). *Doing the right thing: A Catholic's guide to faith, business and ethics.* Cincinnati, OH: St. Anthony Messenger.

Pew Forum on Religion & Public Life. (2008). U.S. religious landscape survey. Retrieved from http://religions.pewforum.org/pdf/report-religious-landscape-study-full.pdf

Pew Forum on Religion & Public Life. (2013). "Nones" on the rise: One-in-five adults have no religious affiliation. Retrieved from http://www.pewforum.org/uploadedFiles/Topics/Religious_Affiliation/Unaffiliated/NonesOnTheRise-full.pdf

Thompson, S. (2015). *Religion and organizational stigma at work.* New York, NY: Palgrave Macmillan.

Tracy, P., Phillips, N., & Lounsbury, M. (Eds.). (2014). Taking religion seriously in the study of organizations. In *Religion and organizational theory* (pp. 3–21). Bingley, England: Emerald Books.

Weber, M. (1958). The Protestant ethic and the spirit of capitalism (T. Parsons, Trans.). New York, NY: Scribner's. (Original work published 1904–05)

Wuthnow, R. (2007). *After the baby boomers: How twenty- and thirty-somethings are shaping the future of American religion.* Princeton, NJ: Princeton University Press.

Zhang, S., Liu, W., & Liu, X. (2012). Investigating the relationship between Protestant work ethic and Confucian dynamism: An empirical test in Mainland China. *Journal of Business Ethics, 106*(2), 243–252.

Zulfikar, Y. (2012). Do Muslims believe more in Protestant work ethic than Christians? Comparison of people with different religious background living in the US. *Journal of Business Ethics, 105*(4), 489–502.

PART I

INDIVIDUAL

CHAPTER 2

ANCIENT SPIRITUALITY AT WORK

Elden Wiebe
The King's University

Cathy Driscoll
Saint Mary's University

Despite a predominant emphasis on finding the "one" definition of spirituality (e.g., Giacalone & Jurkiewicz, 2003; Gotsis & Kortezi, 2008), management spirituality and religion literature has for the most part avoided drawing on grand narratives from faith and wisdom traditions (e.g., Garcia-Zamor, 2003; Miller & Ewest, 2013). Although the meanings of spirituality in a work context have changed over time and will continue to change in different contexts, we base our analysis on the idea that grand narratives not only exist, but that they are displayed in individual understandings and performance of workplace spirituality. We follow Brueggemann's (1978) idea that a prophetic imagination provides symbols from our deepest memories that give us hope for a life-giving order for the present and the future (pp. 63–67). Sandelands (2003, p. 176) likewise describes how the Christian meta-narrative is inscribed in Christian identity, an identity that is expressed in the context of an organization and the work performed there (Ewest, 2015). Actions are rooted in spirituality and

Faith and Work: Christian Perspectives, Research, and Insights Into the Movement
pp. 15–32
Copyright © 2018 by Information Age Publishing

spirituality is rooted in religious beliefs and traditions (Diddams, Whittington, & Davigo, 2006).

RELIGION AND ORGANIZATIONAL AND MANAGEMENT THEORY

Although religion is central to understandings of identity in social sciences(e.g., Wuthnow, 2007, 2012), this work has not widely transferred into organizational and management theory research (Diddams & Daniels, 2008; Tracey, Phillips, & Lounsbury, 2014). Much of the workplace spirituality literature remains focused on spiritual but not religious approaches (Hicks, 2003; King, 2008). In a great deal of the literature published in the 1990s, there is no reference to a particular religion or faith perspective (e.g., Bolman & Deal, 1995; Briskin, 1998; Chappell, 1993; Conger, 1994; Lee & Zemke, 1993). Marcic's (2000) review of 100 books and 100 journals on the topic of workplace spirituality found that less than 20% mentioned God or a Divine presence. Further, most workplace spirituality research has approached the topic from the perspective of organization and management theory rather than from the perspective of spirituality and/or religion (Cunha, Rego, & D'Oliveira, 2006; Fenwick & Lange, 1998).

Approaching spirituality from the perspective of organizational and management theory can distort and/or redefine "spirituality" and "religion" and their practices in ways that are no longer recognizable from the perspective of spirituality and religion. For example, Bartunek and Spreitzer (2006) trace the change in the definition of "empowerment" from its roots in religion as "sharing real power" to its use in organizations as "fostering productivity" with the real danger that only the organization's welfare is in view (see also Giacalone & Thompson, 2006; Steingard, 2005; Wallis, 2010). Indeed, the organization itself can become a secular religion for its employees (Ashforth & Vaidyanath, 2002). Others have combined religion, psychology, and therapy in order to market a pragmatic spirituality that is more appealing to a modern workforce (Sutcliffe & Bowman, 2000; Wedemeyer & Jue, 2002). Critiquing this approach, Hicks (2003, p. 165) concludes that "attempts to translate religiously particular values into common spiritual or secular values are reductionistic at best and inaccurate at worst." Not connecting spirituality to its often religious roots can result in loss of richness and depth found in faith traditions (Driscoll & Wiebe, 2007; Purser & Milillo, 2015).

However, other scholars, following Max Weber, continue to view religion as "a central social force" that influences economies, societies, and organizations (Tracey et al., 2014, p. 6; see also King, 2008). Indeed, scholars are now documenting the analogous influence of other religions, such as Buddhism, Shinshu, and Confucianism, on economic behavior

(Miller & Ewest, 2013). According to Weber's theory of value spheres, all institutions are religious in that their members are bound together through faith, sacrifice, and passion, as well as centered around a loving God (Friedland, 2014, pp. 219–220). Weber moved beyond subject-object, transcendent-immanent dualities and sees God and love as being "immanent" in all institutions (Friedland, 2014).

In a somewhat different, though related, vein, an interest in the relationship between organizational and management theory and theology is growing (e.g., Chan-Serafin, Brief, & George, 2013; Dyck, Starke, & Dueck, 2009; Dyck & Wiebe, 2012; King, 2008; Tracey, 2012). Dyck and Wiebe (2012) note the link between the concept of salvation and organizing, and that the concept of emancipation often found in critical management studies has its origin in the Judeo-Christian concept of salvation. They also note that several issues within organization theory reflect "traditional theological issues" (Dyck & Wiebe, 2012, p. 319). Hence these authors call for a "theological turn" in organization studies that would allow for both the recognition of the theological underpinning of organizational concepts and provide a source of action for organizational actors that is currently either poorly framed (e.g., instrumentally) or entirely unavailable.

While some scholars would suggest that religious precepts cannot "stand against the economic pressures of business with any success over the long term" because good business equates with financially successful business (Bay, McKeage, & McKeage, 2010, p. 673), other scholars suggest the spiritual concerns of religion have relevance for modern day business practice and managerial decision making (e.g., Fernando & Jackson, 2006; Graafland, Kaptein, & Mazererreeuw, 2007; Porth, Steingard, & McCall, 2003), as well as entrepreneurship (Balog, Baker, & Walker, 2014). Religious-based ethical concepts can substantially contribute to our understanding of business ethics and can provide "alternative paradigms for evaluating the meaning and methods of business behavior" (Epstein, 2002, p. 66). Religion can also play a role in the "upholding of human dignity and moral order in a world dominated by voracious state bureaucracies and sprawling transnational corporations that are neither effectively accountable to national law nor effectively answerable to well-established codes of behavior" (McClay, 2000, p. 56).

CHRISTIANITY AND ORGANIZATIONAL AND MANAGEMENT THEORY

Much has been written on the specific influence of the Christian religion on business (Dyck & Wiebe, 2012). For example Stackhouse, McCann, and Roels (1995) compiled 150 articles on the influence of Christianity on business and economics. Many since Weber (1904–05/1958) have critiqued the primary importance of individualism and materialism as the moral under-pinnings of modern management thought (e.g., Dyck & Schroeder, 2005). Martin Luther and John Calvin developed ideas from the biblical text of all work as a calling and service to God through serving others. Christian spir-ituality also deeply "informs and shapes" leadership and leader roles (e.g., servant leadership) (Delbecq, 1999), and the value of stakeholders. Carras-coso (2014, p. 321) suggests that "Creation in the image and likeness of God ground all stakeholder claims." Driscoll, Wiebe, and Dyck (2011) extend that thinking to include the natural environment as a primary stakeholder in all business deliberations. Another central theme is that work is meant to be redemptive. Diddams and Daniels (2008) acknowledge the dark side of humanity and work, but also recognize that individuals can creatively seek out redeeming work. This redemptive theme is also found in Pope John Paul II's (1981) description of a spirituality of work in the encyclical, Laborem Excercens (On Human Work).

METHODS AND ANALYSIS

This qualitative exploratory study draws on data from five Christian-based companies, both Catholic and Protestant, located across Canada. We seek to understand to what extent Christian faith explicitly drawn on to run a business reflects the core Christian narrative. Do the founders/owners/chief executive officers' (CEO) narratives reflect the themes of the ancient biblical text, which is the source of that spirituality? And, second, if they do reflect these themes, how do they evince the Christian world-view within their own narratives?

Data Sources

We utilized our faith networks (both authors adhere to the Christian faith) to find each company and verified that they explicitly identified themselves as operating from a Christian faith base. Upon gaining access through phone or e-mail, we made personal visits to each company where we conducted in-depth semistructured interviews with the founder(s), owner(s), and/or CEO ranging from 30–60 minutes. Each interview was audiotaped and transcribed. See Table 2.1.

Data Analysis

We employed a two-step process in our analysis. To answer our first research question, we did a close reading of Brueggemann's (1977) *The Bible Makes Sense* in which he provides a clear, comprehensive overview of

Table 2.1. Research Participants

Industry	Number of Employees	Key Respondent	Gender	Christian Faith
Industrial farm	60-160 (seasonal)	CEO	M	Protestant
Restaurant	35	Founder/owner/CEO	F	Catholic
Structural engineering	14	Founder/owner/CEO	M	Catholic
Food production	150	Owner/board chair /CEO	M	Catholic
Consulting	2 + project hiring	Founders/owners/CEO	F, M	Protestant

the biblical message by elaborating the relationship of the Old and New Testaments, as well as the relationship between the various types of literature in both testaments to one another. From this we developed codes to analyze the interview data. Each transcript was coded separately either by both authors or by one author and a research assistant, and in some cases by all three. We compared our coding and found our analyses to be highly congruent, providing confidence as to our assessment of the extent the interviews reflected the biblical message. We then further grouped our codes into second-order themes in order to better see the broad thematic focus of each respondent's interview. Since this analysis is not grounded theory in the strictest sense, we do not develop the second-order themes into aggregate dimensions (Gioia, Corley, & Hamilton, 2013); rather we seek to maintain the relative granularity of the analysis.

Our second step was to identify narratives within each interview that described the respondent's faith in relation to business practice. Our goal was to understand how respondents expressed the Christian worldview through their narratives about work. Here we follow Wright (1992, p. 65) who suggests that "the telling of stories ... bring worldviews into articulation." Then, to analyze respondents' stories, we draw on the structural narrative analysis of A. J. Greimas (1966; Wright 1992, pp. 69–80). We do so for two reasons. First, it allows us to readily see the "actants" in the story structure, whether these are concrete (e.g., persons) or abstractions (e.g., an ideology). The basic framework is diagrammed in Figure 2.1.

The "sender" is the initiator of the action, who commissions the "agent" to ... take or convey the "object" to the "receiver." The "agent" is prevented from doing what is required by ... the "opponent," and is, at least potentially, helped by the "helper." (Wright, 1992, p. 71)

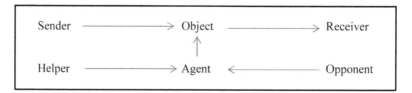

Figure 2.1.

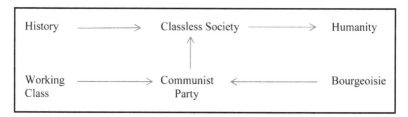

Figure 2.2.

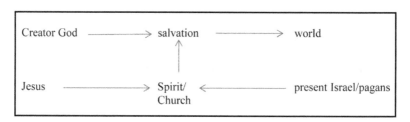

Figure 2.3.

Any story can be diagrammed this way. For example, the basic Marxist story may be diagrammed as shown in Figure 2.2 (Hartz & Steger, 2010, p. 770). The basic Christian story (Gospel of Luke) is very different (Wright, 1992, p. 383). See Figure 2.3.

Second, this narrative structure allows us to probe the narratives at the level of the fundamental values embedded in the story. For example, the business world for the most part expresses a particular worldview, evident in assertions such as "the business of business is business." On the basis of this assertion, business is often seen to operate within its own rationality and values. Conversely, we would expect that business people claiming to run their business from a Christian faith foundation would articulate the Christian worldview and its values in their stories.

RESULTS

Biblical Themes

To what extent do the founder/owner/CEO's narratives reflect the themes of the ancient biblical text? Analysis revealed that each Christian business leader articulates all of the major themes: reorientation of one's life, vital relationship with God, relationship with others, freedom, compassion and suffering for others, memory, hope, and transformation of public institutions. The relative emphasis on each theme varies somewhat.

The breadth found in each respondent was a surprise, given the increasing privatization of Christian faith over the last half century in Canada. Themes which fit a private faith—reorientation of one's life and a personal relationship to God—did not dominate, though they remained vitally important. Each respondent articulated a broader sense of what living out their Christian faith in their workplace meant, including the sense of sacrifice for others and challenging public institutions. We now turn to each of the major themes. Respondents will be referred to by their industry. Biblical references are from the New International Version and provided by the authors to link respondents' narratives to biblical analogues.

Reorientation

The central focus of this theme is conversion to a new way of doing things—a revamping of the way we typically think, speak, and live. From this comes a new lifestyle that turns away from old ways of living and old loyalties to embracing a different story with a different set of promises and demands (e.g., seeking righteousness, faithfulness, justice).

While each respondent expresses reorientation in various ways, a striking characteristic is that each one defines themselves by their Christian faith. Their faith is front and center to who they are and all that they do, including business. Representative of all six business leaders is Engineering. He has a very strong sense of being called by God: "I work around my life based on what God has called me to, to be and to do," and this is not just "daily" but "hourly." He defines "calling" as to love and to serve, which when practiced, develop other godly characteristics and removes selfish ones (see Romans 5:1-5; 2 Peter 1:5-8). From love and service

> you get mercy. Mercy means that, to forgive, to let go, to allow mistakes, whatever, mercy plays that role. To love means that you are called to give up yourself. You become the servant rather than the leader, and as becoming the servant, you become even more powerful than the leader.... It means that when ... I am actually here serving these people, whoever they are, then I lose selfishness ...

... the Christian faith is very different ... the more you give, the more you suffer. The more you suffer, the more you are brought up to have grace which gives you strength, and you become stronger and better.

Calling is living out a higher purpose that takes one "beyond just getting the best result for the client" (consulting) (see Ephesians 4:1).

Relationship With God

Closely related to reorientation is a profoundly intimate relationship with God for each of these business leaders. Life is "in the Spirit," and lived with a deep sense of faith and trust in God (restaurant) (see Romans 8:9; Galatians 2:20). Two business leaders (engineering and food production) go to mass daily, receiving the blessing and intimate relationship of the Eucharistic Lord (see 1 Corinthians 10:16). Work is scheduled around this critical participation in faith. Those in the Protestant context describe living out their faith daily, including weekly church attendance (see Hebrews 10:23-24).

But there is more; each business leader prays regularly (see 1 Thessalonians 5:17)—for their meals (thanksgiving), before or after meetings, during the day, and for guidance and direction especially in difficult situations. "We really defer to a higher power" (Farm) (see Isaiah 55:8-9). All express deep confidence in God, borne out in practice, that God will provide for them (see Genesis 22:14). In some cases it is even described as miraculous (see Galatians 3:5). And this is not idiosyncratic. Farm remarks, it is "surprising how often it happens." The following quote exemplifies each of the business leaders: "I believe in God, the Son and the Holy Spirit. I believe that he is active in my life all the time and he participates with me in everything I do" (Engineering) (see Apostles Creed; Philippians 2:13).

Relationship With Others

The corollary of love for God is love for one's neighbor (see Matthew 22:36-40). This theme captures a sense of responsibility to others, the desire for the well-being of others, honoring the human dignity and worth of others, being reconcilers in relationships of all sorts, and of being in community and bringing others into community.

Relationship with others is variously manifested. Engineering insists on showing respect to all and demanding the same of all in the company. It is important to "care about every single person." Work relationships benefit because issues are worked out sooner and better, even if it means being embarrassed and "eat[ing] my words" (Restaurant). "We remind ourselves we want to be humble and accept the messages we get. And we were able to work it out" (Farm) (see 1 Peter 3:8). Interactions with suppliers and customers are opportunities to build relationship; the interaction is never just transactional. Food Production echoes this orientation and its implications:

> And so marketing, new product development, and quality control all had an importance that went far beyond just their economic importance. In short, those who ate our products were human beings that God lived in and loved.... I knew that this conviction gave us a special, spiritual strength [to make new and better products] but also to give better service to consumers.

Finally, the inherent dignity of humans made in God's image and that each person is loved by God leads to extending God's work of reconciliation, even to those who oppose them:

> one thing about the spirituality in our work ... and this isn't always easy but it's a discipline ... and that's to see our clients and our supporters but also our opposition as children of God ... that they're people loved by God (consulting) (see Matthew 5:44; Romans 12:14)

They work to reconcile people—in imitation of God who is "reconciling the world to himself" (Consulting) (see 2 Corinthians 5:18-19).

Freedom

While this theme could be a subset of the previous, we highlight it because of the nature of business. The mantra of profit maximization and the hierarchical nature of business organizations often place both profit and power above people. Contrary to this, providing freedom, both in participation and in economics, is a hallmark of these Christian business people (see Isaiah 58).

For example, employees are empowered to make decisions and to have frank conversations with one another because of trust that stems from common values (Farm) (see Ephesians 4:15). There is freedom to practice one's faith at work, even if not Christian (e.g., Muslim), which allows openness and mutual respect to flourish (engineering). Food production brings spirituality to the workplace so people are not reduced to "the level of a simple tool, a resource, capital, in the service of prosperity and profit." It is done "not to increase productivity, but out of love for people."

Economic freedom/empowerment comes in several ways. Restaurant is particularly drawn to care for the poor, and staff are given time to help with the poor (see Galatians 2:10). They also work at developing "true community" between the poor and the churches (see 2 Corinthians 8:1-15). Others offer profit sharing across the entire organization (food production, farm), even to Mexican migrant workers (farm) (see Zechariah

7:10). Consulting are committed to ethical behavior, truth-telling (see Psalm 51:6), and community representation so that land development projects are not manipulated by political interests and are truly beneficial to the community (see Proverbs 14:31; 22:16).

Compassion and Suffering for Others

A particularly poignant aspect of following God wholeheartedly, especially in the competitive world of business, is to have compassion for others and willingly embrace suffering to bring benefit to others (see Colossians 3:12; 2 Timothy 1:8; 1 Peter 2:20). Consulting has turned down work that would have been unethical and ultimately bad for a community, creating significant difficulty for them: "if you need the work ... it becomes a more pressing issue for you right?"

Farm persevered through a difficult land rent deal because he discerned that God had "a bigger purpose at stake" in that relationship. He "felt like I needed to stay part of [this person's] life somehow ... as painful as it is for me."

Restaurant gets her staff involved in raising money for people who just lost their home, feeding the poor, helping in a homeless shelter, working with churches to feed the homeless, providing Christmas dinner on Christmas day, "and then they feel good about it—they really do." Food Production does the same (see Isaiah 58).

One particularly unique activity by Food Production is to meet with people who have been laid-off. The responsible manager must meet with the former employee twice in a 12 month period, thus "allow[ing] at least for the beginning of a real reconciliation and for the establishing of a human, authentic, humble, and fraternal relation." His own participation in this activity has given him insight into the exceeding difficulty and suffering involved, but also the very rich rewards.

Memory

This theme is focused on the concrete grounding in history of faith in God and the actions that stem from that faith (see Deuteronomy 8; Ephesians 2). Our respondents often expressed this in shorthand of the primary biblical story and the creeds:

> I like to talk about God, and Jesus (Farm).

> I believe in God, the Son and the Holy Spirit ... to receive God daily through the Eucharist ... believe that God created us all in his image (Engineering).

> We have this incredible gift of Jesus coming as our mediator (Consulting)

Reference is made to the Scriptures (Farm, Consulting), and Bible study is encouraged (Farm). Food Production made many pilgrimages to the Holy Land where he experienced "the concrete discovery of Christ on earth … where Christ himself lived, suffered, and loved." Further reference is made to the Saints: "I believe in what St. Francis Assisi did, and that's through your actions, preach" (Engineering) (see St. Francis of Assisi & El-Bey, 2009). As mentioned earlier, Restaurant and Farm believe in current day miracles and report experiencing them.

These references to an ancient text and to ancient lives concretize and particularize the business leaders' faith and spirituality within a long-standing, historically grounded tradition.

Hope

Linked to the theme above, hope looks forward to the future on the basis of the grounding of faith in a concrete, particular history. It is expressed in a dynamic future filled with possibility and visions of a new humanity because God is still at work in the world (see John 5:17; Revelation 21:5). There is a sense that the world can be a different place.

For example, Restaurant explicitly refers to her business as a "bigger vision" that is "aligned with God" such that "so many other people are being affected in a good way." Farm refers to participating in "kingdom building"—a vision for a humanity characterized by the goodness and grace of God (see Matthew 5:3-12; Romans 14:17; Galatians 5: 13-26). Consulting also understand that "God is in us … reconciling the world to himself." A 'hope founded in memories' provides strength for that hope and a recognition that bigger possibilities exist.

Transformation of Public Institutions

Finally, hope finds further expression in the transformation of public institutions. For example, Engineering underscores the value of respecting all people, leading to good interorganizational working relationships. Rather than seeking profit above all else, this CEO's father created a company that established an excellent work context where the trades could earn good money. Subsequently, their work was done well, abuse was avoided, and the company in turn became even more profitable.

On the basis of their belief that God loves all people and is reconciling the world to himself, Consulting gain access to "authentic community citizens who want to make a difference in their community" and tap into the "hearts and minds of people" rather than "leav[ing] it at the strategic level." Clients have told them that they do their work differently from other consulting companies, which then gives them access to large, complex projects.

Respondents also share even larger visions of transformation. Restaurant's vision is for healing the environment and people through the development of local organic farming. Food Production seeks the renewal of capitalism by making very practical "the grand principles of the Church's doctrine about the dignity of the human person and the meaning of human work." From his perspective, the business world has perfected the economic side of the equation but has increasingly neglected the "human dimension" to the extent that "people are considered only in relation to productivity." With "God-Love" at the center, managers and employees can draw on a greater wisdom and operate from "a heart of flesh" rather than "a heart of stone." To maintain this structure has meant daily the sacrament of the Eucharist and the sacrament of Reconciliation coupled with much prayer:

> How will I be able to manage the business so that there will be no split between the spiritual life and work?… I slowly discovered that work could and should become silent prayer: Ora et labora.

Worldview

How do respondents evidence the Christian worldview within their narratives? Structural analysis reveals respondents believe that God is animating all that they do, and that God is at work even in situations where they were unaware. Furthermore, they believe that God is accomplishing his agenda of reconciliation and restoration in the world. He provides more and more resources to the respondents for their/his work, and over time He produces a proliferation of goodness that goes beyond the initial goal of the business. The contrast between the early and mature phases of Consulting is instructive.

Maintaining integrity to their faith values early in their career provided several key benefits and building blocks for subsequent work. First, it gave them confidence for future circumstances when God provided work after turning down unethical project work. Second, it honed their discernment; they were able "to define a better client for ourselves." Subsequently, other consulting companies are utilizing their ethical discernment, considering them to be the ethical "smell test" of a project. Third, it has led to the development of competitive advantage. They interact with authentic community members and harness their energy to work with developers in creating truly mutually beneficial land developments, something other consulting companies are unable to do because their commitments are elsewhere (e.g., to the developer and/or the money). Consulting's faith commitment, then, has blossomed into a proliferation of goodness, as

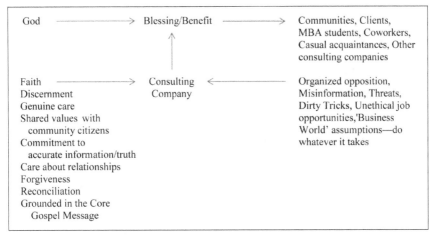

Figure 2.4.   Consultings' overall story: Proliferation of goodness/blessing to others and of resources for the work.

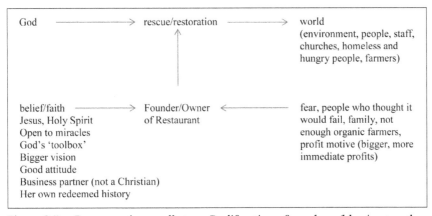

Figure 2.5.   Restaurant's overall story: Proliferation of goodness/blessing to others and of resources for the work.

illustrated in their overall story. The overall story of Restaurant corroborates the conclusions. See Figures 2.4 and 2.5

The practice of authentic Christian spirituality in the workplace results in a proliferation of goodness for many from God's hand, and a proliferation of "God-resources" that he supplies to bring it about. This pattern is reflected in each of our respondents.

DISCUSSION

From our analysis, it is evident that these six Christian business people display ancient Christian spirituality in their workplace. Their interviews manifest the biblical themes, and their stories reflect the Christian world-view. Brueggemann (1977) provides helpful terminology to describe this relationship: primary and derivative narratives. The primary narrative is "that most simple, elemental, and nonnegotiable story line which lies at the heart of biblical faith" (pp. 45–46). Our respondents' narratives are derivative narratives (p. 54) that testify to the veracity and relevance of the ancient biblical faith for their current place and time in history, demonstrating that the God witnessed to by the ancient text is still at work here and now in their lives and in their workplaces. In contrast to the post-modern world of local or personal truth, our respondents' spiritual-ity is anchored in deep history, giving it richness and nuance from millen-nia of practice in a wide variety of settings and circumstances. Yet it is not slavishly replicated; rather, it is creatively implemented through a "histor-ical imagination" (Brueggemann, 1977, p. 33). Historically grounded and imaginatively implemented, the Christian grand narrative is a source of disciplined and yet "liberating energies" (p. 34) because the same God of the primary narrative is believed and confessed to be creatively still at work today in these particular circumstances.

This foundation gives impetus and fortitude to "subversive" behavior in the face of business rationality. Respondents made business subservient within the Christian worldview in which God "plays the central and cru-cial role" (Brueggemann, 1977, p. 54). They display a relationship to the business world that Siker (1989), adapting Niebuhr's typology, character-izes as "Christ the transformer of business."

As such, the Christian worldview is a powerful alternative and antidote to the dominant business- or organization-centered worldview (Giacalone & Thompson, 2006, p. 267), which claims that business is at the center of society, and pursuing the interests of business will also result in meeting society's interests. These worldviews place everything within an economic framework, and judge its value by its instrumentality in achieving finan-cial results. Money holds the highest place in the values hierarchy, along with all that money brings—"power, status, and accumulation of wealth" (Giacalone & Thompson, 2006, p. 267). The Christian worldview chal-lenges this hierarchy and de-centers business, replacing it with love for God and neighbor.

Giacalone and Thompson (2006) argue for a human-centered world-view in place of the business-centered worldview, claiming that placing human and societal well-being above financial considerations will put business in a proper relationship with people and the planet. While perhaps true, we are not confident that the human-centered worldview can be broadly sustained in the face of the immense power of the business-centered worldview. Our respondents note the difficulty of maintaining their faith commitment in the workplace (compare Badaracco & Webb, 1995). Staying true to the Christian worldview has meant fostering an ongoing (daily, hourly), profoundly intimate relationship with God. Christian identity is highly salient for these respondents (Weaver & Agle, 2002, pp. 80-88). There is no bifurcation between business and personal life, with a "bureaucratic ethic" at work and a religious ethic elsewhere. They are intrinsically motivated wherein they resist having faith supplanted by organizational pressures and demands. They exhibit a "stronger link between judgment [of an ethical situation] and behavior [to do the right thing]" (Weaver & Agle, 2002, p. 89).

CONCLUSION

Ancient spirituality (in this case Christianity), holds considerable value for the spirituality in the workplace movement. It can be the source for exercising authentic spirituality in the workplace—a spirituality deeply rooted in ancient story, the character of which is not instrumental nor compartmentalized, but rather foundational and integrated. It is a spirituality that is not concerned with self-actualization but with serving others, including the environment and society. It can become the foundation on which different business practices are built, and it provides resources for imaginative creation and implementation in the here and now of historic precedents and proportions (e.g., Restaurant's imagining growing vegetables on the Church lawn to feed the poor as reminiscent of Biblical Creation). It also supplies the strength to suffer on behalf of others' well-being, becoming a foundation for compassionate organizing (George, 2014).

REFERENCES

Ashforth, B. E., & Vaidyanath, D. (2002). Work organizations as secular religions. *Journal of Management Inquiry, 11*(4), 359–370.

Badaracco, J. L., & Webb, A. P. (1995). Business ethics: A view from the trenches. *California Management Review, 37*(2), 8–28.

Balog, A. M., Baker, L. T., & Walker, A. G. (2014). Religiosity and spirituality in entrepreneurship: A review and research agenda. *Journal of Management, Spirituality, and Religion, 11*(2), 159–186.

Bartunek, J. M., & Spreitzer, G. M. (2006). The interdisciplinary career of a popular construct used in management: Empowerment in the late 20th century. *Journal of Management Inquiry, 15*(3), 255–273.

Bay, D., McKeage, K., & McKeage, J. (2010). An historical perspective on the interplay of Christian thought and business ethics. *Business and Society, 49*(4), 652–676.

Bolman, L. G., & Deal, T. E. (1995). *Leading with soul: An uncommon journey of spirit.* San Francisco, CA: Jossey-Bass.

Briskin, A. (1998). *The stirring of soul in the workplace.* San Francisco, CA: Jossey-Bass.

Brueggemann, W. (1977). *The Bible makes sense.* Atlanta, GA: John Knox Press.

Brueggemann, W. (1978). *The prophetic imagination.* Minneapolis, MN: Fortress Press.

Carrascoso, A. C. (2014). A framework for a Catholic stakeholder core. *Journal of Management, Spirituality, and Religion, 11*(4), 307–330.

Chan-Serafin, S., Brief, A. P., & George, J. M. (2013). How does religion matter and why? Religion and the organizational sciences. *Organization Science, 24*(5), 1585–1600.

Chappell, T. (1993). *The soul of a business: Managing for profit and the common good.* New York, NY: Bantam.

Conger, J. (1994). *Spirit at work: Discovering the spirituality in leadership.* San Francisco, CA: Jossey-Bass.

Cunha, M. P., Rego, A., & D'Oliveira, T. (2006). Organizational spiritualities: An ideology-based typology. *Business & Society, 45*(2), 211–234.

Delbecq, A. (1999). Christian spirituality and contemporary business leadership. *Journal of Organizational Change Management, 12*(4), 345–349.

Diddams, M., & Daniels, D. (2008). Good work with toil: A paradigm for redeemed work. *Christian Scholars Review, 38,* 64–82.

Diddams, M., Whittington, J. L., & Davigo, T. (2006). Creating in the name of God who creates. A whole life model of vocation & work. *Journal of Management, Spirituality and Religion, 2,* 310–331.

Driscoll, C., & Wiebe, E. (2007). Technical spirituality at work: Jacques Ellul on workplace spirituality. *Journal of Management Inquiry, 16*(4), 333–348.

Driscoll, C., Wiebe, E., & Dyck, B. (2011). Nature is prior to us: Applying Catholic social thought and Anabaptist-Mennonite theology to the ethics of stakeholder prioritization for the natural environment. *Journal of Religion and Business Ethics, 3*(1), Article 3.

Dyck, B., & Schroeder, D. (2005). Management, theology, and moral points of view: Towards an alternative to the conventional materialist-individualist ideal-type of management. *Journal of Management Studies, 42*(2), 705–735.

Dyck, B., Starke, F. A., & Dueck, C. (2009). Management, prophets, and self-fulfilling prophecies. *Journal of Management Inquiry, 18,* 184–196.

Dyck, B., & Wiebe, E. (2012). Salvation, theology and organizational practices across the centuries. *Organization, 19,* 299–324.

Epstein, E. M. (2002). Religion and business—The critical role of religious traditions in management education. *Journal of Business Ethics, 38*(1/2), 91–98.

Ewest, T. (2015). Christian identity as primary foundation to workplace ethics. *Religions: A Scholarly Journal, 12,* 22–30.

Fenwick, T., & Lange, E. (1998). Spirituality in the workplace: The new frontier of HRD. *Canadian Journal for the Study of Adult Education, 12*(1), 63–87.

Fernando, M., & Jackson, B. (2006). The influence of religion-based workplace spirituality on business leaders' decision-making: An inter-faith study. *Journal of Management & Organization, 12*(1), 23–39.

Friedland, R. (2014). Divine institution: Max Weber's value spheres and institutional theory. In P. Tracey, N. Phillips, & M. Lounsbury (Eds.), *Research in the sociology of organizations* (pp. 217–258). Bingley, England: Emerald.

Garcia-Zamor, J.-C. (2003). Workplace spirituality and organizational performance. *Public Administration Review, 63*(3), 355–363.

George, J. M. (2014). Compassion and capitalism: Implications for organizational studies. *Journal of Management, 40*(1), 5–15.

Gioia, D. A., Corley, K. G., & Hamilton, A. L. (2013). Seeking qualitative rigor in inductive research: Notes on the Gioia methodology. *Organizational Research Methods, 16*(1), 15–31.

Graafland, J., Kaptein, M., & Mazerereeuw, C. (2007). Conceptions of God, normative convictions, and socially responsible business conduct: An exploratory study among executives. *Business & Society, 46*(3), 331–368.

Giacalone, R. A., & Jurkiewicz, C. L. (Eds.). (2003). Toward a science of workplace spirituality. In *Handbook of workplace spirituality and organizational performance* (pp. 3–28). New York, NY: M. E. Sharpe.

Giacalone, R. A., & Thompson, K. R. (2006). Business ethics and social responsibility education: Shifting the worldview. *Academy of Management Learning & Education, 5*(3), 266–277.

Greimas, A. J. (1966). *Structural semantics: An attempt at a method.* London, England: Faber and Faber.

Gotsis, G., & Kortezi, Z. (2008). Philosophical foundations of workplace spirituality: A critical approach. *Journal of Business Ethics, 78*(4), 575–600.

Hartz, R., & Steger, T. (2010). Heroes, villains and 'honorable merchants': Narrative change in the German media discourse on corporate governance. *Organization, 17*(6), 767–785.

Hicks, D. A. (2003). *Religion and the workplace: Pluralism, spirituality, and leadership.* New York, NY: Cambridge University Press.

John Paul II. (1981). *Encyclical letter: Laborem exercens* (on human work). Retrieved from http://www.catholic-pages.com/documents/laborem_exercens.asp

King, J. E. (2008). (Dis)missing the obvious: Will mainstream management research ever take religion seriously? *Journal of Management Inquiry, 17*(3), 214–224.

Lee, C., & Zemke, R. (1993). The search for spirit in the workplace. *Training, 30*(6), 21–28.

Marcic, D. (2000). God, faith, and management education. *Journal of Management Education, 24*(5), 628–649.

McClay, W. M. (2000). Two concepts of secularism. *The Wilson Quarterly, 24*(3), 54–71.

Miller, D. W., & Ewest, T. (2013). Rethinking the impact of religion on business values: Understanding its reemergence and measuring its manifestations. In S. Rothlin & P. Haghirian (Eds.), *Dimensions of teaching business ethics in Asia* (pp. 29–38). Heidelberg, Germany: Springer.

Porth, S. J., Steingard, D., & McCall, J. (2003). Spirituality and business: The latest management fad or the next breakthrough. In O. F. Williams (Ed.), *Business, religion, and spirituality: A new synthesis* (pp. 249–262). South Bend, IN: University of Notre Dame.

Purser, R. E., & Milillo, J. (2015). Mindfulness revisited: A Buddhist-based conceptualization. *Journal of Management Inquiry, 24*(1), 3–24.

Sandelands, L. E. (2003). The argument for God from organization studies. *Journal of Management Inquiry, 12*(2), 168–177.

Siker, L. van Wensveen. (1989). Christ and business: A typology for Christian business ethics. *Journal of Business Ethics, 8*, 883–888.

St. Francis of Assisi & El-Bey, Z. (2009). *The complete writings of St. Francis of Assisi.* Ilife ebooks.

Stackhouse, M., McCann, D., & Roels, S., with Williams, P. (Eds.). (1995). *On moral business: Classical and contemporary resources for economics in economic life.* Grand Rapids, MI: William Eerdmans.

Steingard, D. S. (2005). Spiritually-informed management theory: Toward profound possibilities for inquiry and transformation. *Journal of Management Inquiry, 14*(3), 227–241.

Sutcliffe, S., & Bowman, M. (2000). *Beyond new age: Exploring alternative spirituality.* Edinburgh, Scotland: Edinburgh University Press.

Tracey, P. (2012). Religion and organization: A critical review of current trends and future directions. *Academy of Management Annals, 6*(1), 87–134.

Tracey, P., Phillips, N., & Lounsbury, M. (Eds.). (2014). *Religion and organization theory: Research in the sociology of organizations.* Bingley, England: Emerald.

Wallis, J. (2010). *Rediscovering values: On Wall Street, main street, and your street.* New York, NY: Howard Books.

Weaver, G. R., & Agle, B. R. (2002). Religiosity and ethical behavior in organizations: A symbolic interactionist perspective. *Academy of Management Review, 27*(1), 77–97.

Weber, M. (1958). *The Protestant ethic and the spirit of capitalism* (T. Parsons, Trans.). New York, NY: Scribner's. (Original work published 1904–05)

Wedemeyer, R. A., & Jue, R. (2002). *The inner edge: How to integrate your life, your work, and your spirituality for greater effectiveness and fulfillment.* Chicago, IL: McGraw Hill.

Wright, N. T. (1992). *The New Testament and the people of God, Vol. 1.* Minneapolis, MN: Fortress Press.

Wuthnow, R. (2007). *After the baby boomers: How twenty-and thirty-somethings are shaping the future of American religion.* Princeton, NY: Princeton University Press.

Wuthnow, R. (2012). *Red state religion: Faith and politics in America's heartland.* Princeton, NJ: Princeton University Press.

CHAPTER 3

THE IMPACT OF COLLEGE TYPE AND OCCUPATIONAL CATEGORY ON FAITH INTEGRATION IN THE COLLEGE WORKPLACE

Sharlene G. Buszka
Daemen College

Timothy G. Ewest
Houston Baptist University

INTRODUCTION

Numerous organizations have acknowledged the importance of workplace faith and spirituality because of observed benefits such as improved customer service, increased productivity and profits, heightened creativity and innovation, and decreased turnover (Sullivan, 2008). In a review of 15 empirical studies on the topic of faith and spirituality in the workplace (Benefiel, Fry, & Geigle, 2014), 5 showed a positive relationship with job satisfaction; 6 with organizational commitment, 3 with job involvement; and 2 with work performance. Other positive relationships were shown to

Faith and Work: Christian Perspectives, Research, and Insights Into the Movement
pp. 33–55

exist with altruism, conscientiousness, self-career management, job identification, and organizational citizenship behavior.

An increased focus on spirituality and faith may also help remedy noted issues such as demoralization and distrust of business organizations and their leaders (Lewin & Regine, 2000) and an overemphasis on maximizing shareholders' value and profits at the expense of mission (López, Ramos, & Ramos, 2009; Vasconcelos, 2015). Alternatively, self-serving organizational agendas can undermine the well-being and rights of employees (Caldwell & Canutu-Carranco, 2010), failing to acknowledge that employees have needs related to body, mind and spirit (McNight, 2005). This results in dispirited workplaces with low morale, high turnover, burnout, frequent stress-related illnesses, and rising absenteeism (Vasconcelos, 2015). Some workers struggle to find time outside of work for meaningful pursuits because of long work hours (Saad, 2014) and the growing time crunch faced by dual income families (Gaddis & Klasen, 2014). With limited leisure time and the distinction between work and nonwork identities fading (Ramarajan & Reid, 2013), employees may find increased meaning and enthusiasm at work if provided guidance in ways to integrate their faith and spirituality in this setting (Dhiman & Marques, 2011; Pawar, 2009).

This research focuses on identifying factors that affect employees' work-related faith integration to provide accurate and helpful information to individuals, and organizations. Miller's (2007) Integration Profile and its related TIP Profile instrument (Miller, 2013; Miller & Ewest, 2013; Miller & Ewest, 2015) provide a useful framework for analyzing specific ways people express their faith through work. This framework is the basis for the present research project.

MILLER'S FRAMEWORK

Miller (2007) developed a common language to facilitate further discussion, research and analysis of the faith at work movement. This language consists of a framework that describes workplace faith integration in four distinct ways: enrichment, ethics, expression, or experience (Miller, 2007). Subsequent research (Miller & Ewest, 2013, 2015) expanded each of these four categories to include the same four manifestations, but bifurcating each manifestation to include two suborientations (see Table 3.1). This framework is theologically legitimate, with none of the four primary categories superior or inferior to each other, individuals or religious groups may manifest one or more simultaneously (Miller & Ewest, 2013), and it can apply to those of different faith backgrounds (Miller & Ewest, 2011). This model "has the capacity to reflect the movement's diverse

Table 3.1. Miller's TIP Manifestations

Manifestation	Orientation	Example
Enrichment type	Group orientation enrichment	Praying with others at work
	Individual orientation enrichment	Meditating by oneself
Ethics type	Community orientation ethics	Supporting organization's efforts to be socially responsible
	Self-orientation ethics	Performing personal work with high levels of integrity
Experience type	Outcome orientation experience	Deriving pleasure from seeing how one's work benefits others
	Process orientation experience	Pleasure inherent from performing the work itself
Expression type	Nonverbal expression	Wearing symbols of one's faith at work
	Verbal expression	Talking openly about one's faith while at work

range of motivations, member profiles and modes of expression, while still recognizing the common organizing principle of a quest for integration" (Miller, 2007, p. 128).

Specific integration types may be the result of one or more of the following: church upbringing, personality type, theological teachings, societal conditioning, gender, geography, and corporate culture (Miller, 2007, p. 128). However, the TIP framework is flexible, allowing workers to possess more than one of the types. Also, an awareness of TIP integration types may help employees and managers become more aware of potential conflicts and problems that could emerge as a result of different integration types existing within the same organization.

The Enrichment Type

The enrichment type focuses on personal improvement through prayer, meditation and nurturing spiritual growth (Miller, 2007; Miller & Ewest, 2013, 2015). The two suborientations within this category are *group orientation enrichment* and *individual orientation enrichment*. These suborientations are similar in that they are both means by which workers may draw strength and comfort to deal with work-related issues. They differ in whether they are practiced alone or with others. Examples include prayer, meditation, scripture study, and yoga.

The Ethics Type

The ethics type (Miller, 2007; Miller & Ewest, 2013, 2015) includes employees primarily interested in integrating faith at work through applying ethical principles to workplace issues and challenges. The two subcategories within this group are *community orientation ethics* and *self-orientation ethics*. *Community orientation ethics* places high importance on organizational, social or structural issues that concern employees and the company. This could include things such as fair compensation, safe working conditions, product safety, environmental or social justice concerns. The second subcategory, *self-orientation ethics*, relates to the worker's personal conduct and behavior. This orientation concerns itself with character traits such as integrity, honesty and showing respect for others (Miller, 2007; Miller & Ewest, 2013, 2015). Those who are personally honest and perform excellent work fall into this category.

The Experience Type

Those with the experience profile look for ways to experience meaning and purpose in work (Miller, 2007; Miller & Ewest, 2013, 2015). Many with this preference view their work as a calling, vocation or ministry. Work provides intrinsic satisfaction and may be viewed as spiritual or divine. The two subcategories in this group were *outcome orientation* and *process/activity orientation*. For the *outcome orientation* type, work is perceived as a means to an end. The work itself may not be particularly rewarding, but the product or service it produces is what provides meaning and satisfaction. The *process/activity orientation* type identifies very closely with the nature of the work itself. Some may describe their work as what they were born to do. This expression can come through the use of specific natural or God-given talents.

The Expression Type

Those whose predominant profile of integration is expression place a high level of importance on the ability to express their faith or worldview to others (Miller, 2007; Miller & Ewest, 2013, 2015). Within the religious traditions of Christianity and Islam, open expression of beliefs and the need to seek converts to their views is part of their theology (Miller & Ewest, 2015). Expression can be exhibited in two different ways, verbally or nonverbally. *Verbal orientation expression* types either wish to engage in conversation about beliefs, or try to persuade others to share similar worldviews. Information from a Gallup poll reported that two thirds of those surveyed believed open expressions of religion would be tolerated or encouraged at their place of work (Gallup, 2002). This suggests a good number of workers would find verbal orientation expression acceptable or even desirable. Those with *nonverbal orientation expression* use attire, symbols such as religious jewelry, or scripture verses left in public places to express their faith to others.

SUMMARY AND APPLICATION OF MILLER'S PROFILE

Because this model can apply to employees of all faiths and spiritual beliefs, it can be particularly helpful to organizations. The application of The Integration Profile (TIP) to the workplace may allow organizations to become aware of the faith manifestations of their employees at work, and respond by developing appropriate policies and practices related to these. Miller and Ewest (2011) suggest that workers will perceive organizations as *faith-friendly* when they are supportive in these ways. The term faith-friendly is consistent with the idea of "respectful pluralism" proposed by Hicks (2003) as a way to be inclusive of all religious faiths and spiritual beliefs. Companies may accrue the benefits of increased diversity and inclusion, fewer religious discrimination lawsuits, increased employee engagement, higher job satisfaction, greater employee loyalty, and improved recruiting and retention (Miller & Ewest, 2015).

FAITH AND SPIRITUALITY IN HIGHER EDUCATION

The specific setting for this research project is within higher education. The majority of present-day colleges and universities in the United States have diverged significantly from their faith-based foundations. Marsden reports (2015) that secular viewpoints are favored in academia while religious views are discouraged. The UCLA Higher Education Institute (Astin, Astin, Lindholm, & Bryant, 2005) reported that even though students were interested in spirituality, professors were not providing the opportunity to discuss these types of issues in class. Gallagher (2007) reported that, though over 80% of faculty reported themselves to be spiritual, only 30% felt colleges should support students' spiritual development.

The study of faith and work within institutions of higher education presents a unique perspective. These institutions were founded to promote religious learning, inquiry, and scholarship. However, many reported that higher education has shifted from "focusing on spirituality and the whole person to becoming a for-profit, economic machine" (Bell-Ellis, Jones, Longstreth, & Neal, 2013, p. 350). The study that follows provides a further investigation into the state of faith integration in higher education. It examines how and if employees integrate their personal views and values in this area depending on whether or not the institution is faith-affiliated or nonsectarian, and depending on the occupation group to which employees belong.

RESEARCH QUESTIONS

This research analyzed how the factors of college type and occupational category affected the ways employees integrate faith and spirituality in the college workplace. These two factors were studied by examining how each impacted the eight modalities of faith work integration measured by The Integration Profile (TIP) Faith and Work Integration Scale (Miller, 2013).

- Hypothesis 1 Category: There are differences in faith integration between employees at a faith-affiliated college and those at a non-sectarian college.
- Hypothesis 2 Category: There are differences in faith integration between those in different occupational categories.

Miller's TIP scale measured faith integration using the four manifestations and eight subcategories: (a) individual orientation enrichment; (b) group orientation enrichment; (c) community orientation ethics; (d) self-orientation ethics; (e) outcomes orientation experience; (f) process/activity orientation experience (g) nonverbal orientation expression; and (h) verbal orientation expression

METHODS

The TIP scale was identified as the most appropriate instrument for the present project as it was designed to remedy some of the gaps in current research on this topic (Miller & Ewest, 2013). The TIP measures eight manifestation dimensions (four categories, each with two subdimensions) of faith, religion and spirituality at the individual level for employees of all faith traditions or worldviews. When analyzed, the eight factors were reported to account for 57% of the total variance and internal consistency with Cronbach's coefficient alpha ranging from .74 to .92 among the eight factors (Miller & Ewest, 2015)

POPULATION AND SAMPLE

Western New York college employees who worked at four different colleges were surveyed. College 1 was nonsectarian, College 2 was Roman Catholic-affiliated, and Colleges 3 and 4 were Protestant-affiliated. Though College 2 was Roman Catholic, it had no requirement that employees believe in or adhere to any specific church doctrines. In contrast, each of the two colleges affiliated with Protestant denominations had an institutional policy and practice to hire only faculty or administrators who profess faith in Jesus Christ. The population included employees falling into the categories of administration, faculty and staff. The number of employees (as counted by the number of names on employee e-mail listserves) were the following: College 1–520; College 2–600; College 3–260; and College 4–318. This resulted in a total population size of 1,707.

DATA COLLECTION AND RESPONSE

The survey was distributed using a Survey Monkey link via e-mail to employees on each institution's listserv during April and May of 2015. There were 500 survey responses from the 1,707 employees who received survey links via employee e-mail. This reflected a 29.3% response rate. Based on Krejcie and Morgan's table (1970), this sample size was sufficient for a valid analysis. Individual college response levels were as follows: College 1–125/520; College 2–152/600; College 3–85/260; and College 4–139/ 318.

MEASURES

There were two independent variables. College type was defined and grouped by Colleges 1 (nonsectarian), 2 (Roman Catholic), 3 (Protestant A) and 4 (Protestant B). Occupational category was defined by Question 3 response to faculty, administration, and staff groupings. Eight dependent variables were measured and equated using the sum of the responses to Likert-type items for: *group orientation enrichment, individual orientation enrichment, community ethics, self-orientation ethics, outcome experience, process/ activity experience, nonverbal expression,* and *verbal expression.*

RESULTS

Demographically, the majority of this sample worked full time (86.6%), were Caucasian (94.9%) aged 41 and older (73.6%), claimed a belief in God, a higher power or gods (88%), reported Christianity as their faith

Table 3.2.   Hypothesis Testing Summary

Hypothesis 1—College Type	Procedure	p Value	Decision
1a group orientation enrichment	Kruskal-Wallis	<0.001	Reject null
1b personal orientation enrichment	Kruskal-Wallis	<0.001	Reject null
1c with community orientation ethics	Kruskal-Wallis	<0.001	Reject null
1d with self orientation Ethics	Kruskal-Wallis	<0.001	Reject null
1e with process/activity orientation experience	Kruskal-Wallis	<0.001	Reject null
1f with outcomes orientation experience	Kruskal-Wallis	<0.001	Reject null
1g with nonverbal orientation expression	Kruskal-Wallis	<0.001	Reject null
1h with verbal orientation expression	Kruskal-Wallis	<0.001	Reject null
Hypothesis 2—Occupational Category	Procedure	p Value	Decision
2a with group orientation enrichment	Kruskal-Wallis	<0.001	Reject null
2b with individual orientation enrichment	Kruskal-Wallis	<0.001	Reject null
2c with community orientation ethics	Kruskal-Wallis	<0.005	Reject null
2d with self-orientation ethics	Kruskal-Wallis	0.958	Accept null
2e with process/activity orientation experience	Kruskal-Wallis	0.113	Accept null
2f with outcomes orientation experience	Kruskal-Wallis	0.313	Accept null
2g with nonverbal orientation expression	Kruskal-Wallis	<0.001	Reject null
2h with verbal orientation expression	Kruskal-Wallis	<0.001	Reject null

(90.2%), and believed their organizations allowed them to freely integrate their faith while at work (88.1%). Two hypotheses were examined, each with eight subhypotheses, for a total of 16 hypotheses. Because surveys measured ordinal data using Likert-type questions, and the hypotheses had three or more measures, they were tested using the Kruskal-Wallis procedure. As shown in Table 3.2, three hypotheses were accepted and thirteen were rejected.

Hypothesis 1 Results and Discussion

The research hypothesis 1 category predicted there would be a statistically significant difference in faith integration between employees working at a faith-affiliated college and those at a nonsectarian college. Miller's (2013; Miller & Ewest, 2013) eight integration dimensions were examined to assess whether differences existed. Hypothesis 1 considered the impact of different work environments on employees' faith integration. Previous research explored differences between faith-affiliated colleges and those that were public or nonsectarian. in aspects such as culture (Bradley & Kauanui, 2003), curriculum (Hodge & Derezotes, 2008), views on student character development (Turi, 2012), faculty organizational commitment and work engagement (Bell-Ellis, et al., 2013) and perceived calling (Thompson & Miller-Perrin, 2003). Results of the analysis of Hypothesis 1 add to the body of research suggesting that working at a faith-affiliated college can be significantly different in a variety of ways from working in other types of colleges. For this project, it was hypothesized that employees working at a faith-affiliated institution would integrate faith differently than those at a nonsectarian institution.

As shown in Table 3.3, Kruskal-Wallace testing supported this hypothesis in each of the eight categories of faith integration with p values of less than 0.05 ($p < 0.001$). The mean rankings for all eight of the integration dimensions were statistically significantly higher for the two Protestant colleges than for the Roman Catholic college. The mean rankings for seven of the eight integration dimensions were statistically significantly higher at the two Protestant Colleges and the nonsectarian college. There was no difference found between the Protestant institutions and the nonsectarian institution in *self-orientation ethics*.

The differences between the Protestant colleges surveyed and the Roman Catholic and nonsectarian colleges surveyed may be, in part, due to the similar employee selection policies held by the two Protestant colleges that required faculty and administrators to state they agreed with the faith positions of these schools. Essentially, the two Protestant colleges were recruiting and hiring faculty and administrators who share their faith views. Also, such views were integrated within college policies and curriculum. Although the Protestant colleges surveyed did not require those hired in staff positions also to agree to this faith statement, it is likely that knowledge of the organizational culture impacts what type of staff employees apply for such positions. Moreover, it is expected that many who choose to work in faith-affiliated organizations do so, at least in part, because they desire to integrate their faith at work.

In contrast, the Roman Catholic institution surveyed required that employees agree to the college's mission, but this did not include professing a belief in a particular faith system. Being a member of the Roman Catholic faith was not a requirement for employment and there was no expectation that administrators or faculty would be promoting the Roman Catholic Church views as part of their work positions. As a result, the Roman Catholic college was not significantly different from the nonsectarian college in seven of the eight ways employees were reported to integrate faith while at work. In the one area it was different, *self-orientation ethics*, the mean rank was lower than at the nonsectarian college. Though

Table 3.3. Kruskal-Wallace Results for Hypothesis 1: Influence of College Type on Faith Integration

Hypothesis 1 Subcategory	Chi-Square	p Value	College Type Mean Rank
Hypothesis 1a: College type w/group orientation enrichment Gp Gp Gp Gp 1 2 3 4 ‾‾	82.2	<0.001	college 1 (nonsectarian) mean rank—165.42 college 2 (Roman Catholic) mean rank—194.38 college 3 (Protestant a) mean rank—285.35 college 4 (Protestant b) mean rank—296.79
Hypothesis 1b: College type w/individual orientation enrichment Gp Gp Gp Gp 1 2 3 4 ‾‾	82.9	<0.001	college 1 (nonsectarian) mean rank—179.02 college 2 (Roman Catholic) mean rank—198.22 college 3 (Protestant a) mean rank—302.45 college 4 (Protestant b) mean rank—305.26
Hypothesis 1c: College type w/community orientation ethics Gp Gp Gp Gp 1 2 3 4 ‾‾	82.8	<0.001	college 1 (nonsectarian) mean rank—177.22 college 2 (Roman Catholic) mean rank—186.72 college 3 (Protestant a) mean rank—288.47 college 4 (Protestant b) mean rank—299.89
Hypothesis 1d: College type w/self-orientation ethics Gp Gp Gp Gp 2 1 3 4 ‾‾	17.1	<0.001	college 1 (nonsectarian) mean rank—238.17 college 2 (Roman Catholic) mean rank—206.55 college 3 (Protestant a) mean rank—262.76 college 4 (protestant b) mean rank—269.73
Hypothesis 1e: College type w/process/activity orientation experience Gp Gp Gp Gp 1 2 3 4 ‾‾	71	<0.001	college 1 (nonsectarian) mean rank—184.45 college 2 (Roman Catholic) mean rank—193.05 college 3 (protestant a) mean rank—282.17 college 4 (protestant b) mean rank—301.08

Hypothesis 1f: College type w/outcomes orientation experience	48.5	<0.001	college 1 (nonsectarian) mean rank—189.81
			college 2 (Roman Catholic) mean rank—209.22
			college 3 (Protestant a) mean rank—290.42
			college 4 (Protestant b) mean rank—284.12
Gp Gp Gp Gp 1 2 3 4 ----			
Hypothesis 1g: College type w/nonverbal orientation expression	60.9	<0.001	college 1 (nonsectarian) mean rank—175.9
			college 2 (Roman Catholic) mean rank—214.58
			college 3 (Protestant a) mean rank—279.73
			college 4 (Protestant b) mean rank—297.27
Gp Gp Gp Gp 1 2 3 4 ----			
Hypothesis 1h: College type w/verbal orientation expression	182.5	<0.001	college 1 (nonsectarian) mean rank—149.12
			college 2 (Roman Catholic) mean rank—178.14
			college 3 (Protestant a) mean rank—334.13
			college 4 (Protestant b) mean rank—337.06
Gp Gp Gp Gp 1 2 3 4 ----			

neither the Roman Catholic nor the nonsectarian college has specific policies about separating faith from work, the employees working in the Roman Catholic and nonsectarian institutions reported integrating faith less than in the two Protestant-affiliated schools. A remaining question is whether the respondents in non-Protestant colleges integrated their faith less because they believed it was not appropriate in these environments or because they did not desire to do so. Employees may refrain from integrating their faith in the absence of explicit and promoted policies about what employees can and cannot do in this area. The nonsectarian and Roman Catholic college employees may mistakenly assume a broader than necessary application of "separation of church and state" (Flax, 2011) applies to their institutions.[1]

Results also indicated that the nonsectarian institution employees exhibited *self-orientation ethics* no differently from employees at Protestant colleges and significantly different from the Roman Catholic institution. This suggests something is happening at the nonsectarian institution to cause employees to act in more individually ethical ways than would be expected based on the results of the other seven integration dimensions. Literature reports that companies are very concerned about employee ethics and frequently seek to instil ethical cultures (Meinert, 2014). Therefore, one obvious explanation for this outcome might be that the nonsectarian college engages in significant ethics training. Another explanation might be that this institution actively seeks to hire ethical employees.

The results of Hypothesis 1 provide additional support for the conclusion that the type of college environment significantly impacts the degree to which employees integrate their faith at work. When a college is faith-affiliated, requires that employees be in agreement with that faith, and openly encourages the integration of faith values into policies and curriculum, employees will feel they can (or even should) integrate their faith while working. Because the Roman Catholic college did not limit hiring to employees who share similar faith views, employment barriers were not created for applicants less interested in integrating faith at work. Another explanation could be that, in the absence of actively promoting the integration of Catholic faith values, employees may not be sure if or how they should integrate their faith in this work environment.

In this study's combined sample, the majority (88%) of the respondents reported belief in a God, gods or higher power. Even though the 100% response rates of the two Protestant institutions skewed this statistic, the majority of employees at the Catholic (78.95%) and the nonsectarian (77.24%) colleges also reported belief in a God, gods or a higher power. These statistics suggest a large majority of employees on all campuses have some basic belief that could translate into positive faith integration.

Therefore, if a college wishes to encourage employees to integrate faith at work, it must be more intentional in communicating this. The Protestant Colleges appear to be doing this through their hiring policies and the integration of faith values in policy and curriculum. Research has suggested that cultures with strong faith-related values can influence even the less spiritually minded employees to engage in behaviors consistent with faith (Parboteeah & Cullen, 2010). For non-Protestant colleges, it may be that in the absence of express encouragement, employees may assume they cannot integrate their faith values and beliefs at work. Also, employees may not be sure how, specifically, to integrate faith in Catholic or non-sectarian work environments.

Hypothesis 2 Results and Discussion

Hypothesis 2 predicted there would be a statistically significant difference in faith integration between those in different occupational categories. This hypothesis was developed to identify how workers in various occupational roles might integrate faith differently from each other. Other research related to occupational faith-work integration found that those with more desirable jobs are more apt to view them as calling (Davidson & Caddell, 1994), professional jobs may result in more discretion over ethical behavior (Donaldson, 2000), and employees in different occupational groups responded differently to ethical situations (Jurkiewicz, 2010).

The three major occupational categories identified in this study were faculty, administration, and staff. The primary responsibilities of the faculty are to teach students, conduct research and serve on committees ("Sociology Teachers, Postsecondary," n.d.). Faculty members possess advanced degrees, many with doctorates. College administrators generally have advanced degrees, have other employees reporting to them, and make key policy and planning decisions ("Education Administrators, Postsecondary," n.d.). In contrast, staff positions at colleges include those who do not fall into the other two categories. Staff positions range from those requiring little to no advanced training and education (e.g., kitchen workers and janitors) to those requiring sophisticated skills and advanced degrees (e.g., grant writers and computer support personnel). Staff positions support the faculty and administrators of the college. We predicted that the three occupational groups would integrate faith at work differently because of the varying nature of the tasks they perform, the different role expectations of their positions (Ahmed, Shahzad, Fareed, Zulfiqar, & Naveed, 2014; Tull, 2014), and their different educational levels.

As shown in Table 3.4, based on Kruskal-Wallace testing of hypothesis 3, the mean ranks of five of the eight areas of faith integration were statistically significantly different with p levels of less than 0.05 ($p < 0.001$). There were differences in the integration dimensions of *group orientation enrichment, individual orientation enrichment, community ethics, nonverbal expression and verbal expression.*

For the first two integration dimensions of *group orientation enrichment* and *individual orientation enrichment*, staff employees were significantly different from the faculty and administration groups. The mean ranks of the staff group were higher for both *group orientation enrichment* and *individual orientation enrichment*. One explanation for this could be the (generally) lower levels of education and responsibility required of employees in staff roles. It may be that those with less education are more apt to perceive the need for such things as prayer or studying scripture. Also, many in staff roles may view themselves as having little direct impact on the students or their organizations. Instead, they may see themselves as helpers and supporters of the faculty and administrative employees who have higher levels of responsibility. Staff employees may perceive that *individual* and *group orientation enrichment* activities are ways to have an unofficial, indirect impact on students, coworkers or organizational outcomes. For example, though staff members may not have a direct impact on the quality of classroom instruction, they may believe that to pray for faculty and students will have a positive effect.

The analysis of the integration dimension of *community orientation ethics* indicated that the faculty group was significantly different from the staff group but not the administration group. Because the mean rank for faculty was lower for *community ethics*, it indicated that faculty reported engaging less in activities aimed at impacting the unethical behaviors of others or the organization than their coworkers in staff positions. Lower *community orientation ethics* may reflect the independent nature of most faculty positions and the personality type that seeks such independence. Two primary faculty roles involve teaching and conducting research in which the faculty member has significant autonomy in deciding content and process. Also, faculty often do not work the same hours as others in the organization and spend less time working with other college employees. Even when interacting with students, it may be perceived that a few hours of classroom time per week may not be sufficient impact students' ethical behaviors or attitudes in any significant way. These same factors help explain why, when examining the integration dimension of *self-orientation ethics*, there were no differences between faculty and the other two groups. In this instance, the faculty group likely perceives as much control over their personal ethics as administrative and staff employees.

Table 3.4. Kruskal-Wallace Results for Hypothesis 2: Influence of Occupational Category on Faith Integration

Hypothesis 2 Subcategory	Chi-Square	p Value	Occupational Category Mean Ranks
Hypothesis 2a: Occupation w/group orientation enrichment Gp Gp Gp F A S ——	26.7	<0.001	a (administration) mean rank—225.56 f (faculty) mean rank—200.07 s (staff) mean rank—272.82
Hypothesis 2b: Occupation w/individual orientation enrichment Gp Gp Gp F A S ——	24.3	<0.001	a (administration) mean rank—219.88 f (faculty) mean rank—215.64 s (staff) mean rank—281.5
Hypothesis 2c: Occupation w/community orientation ethics Gp Gp Gp F A S ——	10.5	<0.001	a (administration) mean rank—224.03 f (faculty) mean rank—214.12 s (staff) mean rank—258.91
Hypothesis 2d: Occupation w/self-orientation ethics Gp Gp Gp S F A ————	.1	0.958	a (administration) mean rank—243.51 f (faculty) mean rank—241.53 s (staff) mean rank—238.81
Hypothesis 2e: Occupation w/process/activity orientation experience Gp Gp Gp A F S ————	4.4	0.113	a (administration) mean rank—215.58 f (faculty) mean rank—239.76 s (staff) mean rank—250
Hypothesis 2f: Occupation w/outcomes experience Gp Gp Gp A F S ————	2.3	0.313	a (administration) mean rank—230.94 f (faculty) mean rank—232.05 s (staff) mean rank—251.24

(Table continues on next page.)

47

Table 3.4. (Continued)

Hypothesis 2 Subcategory	Chi-Square	p Value	Occupational Category Mean Ranks
Hypothesis 2g Occupation w/nonverbal orientation expression	27.2	<0.001	f (faculty) mean rank—212.88
Gp Gp Gp			s (staff) mean rank—214.66
F A S			a (administration) mean rank—281.7

Hypothesis 2h: Occupation w/verbal orientation expression	33.5	<0.001	f (faculty) mean rank—220.62
Gp Gp Gp			s (staff) mean rank—210.29
F A S			a (administration) mean rank—289.48

The integration categories of *outcomes orientation enrichment* and *process/activity orientation enrichment* relate to the meaning or satisfaction employees associate with the work they perform. For *outcomes* and *process/activity orientation enrichment*, there were no significant differences between the faculty, staff and administration groups. We did not expect that the three groups would be similar in the *enrichment orientation* category. We anticipated that faculty who teach and research in areas they are highly interested and educated would experience higher levels of *enrichment* than the other two groups because of meaningful teaching or research processes or outcomes. However, this research suggests that employees of differing education levels, skill requirements, and task responsibilities can see their work processes and outcomes in similarly meaningful ways. Alternatively, it could be that there is something about a college work environment that provides an opportunity for employees of all groups to see the meaning in what they do or the outcomes they achieve.

In the final two categories of *nonverbal orientation expression* and *verbal orientation expression*, individuals falling in the staff category were significantly different from the faculty and administrative groups. The higher mean ranks of the staff employees suggest that this group is more likely to integrate faith by talking about their faith and by wearing or placing faith-related items in the workplace. One explanation for this could be that staff employees do not perceive their roles as officially influencing others in the same ways faculty and administrators do. Because faculty and administrators have direct authority over students and other employees, they may believe expressing faith or spiritual beliefs and values at work might be the misuse of position power. Therefore, faculty and administrators may refrain from overt faith related discussion or the use of symbols or dress in their formal roles. In a similar fashion, faculty and administrators may believe they could be accused more readily of coercive proselytizing because they are more scrutinized in their public roles. Previous research also cited that in recent years, academia has conveyed the idea that faith is to be kept private and not openly discussed in teaching or scholarship (Gross & Simmons, 2007). Certainly, this could cause those in highly visible academic roles to be reluctant to share their faith openly. A final explanation for this could be that as education levels increase (or other factors associated with educational attainment such as intelligence), the level of faith or spirituality decreases (Winseman, 2003; Zuckerman, Silberman, & Hall, 2013).

Recommendations

The fields of human resource management and organizational development have established that employee training can be a powerful tool for developing employee skills, facilitating positive change, and increasing productivity within organizations (Aguinis & Kraiger, 2009; Winfred, Winston, Edens, & Bell, 2003). Also, some have cited the effectiveness of organizations in developing higher levels of workplace spirituality, resulting in changed attitudes and behaviors (Heaton, Schmidt-Wilk, & Travis, 2004) and associated individual and organizational benefits (Baldacchino, 2015; Bandsuch & Cavanagh, 2005; Drenkard, 2008). Therefore, we suggest Miller's (2013) model be used as a tool within a faith-work training curriculum. The results of the present research can assist in further developing the content and delivery of this training. It is expected that such training could result in a number of the positive faith and work related individual and organizational outcomes previously discussed in this paper. Therefore, we make two training-related recommendations to assist those interested in promoting faith-work integration.

The first recommendation pertains to the type of organizational context in which employee's work. This research indicated that faith integration is lower in environments in which faith beliefs and values are not openly encouraged. In the case of the Roman Catholic institution, simply being affiliated with a religion does not mean more faith integration. Therefore, if organizations wish to derive the benefits of faith integration, they must intentionally communicate policies and provide training to encourage integration. Training that provides information about legal protections under Title VII of the 1964 Civil Rights Act and an understanding of religion-related harassment (Cantone & Weiner, 2011; Soni, 2014) may create a more tolerant work environment. If organizations address this deficiency employees will perceive them as *faith-friendly* (Miller & Ewest, 2015) and they may accrue related benefits. Even employees who are not overly spiritual can be influenced and changed by working in spiritual organizations (Heaton et al., 2004; Pawar, 2009). Many of the techniques promoted using Miller's (2007, 2013) model such as *ethics integration* and *experience integration*, can be used by employees without being perceived as part of their personal faith.

The second recommendation relates to occupational position. In this study, it appears that those who have direct authority over others might be more reluctant to express faith verbally or nonverbally. Therefore, training should cover how to integrate faith appropriately when occupying positions of power. Also, research results indicated that employees in all types of positions can view work as related to calling and perceive work-related processes and outcomes as meaningful. Therefore, an important component of this training would be to provide specific and varied examples of meaningful *process/activities* and *outcomes integration* for all types of positions. These could be obtained by interviewing employees in a variety of organizational occupations.

Summary

The majority of working adults claim to have faith or to be spiritual; in this particular study, 88% claimed belief in God, gods or a higher spiritual power. Other research has established that employees integrate this faith or spirituality at work in a variety of ways (Miller, 2007; Mitroff & Denton, 1999; Weaver & Agle, 2002) and that it can be important to them to do so (Ashmos & Duchon, 2000; Mitroff & Denton, 1999). Therefore, the results of this study on two factors related to faith integration can be very helpful in providing organizations with guidance in this area. This research indicates that those employed at Protestant faith-affiliated colleges are more likely to integrate faith than those at Roman Catholic or nonsectarian colleges, and that those in different occupational groups integrate faith differently from each other. These findings can be useful to companies wishing to be faith-friendly in their policies, practices and training. This also suggests that organizations might see beneficial outcomes from using a well-developed faith and work training curriculum.

NOTE

1.   Though the terminology "separation of church and state" is not in the U.S. Constitution, public universities do have some restrictions with respect to religions expressions and displays.

REFERENCES

Aguinis, H., & Kraiger, K. (2009, January). Benefits of training and development for individuals and teams, organizations, and society. *Annual Review of Psychology, 60*, 451–474. doi:10.1146/annurev.psych.60.110707.163505

Ahmed, K., Shahzad, F., Fareed, Z., Zulfiqar, B., & Naveed, T. (2014, September). Impact of relationship, task & role conflict on teaching performance in educational institutes. *International Journal of Management, Accounting & Economics, 1*(2), 101–112.

Ashmos, D. P., & Duchon, D. (2000). Spirituality at work: A conceptualization and measure. *Journal of Management Inquiry, 9*(2), 134–145. doi:10.1177/105649260092008

Astin, A. W., Astin, H. S., Lindholm, J. A., & Bryant, A. N. (2005). *The spiritual lives of college students: A national study of students: Search for meaning and purpose.* Retrieved from http://spirituality.ucla.edu/docs/reports/Spiritual_Life_College_Students_Full_Report.pdf

Baldacchino, D. (2015). Spiritual care education of health care Professionals. *Religions, 6*(2), 594–613. doi:10.3390/rel6020594

Bandsuch, M. R., & Cavanagh, G. F. (2005). Integrating spirituality into the workplace: Theory and practice. *Journal of Management, Spirituality & Religion, 2*(2), 221–254. doi:10.1080/14766080509518581

Bell-Ellis, R., Jones, L. C., Longstreth, M., & Neal, J. (2013). Faith related determinants of organizational commitment. In J. Neal (Ed.), *Handbook of faith and spirituality in the workplace: Emerging research and practice* (pp. 345–379). New York, NY: Springer.

Benefiel, M., Fry, L. W., & Geigle, D. (2014). Spirituality and religion in the workplace: History, theory, and research. *Psychology of Religion and Spirituality, 6*(3), 175–187. doi:10.1037/a0036597

Bradley, J., & Kauanui, S. K. (2003). Comparing spirituality on three southern California college campuses. *Journal of Organizational Change Management, 16*(4), 448–462. doi:10.1108/09534810310484181

Caldwell, C., & Canuto-Carranco, M. (2010). "Organizational terrorism" and moral choices—Exercising voice when the leader is the problem. *Journal of Business Ethics, 97*(1), 159–171. doi:10.1007/s10551-010-0502-5

Cantone, J. A., & Wiener, R. L. (2011). Religion at work: Evaluating hostile work environment religious discrimination claims (Doctoral dissertation). The University of Nebraska-Lincoln). *ProQuest Dissertations and Theses,* 192. Retrieved from http://search.proquest.com/docview/893135238?accountid=12084

Davidson, J. C., & Caddell, D. P. (1994). Religion and the meaning of work. *J Scientific Study of Religion Journal for the Scientific Study of Religion, 33*(2), 135–147. doi:10.1111/jssr.2006.45.issue-2

Dhiman, S., & Marques, J. (2011). The role and need of offering workshops and courses on workplace spirituality. *Journal of Management Development, 30*(9), 816–835. doi:10.1108/02621711111164312

Donaldson, T. (2000). Are business managers "professionals"? *Business Ethics Quarterly, 10*(1), 83. doi:10.2307/3857697

Drenkard, K. N. (2008, January 1). Current models: Integrating human caring science into a professional nursing practice model. *Critical Care Nursing Clinics of North America, 20,* 403–414. doi:10.1016/j.ccell.2008.08.008

Education Administrators, Postsecondary. (n.d.). Retrieved from http://www.onetonline.org/link/summary/11-9033.00#WorkActivities

Flax, B. (2011, July 9). The true meaning of separation of church and state. Retrieved from http://www.forbes.com/sites/billflax/2011/07/09/the-true-meaning-of-separation-of-church-and-state/2/

Gaddis, I., & Klasen, S. (2014, July). Economic development, structural change, and women's labor force participation. *Journal of Population Economics, 27*(3), 639–681. doi:10.1007/s00148-013-0488-2

Gallagher, S. V. (2007). Speaking of vocation in an age of spirituality. *Change: The Magazine of Higher Learning, 39*(3), 32–37. doi:10.3200/CHNG.39.3.32-37

Gallup, G. H., Jr. (2002). Religion for Corporate America. Retrieved from http://www.gallup.com/poll/6679/religion-corporate-america.aspx

Gross, N., & Simmons, S. (2007). *How religious are America's college and university professors?* doi:http://religion.ssrc.org/reforum/Gross_Simmons.pdf

Heaton, D. P., Schmidt-Wilk, J., & Travis, F. (2004). Constructs, methods, and measures for researching spirituality in organizations. *Journal of Organizational Change Management, 17*(1), 62–82. doi:10.1108/09534810410511305

Hicks, D. A. (2003). *Religion and the workplace: Pluralism, spirituality, leadership.* Cambridge, England: Cambridge University Press.

Hodge, D. R., & Derezotes, D. S. (2008). Postmodernism and spirituality: Some pedagogical implications for teaching content on spirituality. *Journal of Social Work Education, 44*(1), 103–124. doi:10.5175/jswe.2008.200500598

Jurkiewicz, C. L. (2010). Ethics and spirituality in crisis. In R. A. Giacalone & C. L. Jurkiewicz (Eds.), *Handbook of workplace spirituality and organizational performance* (pp. 87–98). Armonk, NY: M.E. Sharpe.

Krejcie, R. V., & Morgan, D. W. (1970). Determining sample size for research activities. *Educational and Psychological Measurement, 30*, 607–610. doi:file:C:/Users/Daemen%20College/Downloads/KrejcieandMorgan_article%20(1).pdf

Lewin, R., & Regine, B. (2000). *The soul at work: Listen, respond, let go: Embracing complexity science for business success.* New York, NY: Simon & Schuster.

López, L. H., Ramos, R. R., & Ramos, S. R. (2009). Spiritual behaviour in the workplace as a topic for research. *Journal of Management, Spirituality & Religion, 6*(4), 273–285. doi:10.1080/14766080903290119

Marsden, G. M. (2015). Religious discrimination in academia. *Society, 52*(1), 19–22. doi:10.1007/s12115-014-9853-3

McNight, R. (2005). Spirituality in the workplace. In J. D. Adams (Ed.), *Transforming work*: A collection of organizational transformation readings (2nd ed., pp. 160–169). Alexandria, VA: Miles River Press.

Meinert, D. (2014, April 1). Creating an ethical work: Business decisions aren't always black and white. How can you trust that your workers will do the right thing? Retrieved from http://www.shrm.org/publications/hrmagazine/editorialcontent/2014/0414/pages/0414-ethical-workplace-culture.aspx

Miller, D. W. (2007). *God at work: The history and promise of the faith at work movement.* Oxford, England: Oxford University Press.

Miller, D. W. (2013). *The integration profile (TIP) faith and work integration scale* [Research instrument obtained from www.princeton.edu.faith and work].

Miller, D. W., & Ewest, T. (2011, January). Rethinking the impact of religion on business values: Understanding its reemergence and measuring its manifestations. Retrieved from http://www.princeton.edu/faithandwork/research/tip/current/

Miller, D. W., & Ewest, T. (2013). The integration box (TIB): An individual, and institutional faith, religion and spirituality at work assessment tool. In J. Neal (Ed.), *Handbook of faith and spirituality in the workplace: Emerging research and practice* (pp. 403–417). New York, NY: Springer.

Miller, D. W., & Ewest, T. (2015). A new framework for analyzing organizational workplace religion and spirituality. *Journal of Management, Spirituality & Religion, 12*(4), 305–328. doi:10.1080/14766086.2015.1054864

Mitroff, I. I., & Denton, E. A. (1999). *A spiritual audit of corporate America: A hard look at spirituality, religion, and values in the workplace.* San Francisco, CA: Jossey-Bass.

Parboteeah, K. P., & Cullen, J. B. (2010). Ethical climates and spirituality: An exploratory examination of theoretical links. In R. A. Giacalone & C. L. Jurkiewicz (Eds.), *Handbook of workplace spirituality and organizational performance* (2nd ed., pp. 99–113). Armonk, NY: M.E. Sharpe.

Pawar, B. S. (2009, December 15). Workplace spirituality facilitation: A comprehensive model. *Journal of Business Ethics, 90*(3), 375–386. doi:10.1007/s10551-009-0047-7

Ramarajan, L., & Reid, E. (2013). Shattering the myth of separate worlds: Negotiating nonwork identities at work. *Academy of Management Review, 38*(4), 621–644. doi:10.5465/amr.2011.0314

Russell, M. L. (2007). The secret of marketplace leadership success: Constructing a comprehensive framework for the effective integration of leadership, faith and work. *Journal of Religious Leadership, 6*(1), 71–101.

Saad, L. (2014, August 29). The "40-hour" workweek is actually longer—By seven hours. Retrieved from http://www.gallup.com/poll/175286/hour-workweek-actually-longer-seven-hours.aspx

Sociology teachers, postsecondary. (n.d.). Retrieved from http://www.onetonline.org/link/summary/25-1067.00#WorkActivities

Soni, P. (2014). Title VII religious discrimination and contemporary socio-religious issues in a post-9/11 America: The scope and shortcomings of religious discrimination protection under Title VII. *University of Pennsylvania Journal of Business Law, 16*(2), 599–629.

Sullivan, P. M. (2008). Spirit: A vital key to engagement at work. In M. I. Finney (Ed.), *Building high-performance people and organizations* (Vol. 2, pp. 79–94). Westport, CT: Praeger.

Thompson, D., & Miller-Perrin, C. (2003). Understanding vocation: Discerning and responding to God's call, *Leaven, 11*(1). Retrieved from http://digitalcommons.pepperdine.edu/leaven/vol11/iss1/11

Tull, A. A. (2014). An examination of community college senior student affairs officers', role perception, job satisfaction, and propensity to leave their institutions. *College Student Affairs Journal, 32*(1), 53–65.

Turi, D. M. (2012). *The relationship between student engagement and the development of character in mission driven faith-based colleges and universities as measured by the national survey of student engagement* (Unpublished doctoral dissertation). Thesis (Ph. D.) - Seton Hall University. Seton Hall University Dissertations and Theses (ETDs). Paper 1801.

Vasconcelos, A. F. (2015). The spiritually-based organization: A theoretical review and its potential role in the third millennium. *Cadernos EBAPE.BR, 13*(1), 183–205. doi:10.1590/1679-395110386

Weaver, G. R., & Agle, B. R. (2002). Religiosity and ethical behavior in organizations: A symbolic interactionist perspective. *Academy of Management Review, 27*(1), 77–97. doi:10.5465/amr.2002.5922390

Winfred, J. A., Winston, J. B., Edens, P. S., & Bell, S. T. (2003). Effectiveness of training in organizations: A meta-analysis of design and evaluation features. *Journal of Applied Psychology, 88*(2), 234–245. doi:10.1037/0021-9010.88.2.234

Winseman, A. (2003, February 4). Does more educated really = less religious? Retrieved from http://www.gallup.com/poll/7729/does-more-educated-really-less-religious.aspx

Zuckerman, M., Silberman, J., & Hall, J. A. (2013, November). The relation between intelligence and religiosity: A meta-analysis and some proposed explanations. *Personality and Social Psychology Review, 17*(4), 325–354. doi:10.1177/1088868313497266

CHAPTER 4

WORK AS WORSHIP

Bringing Meaning to Work Through an Integrated Faith

Simone Meskelis and J. Lee Whittington
University of Dallas

The quest for meaning is an innate human need (Emmons, 1999; Frankl, 1959). The workplace has emerged as the primary arena for fulfilling this need (Ciulla, 2000; Conger, 1994; Markiewicz, Devine, & Kausilas, 2000). This quest for meaningfulness and purpose is a core concern of the emerging positive organizational scholarship movement (Cameron & Dutton, 2003; Nelson & Cooper, 2007). Meaningfulness means that both the work itself and the context within which the work is performed is *perceived* as purposeful and significant (Pratt & Ashworth, 2003). The idea of purposeful work extends beyond a focus on profit maximization or increasing shareholder wealth by embracing the idea that the primary purpose of the organization is to improve the well-being of all stakeholders (Mackey & Sisodia, 2013). When people are pursuing a profound purpose or engaging in work that is personally important they experience significant positive effects including increased levels of engagement, commitment, empowerment, satisfaction, and a sense of fulfillment (Cameron, 2012).

Faith and Work: Christian Perspectives, Research, and Insights Into the Movement
pp. 57–76
Copyright © 2018 by Information Age Publishing

This heightened focus on meaning and purpose is converging with an emphasis on the importance of spirituality in organizations. Indeed, there is a growing recognition that employees are seeking to both nourish their inner life through work and to have their inner life inform their work (Ashmos & Duchon, 2000). The contemporary study of spirituality is based on a person's "inner life." Those who study spirituality emphasize the distinction between spirituality and the practices of religion. For these researchers, spirituality has a unifying sense of wholeness that aligns personal values, and the ultimate purposes of life. A person's spirituality allows them to develop strong connections with coworkers and provides a baseline for aligning their core beliefs with the values of the organization (Argyle, 2013; Mitroff & Denton, 1999). Research on the impact of spirituality in the workplace has increased significantly over the years and spirituality has been associated with a variety of positive outcomes including affective commitment, intrinsic work satisfaction, and job involvement (Milliman, Czaplewski, & Ferguson, 2003; Rego & Pina e Cunha, 2008).

The convergence between spirituality and the quest for meaningfulness is reflected in Saks (2011) suggestion that an individual's spirituality would have a direct impact on their experience of meaningfulness at work. This connection was supported by Chan-Serafin, Brief, and George (2013) who found a significant positive relationship between an individual's level of spirituality and the meaningfulness of their work. Saks (2011) also theorized that this spirituality-meaningfulness connection would be the basis for higher levels of employee engagement. Following this suggestion, there has been a recent call to integrate these issues (May, Gilson, & Harter, 2004; Shuck & Rose, 2013). Rather than viewing spirituality, meaningfulness, and engagement as independent constructs, an integration of these research streams would allow each of these topics to be reframed in a broader and more inclusive context (Shuck & Rose, 2013).

We have addressed the call for research that integrates spirituality, meaningfulness and engagement. However, we make a crucial departure from the extant research. Rather than focusing on spirituality, our research examines the impact of an integrated faith on the experience of meaningfulness at work. Our emphasis on faith integration is a distinctively Christian approach to spirituality that is based on our understanding of the biblical perspective although certain things are designated as sacred, everything in life is related to God (Sherman & Hendricks, 1987; Whittington, 2015).

In this chapter, we report the results of field studies that were conducted to examine the relationships among integrated faith, meaningfulness, and engagement. Our model is depicted in Figure 4.1. According to this model, the integrated faith of the individual is the antecedent to the

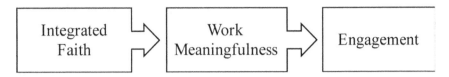

Figure 4.1.   Conceptual model.

experience of meaningful work. Meaningfulness in turn is proposed to have a direct impact on the level of employee engagement.

The focal point of our model is the connection between meaningfulness and engagement, therefore we begin our chapter with a discussion of the various organizational processes that contribute to an employee's experience of meaningful work. While these contextual factors certainly contribute to a sense of meaning, we believe that individuals may also bring a sense of meaning to their work through a sense of calling which is informed by their personal faith. Thus, we explore the role of faith integration as an antecedent to meaningful work. The final stage of our model depicts the relationship between the experience of meaningfulness and the level of employee engagement. We tested this model in two field studies and report the results of those investigations in this chapter.

Meaningfulness

The quest for meaning is an innate human need (Emmons, 1999; Frankl, 1959). The workplace has emerged as the primary arena for fulfilling this need (Ciulla, 2000; Conger, 1994; Markiewicz et al., 2000). For many people, work satisfies the need for significance by allowing both the expression of personal uniqueness and the opportunity to make a purposeful contribution while connecting with others (Diddams & Whittington, 2003; Diddams, Whittington, & Davigo, 2005).

Meaningfulness means that both the work itself and the context within which the work is performed is perceived as purposeful and significant (Pratt & Ashforth, 2003). These perceptions are derived from multiple sources. Pratt and Ashforth (2003) distinguish between meaningfulness *at* work and meaningfulness *in* work. Meaningfulness *at* work can be enhanced through the inspirational motivation of transformational leaders who connect the individual employee's role with the overarching mission and purpose of the organization. These leaders cast a compelling vision that appeals to employees who want to be part of and contribute to something bigger than themselves (Peters & Waterman, 1982: Pratt & Ashforth, 2003).

Meaningfulness in the work involves organizational practices that enrich the job themselves. Among the practices that may increase meaningfulness in the work are job redesign efforts (Hackman & Oldham, 1975; 1976), increased employee involvement, efforts to clarify the connection between meeting performance expectations and rewards. These practices nurture the sense of calling an employee may experience and are designed to enhance the individual employees fit with their job.

In addition to these organizational initiatives, employees may also create meaning in their work through *job crafting* (Wrzesniewski & Dutton, 2001). Job crafting is a form of positive deviance through which employees make physical and cognitive changes to their assigned tasks or in the various relational boundaries of their work. By cognitively reframing and restructuring the tasks and relationships involved in their work, employees may be able to enhance the personal meaningfulness of their work (Wrzesniewski, 2003).

Integrated Faith as an Antecedent to Meaningfulness

In the previous section we argued that organizations may enhance an employee's experience of meaningfulness *in* their work (Pratt & Ashforth, 2003). Job design, and an employee's fit with that job, are important determinants of meaningfulness in work. While organizational aspects and job characteristics are important extrinsic sources of meaningfulness, the actual experience of meaningfulness is based on perceptions. Therefore, the meaning associated with a particular task or organizational purpose may vary widely across individuals (Pratt & Ashforth, 2003).

The subjective nature of meaningfulness is emphasized in the differentiation between jobs, careers, and callings (Wrzesniewski, McCauley, Rozin, & Schwartz, 1997). According to this framework, there are significant differences in how people make meaning of their work. Interestingly, employees who are performing the same job done in the same organization, may view the job from each of these perspectives (Wrzesniewski, 2003).

Those who view their *work as a job* see work as primarily a means to obtaining the financial support they need to live away from work. People who view their work as a job form a compliant relationship with their organization and seek to avoid punishment while focusing on personal gains (Pratt & Ashforth, 2003). For these people, work has only instrumental value.

Those who view their work from the *career* perspective are actively seeking the rewards associated with advancement through an organization or occupational structure. The dominant focus of career-oriented individuals is the increased pay, prestige, and status that accompany promotions. These individuals may have a more engaged relationship with their work than those who see the work as a job (Bakker, Albrecht, & Leiter, 2011; Parker, Bindl & Strauss, 2010). Career oriented individuals identify with their organizations and seek greater levels of involvement and individual contribution (Pratt & Ashforth, 2003). The increased level of involvement may be viewed as instrumental to gaining greater power and status in the organization while improving their visibility with those in the organizational hierarchy who are responsible for the promotion decisions.

The job and career perspectives view work as having only instrumental value. People who view their *work as a calling* see their work as having intrinsic value. They believe that their work contributes to the greater good of not only their organization but society as a whole. These individuals do not work for financial rewards or for advancement, but for the fulfillment that doing the work brings (Cameron, 2012; Wrzesniewski, 2003). This sense of calling usually involves two main elements. Calling involves helping others because of a strong sense of destiny or moral duty, and callings are also intrinsically valued (Dik & Duffy, 2009).

The concept of work as a calling has been further refined by Pratt, Pradies, and Lepistro (2013) who identify three distinct conceptions of work as a calling. In this framework, calling is not viewed as a primary orientation but rather a combination of craftsmanship, serving, and kinship. The *craftsmanship* orientation is based solely on fulfillment that comes from the work itself. The craftsmanship orientation seeks to create meaningfulness through "doing well." A craftsman does his or her work with skill and expertise. For the craftsman developing pride in his or her work is not a means to an end, but is an end in itself.

A sense of calling may also be based solely on helping others. This is referred to as a *serving* orientation. Employees with a serving orientation seek to create meaningfulness through "doing good." This serving orientation focuses on meaningfulness and the perceived effect on the beneficiaries of the work. People with a serving orientation evaluate their work is worth doing when it improves the lives of others or advances a cause.

Finally, a *kinship* orientation suggests a relational or socially based orientation to work. Each of these orientations focuses on the experience of meaningfulness in the workplace (Pratt et al., 2013). The kinship orientation creates meaningfulness through "doing with." This orientation focuses on the quality of relationships one creates for his or her work, not on the work itself. For people with the kinship orientation, the workplace is a venue for creating a sense of community. This view of the workplace has increased importance as traditional sources of social support decline (Ciulla, 2000).

Viewing work as a calling takes on an additional meaning for those who view their *work as an act of worship*. This approach is based on the holistic perspective that seeks to integrate God into every dimension of an individual's life (Diddams et al., 2005; Sherman & Hendricks, 1987). This comprehensive and unifying principle is clearly stated in the *Shema* (Hebrew for *Hear*) recorded in Deuteronomy 6:4-9. The integration of God is called for in the command to "love the Lord your God with *all* your heart and with *all* your soul and with *all* your mind (emphasis added). The practical implications of this commitment include diligently teaching God's principles to the next generation and applying them throughout the daily routines of life—"when you sit in your house and when you walk along the way and when you lie down and when your rise up." According to this passage, God's principles are to permeate our work ("bind them on your hands"), our thoughts ("they shall be as frontals on your forehead"), and guide our family life in the home ("write them on the doorposts of your house and on your gates").

This holistic perspective extends to the New Testament. As described earlier, Paul encouraged people to live their entire lives as an act of worship (Romans 12:2). This perspective on success is also reflected in Paul's frequent admonition to "walk worthy" (Whittington, 2015; Ephesians 4:1; Colossians 1:10; 1 Thessalonians 2:12). This comprehensive integration of life is also described in the "house code" passages of the New Testament letters to the Ephesians and the Colossians where Paul describes the practical implications of being "filled with the Spirit" (Ephesians 5:18) and "letting the word of Christ richly dwell within you" (Colossians 3:16). The comprehensive implication of being filled with the Spirit is expressed in Paul's letter to the Colossian church: "*Whatever* you do in word or deed, do *all* in the name of the Lord Jesus, giving thanks through Him to God the Father" (Colossians 3:17; emphasis added).

The biblical perspective presented here encourages people to integrate their faith in every arena of their lives. As such, this perspective is consistent with intrinsically religious individuals who internalize their faith and use that faith as a guide in all other aspects of their lives (Allport & Ross, 1967). For these people, work is reframed as an act of worship and the workplace becomes a venue for the expression of their faith. Work is both a source of meaningfulness and a vehicle through which individuals can express their faith (Duffy, Reid, & Dik, 2010). Viewing work as worship does not exclude the craftsmanship, serving, or kinship perspective of calling. Indeed, doing work with excellence, serving others, and enjoying the sense of community the workplace provides are consistent with the holistic perspective of life and work as worship. For these individuals, faith is a key component of their identity. Thus we expect that

Hypothesis 1: Integrated faith will be positively related to an individual's experience of meaningfulness in their work.

The Meaningfulness-Engagement Connection

Employee engagement was initially conceptualized as "the simultaneous employment and expression of a person's 'preferred self' in task behaviors that promote connections to work and to others, personal presence, and active full role performances" (Kahn, 1990, p. 700). He identified three psychological conditions that trigger individual engagement: psychological meaningfulness, psychological safety, and psychological availability. Psychological meaningfulness is experienced when individuals feel "worthwhile, useful and valuable—as though they make a difference and are not taken for granted" (Kahn, 1990, p. 700). Results from Khan's ethnographic study showed a positive relationship between psychological meaningfulness and personal engagement. Kahn also identified task characteristics, role characteristics, and work interactions as the critical antecedents of psychological meaningfulness.

Contemporary research supports conceptualization of engagement as a multidimensional construct that captures an individual's cognitive, emotional, and behavioral investment in their work (Macey & Schneider, 2008; Rich, Lepine, & Crawford, 2010). A growing body of evidence links employee engagement to a variety of positive outcomes including performance (Demerouti, Cropanzano, Bakker, & Leiter, 2010), positive emotions (Bakker, 2011), commitment, health, turnover intentions, and performance (Halbesleben, 2010).

Recent research has confirmed a strong positive relationship between meaningfulness and engagement. May et al. (2004) examined the impact of Kahn's three psychological conditions on employee engagement and found that meaningfulness was the strongest predictor of engagement. Consistent with these findings, Olivier and Rothmann (2007) also found a significant correlation between psychological meaningfulness and engagement. Albrecht (2013) found that the satisfaction of the need for meaningful work was related to engagement. Soane et al. (2013) report a significant positive relationship between meaningful work and employee engagement with work. Furthermore, they demonstrated that engagement fully mediated the relationship between meaningfulness and absence from work. Based on this literature we expect that meaningfulness will have a positive relationship with the level of employee engagement.

Hypothesis 2: The experience of meaningfulness will be positively related to the level of employee engagement.

Furthermore, we expect that the relationship between individual's level of faith integration and the level of engagement will be mediated by the experience of meaningfulness. Thus,

Hypothesis 3: The relationship between the integrated faith and employee engagement will be mediated by meaningfulness.

METHOD

Sample

Two field studies were conducted involving participants within the Southwestern United States. The first sample involved students enrolled in a professional MBA program located in the Southwestern United States. The majority of the participants (71%) were full-time employees. As an incentive to participate in the online survey, participants were entered into a random drawing to receive one of several iPads. Two hundred and eighty-two participants took the survey and 172 ($N = 172$) fully completed the questionnaire. The majority of the respondents were male (60.3%) and White/Caucasian (46%). The majority of respondents (62%) reported themselves as Christian, while 10.3% identified themselves as Muslims, and 9.2% reported that they were Hindu.

The second sample was obtained through employees from insurance companies in the Southwestern United States. As an incentive to participate in the online survey, participants were also offered the chance to enter a random drawing to receive one of several iPads. Three hundred and twenty participants took the survey and 260 ($N = 260$) fully completed the questionnaire. The majority of the respondents were female (78.1%), White/Caucasian (82.8%). Finally, most respondents (87%) reported to practice a Christian faith.

Measures

Integrated faith was measured using 14 items from the Mature Religiosity scale developed by Pieper, Van Uden, and De Vries-Schot (2012). This scale captures the degree to which an individual's spirituality is integrated throughout all dimensions of life. A 5-point Likert scale ranging from 1 (*strongly disagree*) to 5 (*strongly agree*) was used to measure responses to statements such as "I have the idea that I entrust myself more and more to God or a Higher Power," "The meaning and significance of my life is in my relationship with God," "My faith is oriented to values that transcend physical and social needs," and "I believe sincerely, not mainly out of obligation or fear." A total score for faith integration was obtained by averaging responses across all of these items. The reliability coefficient for faith integration is 0.98 in both samples.

Meaningful Work was measured using items from the Work and Meaning Inventory (WAMI; Steger, Dik, and Duffy (2012). This self-report instrument assesses three dimensions of meaningfulness: positive meaning (PM), meaning making through work (MMTW), and greater good motivations (GGM). PM captures the idea that individuals evaluate their work to matter and to be meaningful, while MMTW translates the concept of individuals having a broader context of their work. Finally, GGM reflects the perspective that work has more meaning if it impacts other individuals (Steger et al., 2012).

Each item in the WAMI scale was measured in a 5-point Likert scale ranging from 1 (*absolutely untrue*) to 5 (*absolutely true*). Positive meaning (PM) was measured with four items, such as, "I have found a meaningful career." The reliability coefficient for the PM subscale was 0.85 in the first sample and 0.90 in the second sample. Meaning making through work (MMTW) was measured through three items, such as, "I understand how my work contributes to my life's meaning." The reliability coefficient for the MMTW subscale for each of the samples was respectively 0.78 and 0.84. Three items measured greater good motivation (GGM), such as, "The work I do serves a greater purpose." The coefficient for the GGM subscale by sample was 0.78 and 0.80. We did not differentiate among these subscales in our theoretical model, so we consolidated these factors into a single measure by averaging the responses to the three dimensions. This total score for meaningfulness engagement has a reliability of 0.90 and 0.85 for each sample.

Engagement was measured using a self-report scale consisting of 18 items from Rich et al. (2010). This measure captures three distinct dimensions: physical engagement, emotional engagement, and cognitive engagement. Physical engagement refers to the energy exerted and the physical involvement within the job. It was measured through items such as "I exert full effort to my job." Emotional engagement apprehends the level of pleasantness and enthusiasm experienced at work and it was captured through statements such as "I feel energetic at my job." Finally, cognitive engagement measures the level and intensity of focus and concentration applied while performing work related tasks. Cognitive engagement was measured with statements such as "at work, my mind is focused on my job." Each item was measured with a 5-point Likert scale that ranged from 1 (*strongly disagree*) to 5 (*strongly agree*). In our model we did not differentiate among the engagement subscales, so we created a total score for engagement by averaging the responses to the three dimensions. This total score for engagement has a reliability of 0.88 for both samples.

RESULTS

Table 4.1 presents the means, standard deviations, and correlations of the variables tested in both studies. The correlations indicate that the level of faith integration is positively related to the experience of meaningfulness ($r = 0.267$, $p < .01$; $r = 0.318$, $p < 0.01$) and the level of employee engagement ($r = 0.223$, $p < .01$; $r = 0.261$, $p < 0.01$).

Hypotheses 1 and 2 were tested through simple two-variable linear regressions. The usage of this method allows for the identification of a model that can predict results to one variable based on its relationship with another variable (Field, 2013). We anticipated in our hypotheses that faith integration would be related to work meaningfulness (Hypothesis 1), and work meaningfulness would be related to engagement (Hypothesis 2). Hypothesis 3 was tested through a simple mediation model using linear regression through the "Process" tool developed by Hayes (2013), based on the ordinary least squares regression method. This approach also allows for the testing of the size of indirect effects. This test is used to identify the effect of the mediator in transmitting an effect from the independent to the dependent variable. Results of the effects observed through linear regressions are depicted in Figure 4.2.

Results of Hypothesis 1. As shown in Figure 4.2, the level of faith integration is significantly and positively related to their experience of meaningfulness in each of our samples. (Study 1: $\beta = 0.32$, $p < 0.0001$, $R^2 = 0.07$; Study 2: $\beta = 0.27$, $p < 0.0001$, $R^2 = 0.10$).

Results of hypothesis 2. The experience of meaningfulness is significantly and positively related to the level of engagement in both samples (Study

Table 4.1. Correlations and Reliabilities

	Variables	N	Mean	SD	1	2	3
Sample 1	1. Work meaningfulness	172	3.74	0.79	0.94		
	2. Engagement		3.94	0.70	.689**	0.96	
	3. Integrated faith		3.89	0.96	.267*8	.223**	0.97
Sample 2	1. Work meaningfulness	260	3.94	0.68	0.93		
	2. Engagement		4.21	0.55	.574**	0.96	
	3. Integrated faith		4.18	.318**	.261**	0.97	

Note: **Correlation is significant at the 0.01 level (2-tailed). *Correlation is significant at the 0.05 level (2-tailed).

1: $\beta = 0.60$, p <0.0001, $R^2 = 0.47$; Study 2 ($\beta = 0.44$, p <0.0001, $R^2 = 0.34$). Thus, Hypothesis 2 is supported.

Results of Hypothesis 3. As demonstrated in Figure 4.2, integrated faith is positively related to work meaningfulness ($\beta = 0.21$, p <0.000, $R^2 = 0.07$; $\beta = 0.27$, p <0.0001, $R^2 = 0.10$.). Work meaningfulness is in turn positively related to engagement ($\beta = 0.60$, p <0.000, $R^2 = 0.49$; $\beta = 0.44$, p <0.0001, $R^2 = 0.34$). Results from both studies also show that the direct effect of integrated faith on engagement is not statistically significant ($\beta = 0.0273$, p =0.48; $\beta = 0.0570$, p =0.12). Therefore, in support of hypothesis 3, meaningfulness fully mediates the relationship between integrated faith and engagement.

In order to confirm the results in Hypothesis 3, we tested for the size and significance of the indirect effects using the bootstrap of confidence intervals presented by the "Process" tool. Results showed that the confidence intervals for the β did not contain zero (Field, 2013), thus we can conclude that the effects of the mediators in the examined relationships are statistically significant.

Post Hoc Analyses

In their original conception of the mature religiosity scale (MSR), Pieper et al. (2012) explicitly stated that their scale was designed to assess the maturity of Christian's faith. Although the majority of participants declared that they follow a Christian faith, our first sample included people from many faith traditions. Regardless of the religious affiliation variety, results showed a very strong overall measure of reliability. However, we were curious to see if there were any differences on the measure of MSR between the different faith traditions. In order to examine this, we did a t test to see if there was a significant difference between individuals who reported themselves as Christians ($n = 109$) and those who identified themselves as Muslims ($n = 18$) and Hindus ($n = 16$). The result of these tests are depicted in Table 4.2, but these results should be interpreted with a great deal of caution due to the extremely small subsamples of non-Christian faith traditions that made up this sample.

The sample was heavily skewed toward those who professed to be Christians. This is not surprising given the regional location of the school the respondents are attending. Interestingly Muslims reported the highest mean level of MSR, followed by Christians. There is a significant difference in the level of MSR reported by Christians (4.15) and non-Christians (3.97); however, the mean level of MSR for Christians (4.15) and Muslims (4.25) was not significantly different. There was a significant difference between Christians (4.15) and Hindus (3.65). There was also a significant difference between Muslims (4.25) and Hindus (3.65).

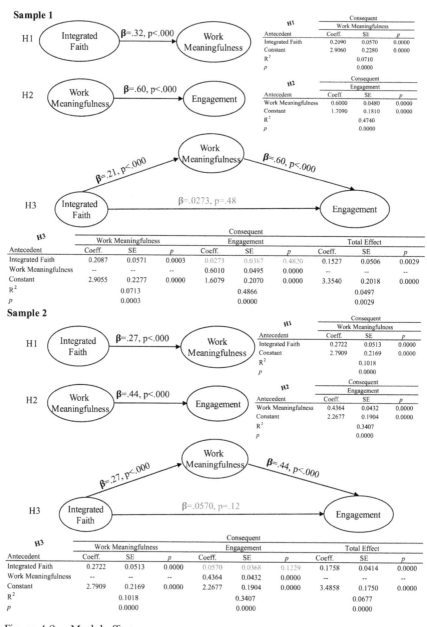

Figure 4.2.   Model effects.

Table 4.2. Comparative Analysis by Religious Affiliation and Gender

Group 1	Mean MRS	SD MRS	N	Group 2	Mean MRS	SD MRS	N	Mean t Test	p
Sample 1									
Christian	4.15	0.80	109	Non-Christian	3.37	1.20	67	Significantly different	$p < 0.0001$
Male	3.65	1.14	105	Female	4.14	0.77	69	Significantly different	0.0022
Sample 2									
Christian	4.29	0.67	217	Non-Christian	3.33	1.10	36	Significantly different	$p < 0.0001$
Male	1.16	0.86	55	Female	4.15	0.81	196	Not significantly different	0.9522

We also tested for significant difference in the result for MRS depending on the country of birth. As shown in Table 4.2, there are no significant differences in the mean level of MSR associated with the country if birth. Based on this analysis we concluded that the country of birth did not affect the level of MRS reported by the participants.

DISCUSSION

There is a growing interest in creating "positive organizations" where employees are encouraged to bring their whole selves to work in an environment where they flourish and thrive (Cameron, 2012; Cameron & Dutton, 2003; Nelson & Cooper, 2007). The foundation for creating positive organizations is the recognition that people have an inherent need for meaning (Frankl, 1959; Emmons, 1999). The desire to live for a higher purpose while connecting with others and making a positive contribution has led many people to reframe their approach to work (Ciulla, 2000; Diddams et al., 2005).

Experiencing work as meaningful involves both the work itself and the context within which the work is performed. Given the importance of meaningfulness, scholars and practitioners alike have identified organizational factors that may enhance the meaningfulness of an individual's work (Pratt & Ashforth, 2003). These interventions include the role of leaders who create meaning at work by connecting the role of individual employees to the purpose of the organization. Meaningfulness in work is achieved through practices such as job redesign that are intended to enhance the fit between the employee and their job. Employees may also engage in their own efforts to reframe their work through the process of job crafting.

Each of these initiatives are specific to the organizational context in which they occur. However, in addition to creating meaning *at* or *in* work, we believe that employees may bring meaning *to* work. This is done by employees who view their work as a calling (Wrezniewksi, 2003). For them, work has intrinsic value and is not dependent on organizational practices or leadership behaviors. The original conception of calling has been extended recently to include the craftsman, serving, and kinship perspectives (Pratt et al., 2013). The *craftsmanship* orientation is based solely on fulfillment that comes from the work itself. People with a serving orientation evaluate their work is worth doing when it improves the lives of others or advances a cause. The *kinship* orientation is a relational or socially based orientation to work. This orientation focuses on the quality of relationships one creates for his or her work, not on the work itself.

In this chapter, we have introduced another perspective on work—*work as worship*. This perspective does not ignore the instrumental value of work. Rather it also explicitly identifies the intrinsic value of work (Duffy et al., 2010; Keller & Alsdorf, 2014; Sherman & Hendricks, 1987, 1989). This view calls for an integrated faith that is similar to the intrinsic religiosity identified by Allport and Ross (1967). This perspective is based on a holistic view of life that seeks to integrate God throughout an individual's life arenas. Individuals who have an integrated faith view their work as a venue through which they can express their inherent creative capacity. Viewing work as worship does not preclude the craftsman's pride in doing excellent work. In fact, the excellence of the work is itself an act of worship. Viewing work as worship also enhances both the service and kinship perspectives.

In this chapter we developed and tested a model that demonstrates that a person's faith may be an important antecedent to the experience of meaningfulness. These results suggest that in addition to creating meaning through organizational practices, people may bring meaning to their work through a sense of calling that leads them to view their work as a "living sacrifice" and a "reasonable act of worship" (Romans 12:1-2).

The purpose of our research was to gain a deeper understanding of the meaningfulness-engagement connection by examining the factors that contribute to each of these important aspects of an employee's experience at work. Taken as a whole our research provides support for a strong connection between meaningfulness and engagement. Thus, those who seek to enhance the level of employee engagement should focus on the factors that first lead to meaningfulness.

We encourage practitioners to recognize the fact that people bring their faith to work with them every day. Along with it they bring a certain level of meaningfulness *to* the work. This should be supported and enhanced through continuous efforts to create meaning at work and meaningfulness in the work itself. Leaders should continue to cast inspiring visions that provide purpose and something significant worth striving for. Leaders should also work hard to demonstrate the contribution an individual's performance makes to that purpose. Furthermore, the efforts to create workplace environments where people can flourish and thrive should also be emphasized. Enhancing the meaningfulness-engagement connection requires a comprehensive approach that embraces each of these dimensions.

Future research should continue to investigate the interaction among individuals who *bring* a certain amount of meaningfulness to their work, and the organization's efforts to create meaningfulness both *in* and *at* work. In Figure 4.3, we suggest one model for such an investigation. In this model we suggest a variety of individual factors, in addition to spiri-

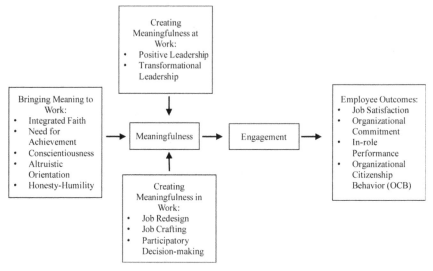

Figure 4.3.   Bringing meaning to work.

tuality, that may contribute to the meaning a person brings to the work-place. Our model suggests that this level of meaningfulness can be enhanced by efforts to inspire through authentic, positive, and transformational leadership. These factors would contribute to the experience of meaningfulness *at* work. Furthermore, job redesign, job crafting, and participatory decision making processes are proposed to enhance the relationship between what an individual brings to work and their experience of meaningfulness. These would contribute to the employee's experience of meaningfulness *in* their work.

Limitations

As with all research, we had several limitations in this study. First, our sample was made up mostly of White/Caucasian individuals who identified themselves as Christians and lived in the United States. Future examinations of the faith-meaningfulness-engagement connection should seek a more diverse sample in terms of race, faith traditions, and cultures. A second limitation is that all of the measures used in this study were obtained from the same source using self-report measures. Future research should examine the impact of faith integration, meaningfulness, and engagement on behavioral outcomes such as performance and organizational citizenship behaviors. This line of research would be strengthened through the use of social-report measures to provide an objective measure of the behaviors associated with the inside-the-head constructs of faith and meaningfulness. Finally, the research reported here is based on a cross-sectional survey. While our results indicate a positive relationship between faith integration and the experience of meaningfulness, we do not fully understand the cognitive and emotional foundations of this connection. Future research should utilize qualitative techniques to provide a deeper understanding of the relationship.

Conclusion

Concerns about the level of employee engagement continue to be raised. Yet, the awareness of the issue has not yet led to an improvement in the reported levels of engagement. Our research suggests that efforts to enhance employee engagement must be comprehensive and integrated. These efforts must begin with what the employee brings with them to the work each day. Rather than stifling spirituality and other individual differences, managers should embrace them and then seek to enhance them by creating positive organizations where the human spirit can flourish and thrive.

REFERENCES

Albrecht, S. L. (2013). Work engagement and the positive power of meaningful work. *Advances in Positive Organisational Psychology, 1,* 237–260.

Allport, G. W., & Ross, J. M. (1967). Personal religious orientation and prejudice. *Journal of Personality and Social Psychology 5*(4), 432–443.

Argyle, M. (2013). *The psychology of happiness.* New York, NY; Routledge.

Ashmos, D., & Duchon, D. (2000). Spirituality at work. *Journal of Management Inquiry, 9*(2), 134–145.

Bakker, A. B. (2011). An evidence-based model of work engagement. *Current Directions in Psychological Science, 20*(4), 265–269.

Bakker, A. B., Albrecht, S. L., & Leiter, M. P. (2011). Key questions regarding work engagement. *European Journal of Work and Organizational Psychology, 20*(1), 4–28.

Cameron, K., & Dutton, J. (2003). *Positive organizational scholarship: Foundations of a new discipline.* San Francisco, CA: Berrett-Koehler.

Cameron, K., Dutton, J., & Quinn, R. (2003). An introduction to positive organizational scholarship. In K. Cameron & J. Dutton (Eds.), *Positive organizational scholarship* (pp. 3–13). San Francisco, CA: Berrett-Koehler.

Cameron, K. S. (2012). *Positive leadership: Strategies for extraordinary performance.* San Francisco, CA: Berrett-Koehler.

Chan-Serafin, S., Brief, A. P., & George, J. M. (2013). Perspective—How does religion matter and why? Religion and the organizational sciences. *Organization Science, 24*(5), 1585–1600.

Ciulla, J. B. (2000). *The working life: The promise and betrayal of modern work.* New York, NY: Three Rivers Press.

Conger, J. A. (1994). *Spirit at work: Discovering the spirituality in leadership.* San Francisco, CA: Jossey-Bass.

Demerouti, E., Cropanzano, R., Bakker, A., & Leiter, M. 2010. From thought to action: Employee work engagement and job performance. *Work engagement: A handbook of essential theory and research* (pp. 147–163). New York, NY: Psychology Press.

Diddams, M., & Whittington, J. L. (2003). Revisiting the meaning of meaningful work. *Academy of Management Review, 28*(3), 508–512.

Diddams, M., Whittington, J. L., & Davigo, T. (2005). Creating in the name of God who creates: A whole-life model of spirituality within work. *Journal of Management, Spirituality & Religion, 2*(3), 310–331.

Dik, B. J., & Duffy, R. D. (2009). Calling and vocation at work definitions and prospects for research and practice. *The Counseling Psychologist, 37*(3), 424–450.

Duffy, R. D., Reid, L., & Dik, B. J. (2010). Spirituality, religion, and career development: Implications for the workplace. *Journal of Management, Spirituality and Religion, 7*(3), 209–221.

Emmons, R. A. (1999). *The psychology of ultimate concerns: Motivation and spirituality in personality.* New York, NY: Guilford Press.

Field, A. (2013). *Discovering statistics using IBM SPSS statistics.* Thousand Oaks, CA: SAGE.

Frankl, V. (1959). *Man's search for meaning: An introduction to logotherapy.* New York, NY: Simon &Schuster.

Hackman, J. R., & Oldham, G. R. (1975). Development of the job diagnostic survey. *Journal of Applied Psychology, 60*(2), 159.

Hackman, J. R., & Oldham, G. R. (1976). Motivation through the design of work: Test of a theory. *Organizational Behavior and Human Performance, 16*(2), 250–279.

Halbesleben, J. R. (2010). A meta-analysis of work engagement: Relationships with burnout, demands, resources, and consequences. In *Work engagement: A handbook of essential theory and research* (Vol. 8, pp. 102–117). New York, NY: Psychology Press.

Hayes, A. F. (2013). *Introduction to mediation, moderation, and conditional process analysis: A regression-based approach.* New York, NY: Guilford Press.

Kahn, W. A. (1990). Psychological conditions of personal engagement and disengagement at work. *Academy of Management Journal, 33*(4), 692–724.

Keller, T., & Alsdorf, K. L. (2014). *Every good endeavor: Connecting your work to God's work.* New York, NY: Penguin.

Macey, W. H., & Schneider, B. (2008). The meaning of employee engagement. *Industrial and Organizational Psychology, 1*(1), 3–30.

Mackey, J., & Sisodia, R. (2013). *Conscious capitalism: Liberating the heroic spirit of business.* Cambridge, MA: Harvard Business Review Press.

Markiewicz, D., Devine, I., & Kausilas, D. (2000). Friendships of women and men at work: Job satisfaction and resource implications. *Journal of Managerial Psychology, 15*(2), 161–184.

May, D. R., Gilson, R. L., & Harter, L. M. (2004). The psychological conditions of meaningfulness, safety and availability and the engagement of the human spirit at work. *Journal of Occupational and Organizational Psychology, 77*(1), 11–37.

Milliman, J., Czaplewski, A. J., & Ferguson, J. (2003). Workplace spirituality and employee work attitudes: An exploratory empirical assessment. *Journal of Organizational Change Management, 16*(4), 426–447.

Mitroff, I., & Denton, E. A. (1999). *A spiritual audit of corporate America: A hard look at spirituality, religion, and values in the workplace*. San Francisco, CA: Jossey-Bass.

Nelson, D., & Cooper, C. L. (2007). *Positive organizational behavior*. Thousand Oaks, CA: SAGE.

Olivier, A., & Rothmann, S. (2007). Antecedents of work engagement in a multi-national company. *SA Journal of Industrial Psychology, 33*(3), 49–56.

Parker, S. K., Bindl, U. K., & Strauss, K. (2010). Making things happen: A model of proactive motivation. *Journal of management, 36*(3), 827–856.

Peters, T. J., & Waterman, R. H. (1982). *In search of excellence: Lessons from America's best-run companies*. New York, NY: HarperCollins.

Pieper, J. Z., Van Uden, M. H., & De Vries-Schot, M. R. (2012). Mature Religiosity scale: Validity of a new questionnaire. *European Journal of Mental Health, 1*, 57–71.

Pratt, M. G., & Ashforth, B. E. (2003). Fostering meaningfulness in working and at work. *Positive organizational scholarship: Foundations of a new discipline* (pp. 309–327). San Francisco, CA: Berrett-Koehler.

Pratt, M. G., Pradies, C., & Lepisto, D. A. (2013). Doing well, doing good, and doing with: Organizational practices for effectively cultivating meaningful work. In B. Dik, Z. Byrne, & M. Steger (Eds.), *Purpose and meaning in the workplace* (pp. 173–196). Washington, DC: APA.

Rego, A., & Pina e Cunha, M. (2008). Workplace spirituality and organizational commitment: An empirical study. *Journal of Organizational Change Management, 21*(1), 53–75.

Rich, B. L., Lepine, J. A., & Crawford, E. R. (2010). Job engagement: Antecedents and effects on job performance. *Academy of Management Journal, 53*(3), 617–635.

Saks, A. M. (2011). Workplace spirituality and employee engagement. *Journal of Management, Spirituality & Religion, 8*(4), 317–340.

Sherman, D., & Hendricks, W. (1987). *Your work matters to God*. Colorado Springs, CO: NavPress.

Sherman, D., & Hendricks, W. (1989). *How to balance competing time demands*. Colorado Springs, CO: NavPress.

Shuck, B., & Rose, K. (2013). Reframing employee engagement within the context of meaning and purpose: Implications for HRD. *Advances in Developing Human Resources, 15*(4), 341–355.

Soane, E., Shantz, A., Alfes, K., Truss, C., Rees, C., & Gatenby, M. (2013). The association of meaningfulness, well-being, and engagement with absenteeism: A moderated mediation model. *Human Resource Management, 52*(3), 441–456.

Steger, M. F., Dik, B. J., & Duffy, R. D. (2012). Measuring meaningful work: The work and meaning inventory (WAMI). *Journal of Career Assessment, 20*(3), 322–337.

Whittington, J. L. (2015). *Biblical perspectives on leadership and organizations.* New York, NY: Palgrave Macmillan.

Wrzesniewski, A. (2003). Finding positive meaning in work. In K. Cameron & J. Dutton (Eds.), *Positive organizational scholarship* (pp. 296–308). San Francisco, CA: Berrett-Koehler.

Wrzesniewski, A., & Dutton, J. E. (2001). Crafting a job: Revisioning employees as active crafters of their work. *Academy of Management Review, 26*(2), 179–201.

Wrzesniewski, A., McCauley, C., Rozin, P., & Schwartz, B. (1997). Jobs, careers, and callings: People's relations to their work. *Journal of Research in Personality, 31*(1), 21–33.

CHAPTER 5

PRIESTS OF CREATION, MEDIATORS OF ORDER

Taking God to Work

Peter McGhee
Auckland University of Technology

Myk Habets
Carey Graduate School

She: "What do you do for a living?"
*He: "I work for a company that makes bottle caps, but it's not as
exciting as it sounds"*

—Anonymous

SPIRITUALITY AND THE WORKPLACE

Labor is an inherent part of what we do and sometimes who we are; it can affect our lives both at work and at home. Unfortunately, much of how we understand work "is a modern invention, a product of industrialization and governed by the laws of economic rationality" (Casey, 1995, p. 28).

Faith and Work: Christian Perspectives, Research, and Insights Into the Movement
pp. 77–96
Copyright © 2018 by Information Age Publishing
77

These "laws" ensure that labor is reorganized in the interests of efficiency and profits. Workplaces, and the individuals within them, have come to be seen as machines—tools created to achieve instrumental ends (Morgan, 1997). Perhaps, it is not surprising therefore, that interest in spirituality in the workplace (hereafter SWP) has developed not only as a bulwark against such thinking (Benefiel, Fry, & Geigle, 2014) but also to meet existential needs for greater connectedness and meaning through work (Ashar & Lane-Mahar, 2004). As Mitroff (2003) has noted, "whether we like it or not, work is inextricably intertwined with our perpetual search for meaning. Work is an integral part of our spirituality, our search for ultimate meaning" (p. 375).

Much has been written about SWP in the last 2 decades. Organizational scholars have found beneficial relationships between SWP and employee well-being (Harrington, Preziosi, & Gooden, 2001; Karakas, 2010; Trott, 1996), motivation (Fry, Hannah, Noel, & Walumbwa, 2011; Nur & Organ, 2006; Rego & Cunha, 2008), and sense of community (Crawford, Hubbard, Lonis-Shumate, & O'Neill, 2009; Kolodinsky, Giacalone, & Jurkiewicz, 2008; Milliman, Czaplewski, & Ferguson, 2003). Despite these findings however, much of the SWP literature is still in the initial concept/ development stage (Pawar, 2009; Sass, 2000).

Unfortunately, spirituality has been labeled an applause word (Carson, 1994)—it is the kind of word that generates applause whenever it is stated. In this sense, the modern understanding of the term depends on whoever is using it. The same may be said about the plasticity of SWP, which is also yet to uncover a definitive understanding (Fornaciari & Dean, 2001; Giacalone & Jurkiewicz, 2003) although progress is occurring (Benefiel et al., 2014). Such uncertainty, however, suggests that locating SWP within a wider religious system such as Christianity, with its long history and analysis of work (Volf, 1991) may produce better insights (McGhee, 2010). Indeed, recent Christian thought and writing in this area typically refutes the machine mentality and the dehumanization of labor that is so prevalent in modern organizations (Jensen, 2006; Morgan, 1997). This is evidenced, for example, in much of the scholarship by the Faith at Work movement (Miller, 2007).

This chapter builds on the notion that people want to integrate their Christianity into their work. It realizes this using the work of Scottish theologian Thomas Torrance, and in particular, his view of human beings as "priests of creation" and "mediators of order." The chapter begins with an overview of what such roles entail, what relevance they are to our labors, and how we might enact these callings in and through our work. These ideas are formulated into a methodological framework which forms the basis for a deductive analysis of Christians enacting their spirituality in several large New Zealand service organizations.

ON BEING PRIESTS OF CREATION AND MEDIATORS OF ORDER

According to Thomas Torrance, human beings require others to fulfil their end or *telos*. Thus, he contends we are "defined by, and sustained within our relations to God, the created order and fellow human beings" (Flett, 2005, p. 163). Several pertinent ideas arise from this claim. First, human beings are created by and contingent upon God and as such have both physical and spiritual aspects that are "essentially complementary and ontologically integrated" (Torrance, 1984, p. 105). Consequently, differentiating between the physical (e.g., labor) and the spiritual is a non sequitur; rather these are two basic aspects of the Christian life, albeit different in form but irreducible to one another; together they are an inseparable unity (Volf, 1991).

Second, because we are addressed and constituted by God, all that we are, and indeed can become, is dependent upon "a continuing relation and proper orientation toward that same God" (Flett, 2005, p. 169). However, such a relationship is possible only through the person and work of Jesus Christ who Torrance (1992) labels, the "personalising person" (p. 67) and "humanizing man" (p. 69), and upon the Holy Spirit who continually sustains "communion between man and God" (Torrance, 1989, p. 112). Thus, the work of Christ and the Spirit does not override humanity but recreates, reaffirms, and enables us to stand before God as his beloved child. Accordingly, in accepting the truth of Jesus Christ, we become more human not less; our lives, and therefore our labor, takes on new meaning and importance as we participate in God's divine love and plan for creation.

Finally, this ontological change from self-will and self-understanding to loving God for his own sake liberates us from ourselves such that we can love our neighbor objectively (Torrance, 1965). Restored vertical relations with God ensures comparable horizontal relations with others. According to Torrance, this network of redeemed relationships (e.g., family, church, and society) enables humanity (and the created order of which we are part) to image or mirror God back to God though Christ by the Holy Spirit—this is the true telos of being human. Flett (2005) labels this a dynamic image; it is "not only a creaturely reflection, or a spiritual reflection, but also a social reflection" (p. 170). Without social contexts, such as workplaces, it is not possible "for humanity in the image God to fulfil its calling and vocation as such a being" (p. 171). Solitary confinement is, in other words, the opposite of what a life well-lived looks like. Rather, a human person involved in a rich nexus of rightly ordered social relationships at church, at home, at work, and at play, provides the context for life to flourish.

These onto-personal relations (i.e., being constituting relations between persons and objects that are necessary for the healthy development of the self) (Torrance, 1982) ensure that the image of God in humanity is both a description and an action, it is both one's nature and calling. Interestingly, work has often been viewed from a vocational perspective in Christian thought (Cosden, 2005). However, as Volf (1991) has noted, this understanding often allows any type of work, no matter how dehumanizing, to be a calling. Moreover, there can be ambiguity between one's spiritual and external call when the two conflict. This can lead to a compromising synthesis whereby one's external vocation becomes their spiritual one. Finally, Jensen (2006) has argued that such thinking has furthered the elevation of work to the status of a religion. So what notion might conceptualize the image of God in a work context if the concept of vocation as historically understood has limitations? The concept of humanity created to become *priests of creation* recommends itself.

Reflecting a unified view of creation and humanity under the triune creator God, Russian Orthodox theologian Alexander Schmemann (1973) writes:

> In the Bible the food that man eats, the world of which he must partake in order to live, is given to him by God, and it is given as *communion with God*. The world as man's food is not something "material" and limited to material functions, thus different from, and opposed to, the specifically "spiritual" functions by which man is related to God. All that exists is God's gift to man, and it all exists to make God known to man, to make man's life communion with God. (pp. 14–15, emphasis in original)

In addition to eating—clearly a metaphorical use of the term—humanity is given the task of naming the animals, something which Schmemann further comments on:

> To name a thing is to manifest the meaning and value God gave it, to know it as coming from God and to know its place and function within the cosmos created by God. To name a thing, in other words, is to bless God for it and in it. And in the Bible to bless God is not a "religious" or a "cultic" act, but the very *way of life*. God blessed the world ... and this means that He filled all that exists with His love and goodness ... So the only *natural* (and not "supernatural") reaction of man, to whom God gave this blessed and sanctified world, is to bless God in return, to thank Him, *to see the world as God sees it* and—in this act of gratitude and adoration—to know, name and possess the world. (p. 15, emphasis in original)

To see the world as God sees it. That is the vision for everyday life we require today. In order to see the world as God sees it, we must be God-like; and that means not only giving but also receiving. Such a gift is possible only as we are in communion with God. The Gift cannot be abstracted from the Giver. All of this, the Orthodox, and many Western thinkers, subsume under the grand idea that humans are the God-ordained "priests of creation." The spirit of God woos and entices us into this priestly vocation. Again, Schmemann (1973, p. 15) writes:

> The first, the basic definition of man is that he is *the priest*. He stands in the center of the world and unifies it in acts of blessing God, of both receiving the world from God and offering it to God—and by filling the world with his Eucharist, he transforms his life, the one that he receives from the world, into life in God, into communion with Him. (emphasis in original)

Romanian Orthodox theologian, Dumitru Staniloae (2000), prefers to describe men and women as creation's "master" (*archon*), its created "cocreator," "coworker" or "continuator" (p. 21–112). Staniloae considers the world as God's gift to humanity in order that humanity may gift it back to God. In this way, argues Staniloae (1969), the sacrifice offered to God by men and women is a Eucharist, making every person a priest of God for the world. The language of Eucharist reminds us of priestly duty, specifically the priestly duty of humanity to present the world to God.

Such is a vision for a rightly ordered concept of work; it is priestly labor, freely offered to God. In the hands of Thomas Torrance (1980), the concept of priest of creation captures what he means by the image of God being a calling. As its priest, humanity's vocation is to "assist the creation as a whole to realize and evidence its rational order and beauty and thus to express God" (Habets, 2009, p. 45). "Nature itself is mute," writes Torrance (1996), "but human being is the one constituent of the created universe through whom its rational structure and astonishing beauty may be brought to word in praise of the Creator" (p. 213). As such humanity is the *mediator of order* and the priest of creation, a creation "freely brought into being by the will of God and graciously entrusted to a creature crafted after the image of God" (Flett, 2005, p. 182).

Torrance views redeemed humanity as cocreators with God. Our work brings forth "forms of order and beauty of which it would not be capable otherwise" (Habets, 2009, p. 45). This is our priestly call to cocreate and act as stewards of creation. For Torrance (1982), the primary way this occurs is through the natural sciences. However, as both Habets (2009) and Flett (2005) note, this seems too narrow an approach. If we take this idea into the workplace (a social context), then our daily labors also enact our priesthood.

We see this in the original creation story of the Garden of Eden. We must ask ourselves, is Eden merely a Mesopotamian farm and Adam and Eve its first gardeners? If so, does Genesis 1–2 then provide human creatures with a work ethic—to till the ground, multiply, and steward? Quite simply, no.

Adam's responsibility is not so much farming as priestly. The Garden of Eden functioned as the earthly archetypal temple and Adam and Eve are its first priests (Fesko, 2007). The combined evidence suggests that the Genesis narrative identifies the garden as the holy of holies, in which human creatures had access to the presence of God. And so we return to ask what the "work" was that Adam and Eve, and all their sons and daughters, were created for. God placed humans "in the garden to work it and keep it" (Genesis 2.15). Many simply read this as "cultivation"—thus "farming." God meant for us all to be farmers! But that is not what the text is saying at all. The exact same vocabulary— "work" and "keep" is used to describe the priestly responsibilities in the tabernacle: "They shall keep guard over him ... before the tent of meeting as they minister/work at the tabernacle" (Numbers 3:7-8; 8:26; 18:5-6 cf. 4:23-24, 26). This is the only other time in the Pentateuch these words are used together—something the rabbi's noticed in their midrash. Thus we are on safe ground to assert that Adam and Eve's responsibilities in the garden are primarily priestly rather than agricultural! As John Fesko (2007) has stated:

> Adam was an archetypal priest, not a farmer. Scanning the horizon of redemptive history, we find further confirmation of the garden-temple thesis. At the end of redemptive history, it is not a massive city-farm that descends out of the heavens, but a city-temple. If the end of redemptive history represents God's intentions from the beginning, then he planted a temple in Eden, not a farm. (p. 75)

It is from this relationship of Creator to creature that the human being derives their significance and responsibility in the formation of the world toward its final consummation. As Flett (2005) notes, "*this* creature is peculiarly constituted and uniquely called to improvise with God "as 'scientist,' 'midwife,' 'priest,' and 'instrument,' in order to draw the created order toward its liberating telos" (p. 182).

Telling the story of God's work in the world involves the embodiment and expression of God's purposes for it. This story cannot be told apart from the formation of specific communities and their concrete action *in the world*. When human persons act in the world they function, implicitly or explicitly, as "mediators of order." They cannot escape the fact that their actions have a purpose and that purposeful action is rooted in an overarching and comprehensive conception of order. Consequently, the way in which human communities order their social and physical environments becomes a form of embodied worship, a living and concrete witness to their most comprehensive ideas of order, value, and purpose formed in conversation with a real and objective world. Our relationships with others, the created order, and God, form the fundamental basis upon which this activity takes place. The quality of these relationships will also determine whether the result of that activity will sustain or subvert the very relations upon which it is built. Those relations, and the cultural environments they produce and sustain, can only be morally legitimated as they enable the embodiment of God's purposes for the created order and by so doing sustain the personhood and integrity of human agents created in God's image. And this can only be done when life is lived in relation to Jesus the Son of God incarnate.

In other words—when men and women function in their God-given roles as priests of creation and mediators of order, they initiate the great shalom of God, they embody worship (Romans 12:1), and they represent the world to God in their representation of God to the world. As such we work toward creating the "order that ought to be"—the nudging of creation toward its intended telos. Eric Flett (2011) correctly argues that:

> If that relation is construed properly, that identity and mission will thrust [the church] into the world as a royal priesthood, whose activity in the world of culture will not only bear witness to the God she worships, but will advance God's mission in the world through cultural transformation. (p. 222)

As uniquely created beings in the image of God, humanity occupies an exclusive place on the boundary between the natural and the super natural (Torrance, 1985, 1988). As priest of creation, humanity has the function and privilege to assist the creation to realize and evidence its rational order and beauty and thus to express God's beauty and being back to God. According to Torrance (1981, p. 130), "through human cultivation and development nature should bring forth forms of order and beauty of which it would not be capable otherwise." True priestly functions of humanity include caring for the poor and the oppressed, developing sustainable farming practices, implementing ethical labor practices, and generally working in ways which respect God, creation, and humanity.

Through their work, Christians participate in God's new creation. This involves our labor reflecting God back to himself. Through their work, Christians also cooperate with God in the redemption of the world. Our mundane labors empowered by the Holy Spirit contribute to God's eschatological transformation of the present (Volf, 1991). These expectations ensure that legitimate forms of work have intrinsic value and invests it with ultimate meaning via its relation, indirectly through sanctification and directly through what humans create, to the new creation. Not all work, however, qualifies. Criteria in 1 Corinthians 3:12-15 suggests that under judgment, work that has ultimate significance, work that reflects and cooperates with the triune nature of God, is purified (is good). Insignificant work, on the other hand, work done counter to God's nature or in cooperation with powers that wish to ruin God's plan for creation, is illegitimate. Combining the ideas above into a methodological framework applicable to a real-life work context resulted in Figure 5.1.

A STUDY OF CHRISTIAN SPIRITUALITY AT WORK

Using the framework in Figure 5.1 as the basis for deductive analysis, and as part of a larger study (McGhee, 2015), 21 Christians from several New Zealand service organizations were interviewed about their spirituality and its relationship to their work. Their answers were analyzed using the two key themes identified in Figure 5.1: (1) Christians are cocreators and coredeemers with God in and through their work and (2) that such work has the ultimate meaning and value in and of itself separate from other external goods.

As a result of this analysis, we found participants frequently acted as "embodied witnesses to the glory and eternal purposes of God" (Flett, 2005, p. 176) and in doing so brought another dimension to their organizations. This dimension encouraged serving humanity's real needs, developed a corporate distinctiveness that focused on character and virtues, and made decisions that transcended individual and organizational selfishness. This resonates with the Spirit's work in creation and contributes to the long-term flourishing of all (Volf, 1991). Such behavior was worship made flesh; an incarnate and tangible sign of God in the world through their work.

A good example of these ideas in action comes from a privacy manager in a government organization. In response to questions about his influence in the workplace, he provided a clear indication that his Christian spirituality played a significant role. When asked how, he stated it helped set the ethical tone at work and contributed momentum for sustainable ethical change:

> Well I believe it [Christianity] enhances it [the organization] significantly ... I believe I help set the tone. I believe that being a spiritual person, and having that as a value means that I do my job different, better; more efficiently, more thoroughly than I would if I didn't have that. And that does effect the organization. And I think that having people who get that, who do value spirituality, it does create momentum toward making the organization a better place.

He referenced improved working outcomes including caring about his team, looking out for broader interests besides his own and working with integrity:

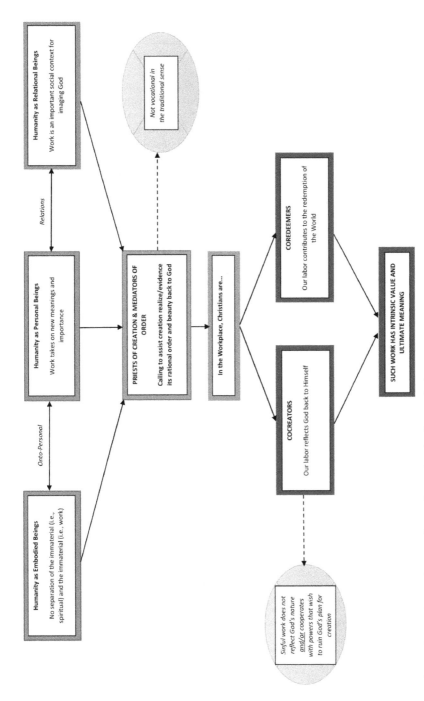

Figure 5.1. Humanity as priests of creation in the workplace.

I take a more a team oriented perspective. You know, rather than just, "Well how am I gonna get ahead? What am I gonna do to get that next position?" To more a, "Well what's best for our clients and for society?" As an organization we have a responsibility to look after the care and protection of the children of New Zealand And to me that is a very important role in a society and foundational to our future ... I guess also this whole thing of you know, not only looking out for your own interests but for the interests of others—I guess to me it means that as an employee I'm not only looking out for my interests as an employee but I am saying: "What would the employer want from me?" "Well hold on here, if I was the employer would I be happy about the way you've done your time sheet? You know, taking 15 minutes off here or there?", or even the quality of work going that extra mile to me makes the organization a better place.

Unfortunately, organizational misbehavior continues to make headlines around the world. Since the collapse of Enron and WorldCom in 2001 through to Volkswagen's recent admission that 11 million of its vehicles were equipped with software to cheat emissions tests (Gates, Ewing, Russell, & Watkins, 2016), there have been many well-known cases. A sample of these include Chiquita's funding of Columbian paramilitary groups in 2007 (Brodzinsky, 2007), Siemen's Greek bribery scandal in 2008 (Schubert & Miller, 2008), the BP Gulf of Mexico oil spill in 2010 (Lean, 2010), Olympus' loss-hiding arrangement, the largest in Japanese history, in 2011 (Inagaki & Dvorak, 2011) and GlaxoSmithKline's $3 billion fine, at that time the highest ever imposed, for criminal activity in 2012 (Thomas & Schmidt, 2012).

Why are such transgressions a prevalent and continuing blight in organizations? The simple answer is that we are, as Paul writes in Romans 3:9-10, "all under sin ... there is no one righteous, not even one." This response, appropriate as it is, does not explain such incident's frequent occurrence. Many modern organizations operate within a pervasive economic system that is individualistic, self-interested, focused on pecuniary ends while rationalizing such behavior as conducive to greater well-being (Berry, 2013; Hamilton, 2003; Kasser, 2002; Lips-Wiersma & Nilakant, 2008). This ensures organizations image this dominate paradigm and strive to realize its ends (Ghoshal, 2005; Giacalone, 2004). Sadly, this often fosters policies, procedures and practices that bolster unethical conduct (Anand, Ashforth, & Joshi, 2004; Bakan, 2004; Buchanan, 1996; Darley, 1996; Jackall, 1988; McKenna & Tsahuridu, 2001; Trevino & Youngblood, 1990).

The potency of self-interest in many organizations suppresses moral choices, ensures means are more important than ends and regularly ignores externalities as part of operational processes (Moore, 2008). This incentivizes individuals to view their organization as a separate entity from society; an entity that priorities economic goals over other concerns (Lips-Wiersma & Nilakant, 2008). Indeed, Schwartz, writing in his book *Narcissistic Process and Corporate Decay,* argues that organizations could not be the "bastions of benign community oriented ethical reasoning we wished them to be because of the demands and requirements of the market." Accordingly, organizations, and the people within them, create for themselves a "self-contained, self-serving worldview, which rationalizes anything done on their behalf and does not require justification on any grounds outside of themselves" (cited in Gini, 2011, p. 9). This worldview, Schwartz suggests, imposes a survival of the fittest requirement on all participants in organizational life that in turn ensures that to get ahead all must conform.

As embodied created beings living in community, human action has bearing not only on others, but on creation itself. As Paul writes in Romans 8:19-22, creation is frustrated by our sin. It bears the scars of humanity's disobedience. Unfortunately, business and industry often plays a conspicuous role in such wounding (Ehrenfeld & Hoffman, 2013; Klein, 2014). The church's mission, states Flett (2005) is "not spiritual in any narrow sense, but cultural, since it is her function to stand as an embodied witness of the glory and eternal purpose of God" (p. 176). Christians in the workplace are to image God, not the dominant economic ideology. Our purpose, and labors, help liberate creation from its "bondage to decay"; this is the true calling of Christ since it brings our work life into "conformity with the way it has been ordered by the Father and redeemed by the Son" (p. 178).

When was asked why the privacy manager acted thus, his answer reflected this calling. For him, work was more than just a job—it was also about making a difference. Note the reference to imaging God in and through his work. His spirituality acts as a compass pointing him back to Christ. This ensures his work reflects God's nature and desires for creation:

> I like to think what I do, it's not about getting information to parties, it's ultimately about the best interests of the parties that are involved … I know sometimes in meetings and things you hear other employees talking about, "Well it's just about this request or whatever" and I always say, "Well no it's not just about that request; it's about what is the best long term decision for these parties." Many times, we can lose that perspective. But I think spirituality and understanding, for me, what God means and what Jesus has done in my life means that I do always get reminded: well look it's about more than just this … I think well when you're not tired and you are fresh you get reminded that no, this counts, this actually is making a difference for God's world. It might not be huge and it might not hit the media in a positive way but it's important and it counts.

As mentioned earlier, interpreting work from a traditional calling stance may be problematic. Several authors, writing in the theology of work literature, provide varied limitations of this approach (see, e.g., Cosden, 2005; Jensen, 2006; Volf, 1991). While their criticisms differ, they share a belief that underpinning much of this perspective is the notion of individualism. Perhaps this not surprising given its ascetic roots, Protestant emphasis on freedom and close links to capitalism (Nadesan, 1999). Unfortunately, such a focus shifts our attentiveness from the object of our faith, which is the triune *redemptor* and *recreator* God, to the subjective requirements of persons (or organizations). Our faith becomes primarily a transaction between an individual and God often at the expense of the wider community (Grenz, Guretzki, & Nordling, 1999). Within the work context, this typically involves co-opting notions of faith, spirituality and calling to serve instrumental ends (Carrette & King, 2005; Lips-Wiersma, Dean, & Fornaciari, 2009). As redemptor, God frees us from sin. His spiritual presence enables us to reject evil and to choose his desires (2 Corinthians 3:17) and "not to be instigators or active practitioners of degrading or debasing work either for ourselves or others" (McGhee, 2010, p. 190). As recreator, God makes all things new. In adopting us through Christ by the Holy Spirit, God humanizes our labors fully such that they participate in the completion of his new creation. Work that fails in these aspects, that fails to cooperate with God in his eschatological *transformation mundi,* has no place in this new creation (Volf, 1991).

The participants in this study rejected any such co-optation and enacted their spirituality often in the face of counterforces which encouraged dehumanizing work practices (Ghoshal, 2005; Giacalone, 2004). They reframed their circumstances from a transcendent perspective and acted accordingly. This involved considering the impact of their decisions on a range of stakeholders as well as God's desire for His creation. Again, we turn to the privacy officer for an example of such praxis in his refusing a superior's request to withhold documentation from its rightful owner because she feared compromising the organization's reputation and/or a having a potential claim against the organization from the client:

> Well I think to me the question becomes, if we remove documents for this reason, then what stops us from removing other documents for other reasons? I mean where does it end? And then you know even do we go further? Do we go through all the files, and start sort of rummaging through files and say "Anything that doesn't make us look good?" I simply can't do that! She [his manager] wasn't happy but we ended up getting someone else involved—another executive manager—and they decided not to remove the document from the file.... As Christian I would have to say that they [his choices here] would have something to do at least with the teachings and the life and the death of Jesus of Nazareth. And that would certainly

include—but not be limited to—things like caring about others, loving our neighbor as ourselves, being in touch with God, through things like prayer and reading the bible. So yeah, those kind of principles upon which we build our lives—I think—that help us to make decisions to live how God wants us to.

Many times, other participants told the story of God's work in the world via their concrete embodied actions. And these actions helped shape their world in ways that effect creation's intended telos, the purpose for which God created it. Interestingly, these benefits were not limited to our participants alone. Through their conduct, they initiated the great *shalom* of God as they helped others (often unbeknownst to them) represent themselves to God and God back to them (Flett, 2005). This participant, for example, influenced his fellow privacy officers to act in similar redemptive ways. Referring to the incident above, he stated:

> I think spirituality does [influence the behavior of others] and especially that second incident with the files. Again, when it was clear what was happening—I mean everybody got on board to say, "No, this is not right. Something needs to clearly change here"—so everybody got on board with that. I mean of course sometimes you do think, "Well look, is this really making any difference on other people" but I certainly like to think it is in some way. I mean surely if we could have more people making decisions based on spirituality that has to make a difference to organizations and on our society as a whole.

Participants found such priestly work brought significant meaning and value to their lives. Indeed, many reported a deep-seated sense of fulfilment and wholeness. Recall that for Torrance (1982), human beings are constituted by their relations with God, creation and others. As instruments in the hand of God, human beings are in tune when these three onto-relations are transcendentally determined (Torrance, 1989). When we choose freely to image God in our labors by, for example, treating others as ends not means (e.g., opposing sweatshop labor) and stewarding God's creation as opposed to diminishing it (e.g., reducing pollution), then we "are being transformed into His likeness with ever-increasing glory, which comes from the Lord, who is the Spirit" (2 Corinthians 3:18). This progression, through Christ and by the Spirit, ensures we are no longer alienated from God, from each other, or from creation. Instead of being less, we are becoming more complete, more in-tune, indeed we are becoming more human. It is no surprise perhaps that these participant's felt and articulated enhanced well-being, "a sense of peace that transcends all understanding" (Philippians 4:7), when they labored objectively for God as opposed to subjectively for themselves.

We see a good example of this in insurance agent in a large multinational company. He choose to circumvent rules and policies to pay out clients who had suffered during the Christchurch earthquake and who had been unjustly rejected by his insurance company, even at the risk of his own job position and financial security. He transcended his role and the organizational culture to help these people:

> So quite often I batted for the client, I looked for opportunities wherever I could to pay claims for the client, even though that actually went away from the rules and regulations of the company.... There was some wheeling and dealing and maybe, as I say, when I was younger there's no way I would do that because I was probably more black and white. Now I would, I've changed in the fact of wanting to help people so how can I pay something, get under the radar and yet it [the claim] still lines up.

When asked why he did this, his answer reflected his desire to live an authentic Christian life, a life not compromised by inauthentic action. He interpreted this authentic life using a phrase "living for God, living for the kingdom," which essentially means being true to your priestly calling daily. Interestingly, for him, this was primarily about loving God and his neighbor objectively (Torrance, 1965):

> It's [Christianity] everything, so every day you want to be living for God, living for the kingdom. If it's not of the kingdom then you don't want to be doing it, so that's part of who I am, so every day is, yeah, it is a part of everyday life. So to me, [it is about] helping others, in this case we're to help other people, you know, their lives are decimated, so common sense tells us to pay what we can to get their house repaired, to put them in temporary accommodation, to get them some help. So what is living for Kingdom? [It is] loving God and others.

The consequence of these types of transcendent actions and this authentic living was an enhanced sense of well-being and the repetitive likelihood of such behaviors happening in other contexts:

> I felt good about doing it, the client was happy. You know, the company should've paid it anyway; it's just that common sense went out the window.... Maybe it [spiritually informed action] just reinforces where I'm at. When you make a decision and do things like that it reinforces that this is where I am at, this is how I operate, these are the decisions that I make and that I'm comfortable doing it and this is in the zone. Therefore, I will continue to operate like that even in new roles, if I can, [because] you take that with you wherever else you go.

This differs significantly from contemporary views of spirituality which is primarily about satisfying individual existential desires and organization instrumental needs. This discourse simply "reinforces the idea of work providing a path to enlightenment through the notion of self-actual-ization" (Bell & Taylor, 2003, p. 336) instead of through Christ, the per-sonalizing person and the humanizing human (Torrance, 1992), and the Holy Spirit. As Herrick (2003) puts it, such a limited perspective "calls for a self-adoration and exaltation of our own rational self-awareness—the divinity operating within us [and ...] arrives at no more interesting desti-nation than spiritual narcissism" (p. 259).

Interestingly, those that failed in their "priestly duties" often conveyed feelings of discontent, anxiety and meaninglessness dependent on the extent of their inauthenticity in action. Communication of this was often in terms of damage to the self. If imaging God is the central aspect of a Christian's identity, then not acting thus may cause significant conative conflict and affective distress (Rozuel & Kakabadse, 2010). Several extracts which capture participant's descriptions of their feelings when they failed to act spiritually are provided as evidence of this:

> I think I acted somewhere in between because if it was ethically and spiritu-ally right I wouldn't feel bad about it ... I don't think I have come to terms with it all in my head ... the good thing is you prepare for that sort of manipulation in the future and that strengthens your spirituality. (Sales engineer)

> Oh, I felt awful; it was really difficult, I felt disconnected from my spiritual self like someone else was doing it. (Communications consultant)

> I feel frustrated. I feel really frustrated. I sit in those meetings and I listen to people talk poorly of students based on, you know, in a humorous way, or even if they're being serious, I just feel like there's nothing I can do. And I feel quite powerless ... I'm not quite ready to properly affect change or to do something so I feel kind of a bit spiritually weak and frustrated. (Teacher)

> You're going to feel discomfort because you're dealing with people and their futures and all the rest of it. If you take that stuff [Christianity] seriously, if you have a sense of care for people and their wellbeing then some situations inevitably are uncomfortable because the outcomes have quite strong effects. (Company director)

Moreover, such individuals "yield more easily to the pressure of social conformity, relinquishing their personal responsibility by claiming to be just an agent within a system" (Rozuel & Kakabadse, 2010, p. 426). Being inauthentic ensures the ego takes precedence so "moral decisions may no longer be genuine and in accordance with our values; instead, they may respond to our personal interests or to collective expectations" (p. 426).

Such individuals can become compartmentalized, ignore they are *imago Dei* and risk developing psychopathologies.

CONCLUSION

Writing in the *Journal of Management Inquiry,* Gull and Doh (2004) argued that organizations need transmutation toward more spiritual workplaces. They contend that rationalism, power, self-will, and greed are rampart and as such, limits our capacity for connectedness with and compassion for others. This encourages a "me" over the "we" mentality which eventually corrupts behavior. The solution to this problem, they argue, is to change the organization's dominant schema. This, however, cannot occur by simply espousing spirituality or by including a few spiritual mantras as part of the company's values statement. Training and incentives programs will also be ineffective. Such a transmutation, according to Gull and Doh, will only happen if employees are permitted and encouraged to enact their spirituality fully in the life of the organization.

Despite these lofty goals, Gull and Doh offer a very humanistic/existentialist solution that cannot achieve what they desire. This proposal, on the other hand, provided a short overview of the work of Torrance and its application to Christian faith in the workplace. It briefly discussed the findings of a deductive qualitative study that applied this framework to Christians in New Zealand Organizations. It found that humans created in the *imago Dei* flourish when they fully live out their roles as mediators of order and priests of creation, ordering creation and presenting it back to God in worship. Labor, which has so often instrumentalized humans and has been co-opted for power relations and economic control, must be seen, rather, as a key aspect of humanity's priestly duty toward God. Once this shift occurs, as the qualitative study described above highlights, human beings can become the human persons God intended them to be, in harmony with God, with each other, and with all of creation.

REFERENCES

Anand, V., Ashforth, B. E., & Joshi, M. (2004). Business as usual: The acceptance and perpetuation of corruption in organizations. *Academy of Management Executive, 18*(2), 39–53. doi:10.5465/AME.2004.13837437

Ashar, H., & Lane-Mahar, M. (2004). Success and spirituality in the new business paradigm. *Journal of Management Inquiry, 13*(3), 249–260. doi:10.1177/1056492604268218

Bakan, J. (2004). *The corporation: The pathological pursuit of profit and power.* New York, NY: Free Press.

Bell, E., & Taylor, S. (2003). The elevation of work: Pastoral power and the New Age work ethic. *Organization, 10*(2), 329–349. doi:10.1177/1350508403010002009

Benefiel, M., Fry, L. W., & Geigle, D. (2014). Spirituality & religion in the workplace: History, theory, and research. *Psychology of Religion & Spirituality, 6*(3), 175–187. doi:10.1037/a0036597

Berry, P. (2013). *Fostering spirituality in the workplace: A leader's guide to sustainability.* New York, NY: Business Expert Press.

Brodzinsky, S. (2007, May 2). Terrorism and bananas in Colombia. *Time.* Retrieved from http://www.time.com/time/world/article/0,8599,1616991,00.html

Buchanan, A. (1996). Toward a theory of the ethics of bureaucratic organizations. *Business Ethics Quarterly, 6*(4), 419–440.

Carrette, J., & King, R. (2005). *Selling spirituality: The silent takeover of religion.* Abingdon, Oxfordshire, England: Routledge.

Carson, D. A. (1994). When is spirituality spiritual? Reflections on some problems of definitions. *Journal of the Evangelical Theological Society, 37*(3), 381–394.

Casey, C. (1995). *Work, self and society.* London, England: Routledge.

Cosden, D. (2005). *Theology of work: Work & the new creation.* Eugene, OR: Wipf & Stock.

Crawford, A., Hubbard, S. S., Lonis-Shumate, S. R., & O'Neill, M. (2009). Workplace spirituality and employee attitudes within the lodging environment. *Journal of Human Resources in Hospitality & Tourism, 8*(1), 64–81. doi:10.1080/15332840802274445

Darley, J. M. (1996). How organisations socialize individuals into evil doing. In D. Mesick & A. E. Tenbrunsel (Eds.), *Codes of conduct: Behavioral research into business ethics* (pp. 13–42). New York, NY: Russell Sage Foundation.

Ehrenfeld, R., & Hoffman, A. J. (2013). *Flourishing: A frank conversation about sustainability.* Stanford, CA: Stanford Business Books.

Fesko, J. V. (2007). *Last things first: Unlocking Genesis 1–3 with the Christ of Eschatology.* Fern, Scotland: Mentor.

Flett, E. G. (2005). Priests of creation, mediators of order: The human person as a cultural being in Thomas F. Torrance's theological anthropology. *Scottish Journal of Theology, 58*(2), 161–183. doi:10.1017/S0036930605000992

Fornaciari, C. J., & Dean, K. L. (2001). Making the quantum leap: Lessons from physics on studying spirituality and religion in organizations. *Journal of Organizational Change Management, 14*(4), 335–351. doi:10.1108/EUM0000000005547

Fry, L. W., Hannah, S. T., Noel, M., & Walumbwa, F. O. (2011). Impact of spiritual leadership on unit performance. *The Leadership Quarterly, 22*(2), 259–270. doi:10.1016/j.leaqua.2011.02.002

Gates, G., Ewing, J., Russell, K., & Watkins, D. (2016, June 1). Explaining Volkswagen's emissions scandal. *New York Times.* Retrieved from http://www.nytimes.com/interactive/2015/business/international/vw-diesel-emissions-scandal-explained.html?_r=0

Ghoshal, S. (2005). Bad management theories are destroying good management practices. *Academy of Management Learning & Education, 4*(1), 75–91. doi:10.5465/AMLE.2005.16132558

Giacalone, R. A. (2004). A transcendent business education for the 21st century. *Academy of Management Learning & Education, 3*(4), 415–420. doi:10.5465/AMLE.2004.15112547

Giacalone, R. A., & Jurkiewicz, C. L. (Eds.). (2003). Toward a science of workplace spirituality. In *Handbook of workplace spirituality* (pp. 3–28). Armonk, NY: M.E. Sharpe.

Gini, A. (2011). A short primer on moral courage. In D. R. Comer & G. Vega (Eds.), *Moral courage in organizations: Doing the right thing at work* (pp. 3–12). Armonk, NY: M.E. Sharpe.

Grenz, S., Guretzki, D., & Nordling, C. F. (1999). *Pocket dictionary of theological terms* Downers Grove, IL: InterVarsity Press.

Gull, G. A., & Doh, J. (2004). The "transmutation" of the organization: Towards a more spiritual workplace. *Journal of Management Inquiry, 13*(2), 128–139. doi:10.1177/1056492604265218

Habets, M. (2009). *Theosis in the theology of Thomas Torrance*. Surrey, England: Ashgate.

Hamilton, C. (2003). *Growth fetish*. Crows Nest, New South Wales, Australia: Allen & Unwin.

Harrington, W. J., Preziosi, R. C., & Gooden, D. J. (2001). Perceptions of workplace spirituality among professionals and executives. *Employee Responsibilities and Rights Journal, 13*(3), 155–163. doi:10.1023/A:1014966901725

Herrick, J. A. (2003). *The making of the new spirituality*. Downers Grove, IL: InterVarsity Press.

Inagaki, K., & Dvorak, D. (November 8, 2011). Olympus admits to hiding losses. *Wall Street Journal*. Retrieved from http://online.wsj.com/article/SB10001424052970204190704577024680506345936.html

Jackall, R. (1988). *Moral mazes: The world of corporate managers*. New York, NY: Oxford University Press.

Jensen, D. H. (2006). *Responsive labor: A theology of work*. Louisville, KY: Westminster John Knox Press.

Karakas, F. (2010). Spirituality and performance in organizations: A literature review. *Journal of Business Ethics, 94*(1), 89–106. doi:10.1007/s10551-009-0251-5

Kasser, T. (2002). *The high price of materialism*. Cambridge, MA: MIT Press.

Klein, N. (2014). *This changes everything*. New York, NY: Simon & Schuster.

Kolodinsky, R. W., Giacalone, R. A., & Jurkiewicz, C. L. (2008). Workplace values and outcomes: Exploring personal, organisational and interactive workplace spirituality. *Journal of Business Ethics, 81*(2), 465–480. doi:10.1007/s10551-007-9507-0

Lean, G. (2010, May 4). BP's Gulf of Mexico oil spill: The crude facts of an oil disaster. *The Telegraph*. Retrieved from http://www.telegraph.co.uk/earth/environment/7676018/BPs-Gulf-of-Mexico-oil-spill-the-crude-facts-of-an-oil-disaster.html

Lips-Wiersma, M., Dean, K. L., & Fornaciari, C. J. (2009). Theorizing the dark side of the workplace spirituality movement. *Journal of Management Inquiry, 18*(4), 288–300. doi:10.1177/1056492609339017

Lips-Wiersma, M., & Nilakant, V. (2008). Practical compassion: Toward a critical spiritual foundation for corporate responsibility. In J. Biberman & L. Tischler (Eds.), *Spirituality in business: Theory, practice, and future directions* (pp. 51–72). New York, NY: Palgrave Macmillan.

McGhee, P. K. (2010). Taking the spirit to work. In M. Habets (Ed.), *The spirit of truth: Reading scripture and constructing theology with the Holy Spirit* (pp. 179–205). Eugene, OR: Wipf & Stock.

McGhee, P. K. (2015). *The role of spirituality in ethical decision-making and behaviour and the benefits to organisations: A critical realist analysis* (Doctoral dissertation). University of Auckland, Auckland, New Zealand.

McKenna, R., & Tsahuridu, E. (2001). Must managers leave ethics at home? Economics and moral anomie in business organisations. *Reason in Practice, 1*(3), 67–76. doi:10.5840/pom2001138

Miller, D. W. (2007). *God at work: The history and promise of the faith at work movement.* New York, NY: Oxford University Press.

Milliman, J. F., Czaplewski, A. J., & Ferguson, J. (2003). Workplace spirituality and employee work attitudes: An exploratory empirical assessment. *Journal of Organizational Change Management, 16*(4), 426–447. doi:10.1108/09534810310484172

Mitroff, I. I. (2003). Do not promote religion under the guise of spirituality. *Organization, 10*(2), 375–382.

Moore, G. (2008). Re-imagining the morality of management: A modern virtue ethics approach. *Business Ethics Quarterly, 18*(4), 483–511. doi:10.5840/beq200818435

Morgan, G. (1997). *Images of organizations.* Thousand Oaks, CA: SAGE.

Nadesan, M. H. (1999). The discourses of corporate spiritualism and evangelical capitalism. *Management Communication, 13*(1), 3–42. doi:10.1177/0893318999131001

Nur, Y. A., & Organ, D. W. (2006). Selected organizational outcome correlates of spirituality in the workplace. *Psychological Reports, 98*(1), 111–120. doi:10.2466/pr0.98.1.111-120

Pawar, B. S. (2009). Some recent organizational behaviour concepts as precursors to workplace spirituality. *Journal of Business Ethics, 88*(2), 245–261. doi:10.1007/s10551-008-9961-3

Rego, A., & Cunha, M. P. (2008). Workplace spirituality and organizational commitment. *Journal of Organizational Change Management, 21*(1), 53–75. doi:10.1108/09534810810847039

Rozuel, C., & Kakabadse, N. (2010). Ethics, spirituality and self: Managerial perspectives and leadership implications. *Business Ethics: A European Review, 19*(4), 423–436. doi:10.1111/j.1467-8608.2010.01603.x

Sass, J. S. (2000). Characterizing organizational spirituality: An organizational communication culture approach. *Communication Studies, 5*(3), 195–217. doi:10.1080/10510970009388520

Schmemann, A. (1973). *For the life of the world: Sacraments and orthodoxy* (2nd ed.). Crestwood, NY: St. Vladimir's Seminary Press.

Schubert, S., & Miller, C. T. (December 20, 2008). At Siemens, bribery was just a line item. *New York Times*. Retrieved from http://www.nytimes.com/2008/12/21/business/worldbusiness/21siemens.html?pagewanted=all&_r=0

Thomas, K., & Schmidt, M. S. (2012, July 2). Glaxo agrees to pay $3 billion in fraud settlement. *New York Times*. Retrieved from http://www.nytimes.com/2012/07/03/business/glaxosmithkline-agrees-to-pay-3-billion-in-fraud-settlement.html?pagewanted=all

Torrance, T. F. (1965). *Theology in reconstruction*. London, England: SCM Press.

Torrance, T. F. (1980). *The ground and grammar of theology*. Edinburgh, Scotland: T & T Clark.

Torrance, T. F. (1981). *Divine and contingent order*. Oxford, England: Oxford University Press.

Torrance, T. F. (1982). *Reality & evangelical theology*. Philadelphia, PA: Westminster.

Torrance, T. F. (1984). *Transformation & convergence in the frame of knowledge: Explorations in the interrealations of scientific and theological enterprise*. Grand Rapids, MI: Eerdmans.

Torrance, T. F. (1989). The soul and person. In T. Roberts & S. Sutherland (Eds.), *Religion, reason and the self* (pp. 103–118). Cardiff, Wales: University of Wales.

Torrance, T. F. (1992). *The mediation of Christ* (2nd ed.). Edinburgh, Scotland: T & T Clark.

Torrance, T. F. (1996). The Christian Doctrine of God: One being three persons. Edinburgh, Scotland: T. & T. Clark.

Trevino, L. K., & Youngblood, S. A. (1990). Bad apples in bad barrels: A causal analysis of ethical decision-making behavior. *Journal of Applied Psychology, 75*(4), 378–385. doi:0021-9010/90/$00.75

Trott, D. C. (1996). *Spiritual well-being of workers: An exploratory study of spirituality in the workplace* (Doctoral dissertation). The University of Texas, Austin, TX.

Volf, M. (1991). *Work in the spirit: Toward a theology of work*. London, England: Oxford University Press.

CHAPTER 6

"AS THE BIRDS TO FLYING, SO IS MAN BORN UNTO WORK"

Martin Luther's Notion of Work as an Individual Source for Meaning

Lucas Zapf and Peter Seele
Institute of Marketing and Communication Management

Introduction[1]

This chapter addresses the reformatory notion of work as put forward by Martin Luther as a source for producing meaning on the individual level in organizational work environments. We chose Luther, founder of German Protestantism in the 16th century, for his central significance in reformatory history and the extensive examination of work in his writings. Spiritual positions such as Luther's are prone to nourish meaningful notions of work by framing them as a contribution to a higher level order (Zapf, 2015). This holds true even for secularized contexts in modern day market economy (McCleary & Barro, 2003), which is why the knowledge of such backgrounds contributes to a fuller picture of how a meaningful work environment is comprised.

We understand work as purposeful, economically oriented action, thereby not focusing on the work's content, but rather on the action itself

Faith and Work: Christian Perspectives, Research, and Insights Into the Movement
pp. 97–114

97

and its individual implications. Work in this sense has several manifest functions, such as the production of goods and providing for the worker's subsistence. There are, however, a number of latent functions that exceed this practical dimension (cf. Jahoda & Rush, 1980, pp. 10–12). We are going to research these latent functions—or, as we call them, interpretations of work—through the lens of the reformer Martin Luther. We focus on the attribution of meaning to work as promoted by the reformer's interpretations. We find that even without the theological superstructure, Luther's interpretations of work are commensurable for today's working-environments by offering a structure helping to produce meaning on the individual level.

For this argument, we start with some theoretical remarks on the economics of religion from a religious-studies perspective and outline a systematic approach to describe the influence of religion on individual economic action. We then turn to Martin Luther and his historical and socioeconomic context before we describe the three pillars of the reformer's interpretations of work (work as social activity, work as a law of nature, work as self-realization). We then apply these findings to the production of meaning both in religious and organizational contexts, describing the commensurability of Luther's interpretations of work for secular contexts.

An Economics-of-Religion Framework

The link between Protestantism and capitalism has been en vogue since Max Weber published his famous essay "The Spirit of Capitalism" first published in German in 1920 (Weber, 2001). Besides Weber's description of the elective affinities between confession and the economic system, he did not elaborate how to theoretically and methodologically address the connection between religion and the economic system. If we want to shed light on the connection between Luther's theology as a source for contemporary working environments, we first need a framework for describing the influence of religion on individual economic action. This topic of research falls within the economics of religion (EoR).

EoR has been part of the economics' discourse since the 1970s (starting with Azzi & Ehrenberg, 1975) and has been elaborated steadily since. However, there still is a certain lack of conceptual overview. In general, EoR analyzes the interplay between religion and the economy from various disciplinary standpoints. Religion and religious phenomena are analyzed and validated empirically with a focus on methodological concepts of the economics sciences (Iannaccone, 1998, p. 1465). Scholars in the tradition of Gary Becker applied their paradigm and axioms on religion, a common starting point being rational choice theory, describing religious and economic action as the result of rational considerations (Iannaccone, 1997).

The underlying interest of the field is the systematic description of economic impact on and of religion. In doing so, EoR is not an economics subdiscipline, but rather an interdisciplinary endeavor. It is not the disciplinary background, but the topics and theories that shape the various approaches to EoR:

> Economics of religion cannot be understood as a discipline in itself, but rather as a research agenda partly rooted within the framework of established disciplines and partly interdisciplinary. (Seele, Gatti, & Lohse, 2014, p. 74)

This thought serves as the starting point to map EoR along its subjects of research, not its disciplinary affiliations. Rachel McCleary, Harvard economist and Robert J. Barro, for example, distinguish between two roles of religion within EoR (McCleary & Barro, 2006):

- *Religion as an dependent variable*, that is, how economic circumstances influence religion and belief. The alterations of religious supply and demand, market- and choice-models are employed as well as institutional analysis of religious environments. And:
- *Religion as an independent variable:* How religion and belief shape economic action. The influence of religion on economic processes, and of religious structures of interpretation on economic behavior is researched. Religious attitudes toward inner worldly action are especially considered.

We combine these findings with the two central economic perspectives (demand-side and supply-side). Now, the roles of religion define the approaches to EoR, as shown in Figure 6.1.

The matrix organizes the approaches of EoR according to the role of religion (dependent/independent variable) and the form of religion analyzed (supply-/demand-side). The disciplines involved are layers to the matrix. Feuilletonist approaches differ from scientific approaches (mainly in their tone, depth and sometimes normative intention) and are hence marked blue. However, as a common appearance at the crossroads of economics and religion, they have earned their spot.

The research present and its disciplinary starting point are highlighted in red. Our topic of interest is the influence of religion on economics (independent variable) on the demand-side (individual level). We apply a descriptive, studies-of-religion, outside perspective, using Luther's theo-

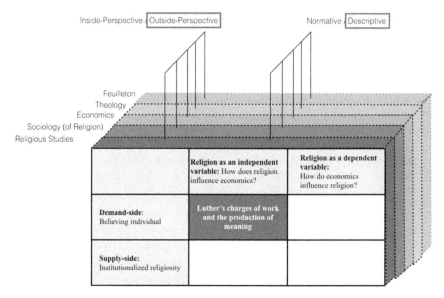

Figure 6.1.   Approaches of EoR.

logical texts as sources while maintaining the analytical distance toward the theological contents.

If we assume a religious influence on economic action, we implicitly accept the existence of two distinct spheres: "religion" and "economy." The spheres seem to be separated; otherwise, they could not influence each other. It is important to note however, that these spheres are an artificial classification—in life and practice, they are probably not selective, but implicit and overlapping. In theory, however, they make it possible to analyze and describe the manifold interests and influences that constitute individual action and decisions—as it seems to be the case with religion's effect on economic action.

With this systematic approach at hand, we now turn to our subject matter: Martin Luther and his reformatory notions of work.

HISTORICAL-THEOLOGICAL BACKGROUND: HOW LUTHER MADE WORK PART OF RELIGION

The significance of work in Lutheran theology is attached to the historic circumstances of 16th century Western Europe, the time and place of the reformer's work. Then, the economy was bound by a feudal-agrarian social structure: Few owned land and many worked on this land.

Economic and social status depended on this property. The Catholic Church declared itself caretaker of this property, controlling cultivation and distribution of the yields. For its financing, the church, was accustomed to this feudal system and to upkeep this socioeconomic *status quo*, clergy proscribed incomes by trade or money operations (cf. Pirenne 1986, pp. 16–19). Sales of indulgences and church taxes burdened the trading population, while the ruling class overall was financially spared (cf. Seele, 2010). With a damping effect on broader economic action: Spiritual betterment was religiously encouraged for all parts of the population, economic betterment however was restricted to the ruling class. The church proclaimed monkish austereness (*vita contemplativa*) as the spiritual and economic ideal. Private business was no part of this ideal.

This changed with a fresh economic development: The rise of the monetized economy. Labor, property, land and commodities now were measured by prices, became fluid, feudal structures crumbled. As everything now had a price, economic thought began to adapt and money moved into the realm of religion (cf. Seele, 2009). Interests were claimed for loans. The former sinfulness of monetary profit seemed in retreat (cf. Wood, 2002, pp. 206–209). The church-sanctioned economic inequalities combined with the promise of social betterment for the lesser fortunate parts of the population created an atmosphere of change, economically and religiously.

It was in this situation that Luther developed his revolutionary ideas to reform Christianity. While reforming, Luther was not fond of the social and economic changes occurring around him (cf. Zapf, 2015). He neither promoted Renaissance's humanism, nor the aspiring bourgeoisie or the accompanying decline of the estate-based society. He considered the developments a threat to feudal society, which he was accustomed to. He was critical against the aspiring private markets, and overall Luther was far from being an advocate of capitalism. As Weber put it, Luther's mission was to promote a new understanding of Christian theology—not new forms of business:

> Once and for all it must be remembered that programs of ethical reform never were at the centre of interest for any of the religious reformers.... They were not the founders of societies for ethical culture nor the proponents of humanitarian projects for social reform or cultural ideals. The salvation of the soul and that alone was the centre of their life and work. Their ethical ideals and the practical results of their doctrines were all based on that alone, and were the consequences of purely religious motives. (Weber, 2001, p. 48)

The Reformation did not aim to develop a "capitalist religion." However, reformatory thought was influenced by the simmering social, political, and economic changes of the time and, vice versa, the theological change transformed the economic circumstances.

Reformatory theology offered concepts that fit the economic needs and opportunities better than these of the established church (Anderson, 1988). An expression of the mutual influence between socioeconomic and theological ideas is the reformulation of the churches' role for individual redemption: Luther found that faith alone justifies the believer before God: *iustificatio sola fide*. God's show of mercy does not depend on human or financial considerations—rendering the Catholic practice of confession, the sales of indulgences, and the forgiving of sins through settlement dysfunctional. Luther struck the church, formerly the intermediary between the believer and his salvation, off the transaction. Before the reformation, the church had generated trust in Godly salvation, forgiveness, and mercy. Now, in reformed Christianity, it is the believer's own task to generate this trust. The new salvation economy drives the church out of the salvation business, handing it over to the believing individual.

As a consequence, religiously relevant action is not bound to the monastery, Sunday service or any religious authority anymore. Every human action is considered probation of God's trust. It is life on this earth and the processing and shaping of this world along a Christian ethic that is considered the God-given task of man (Troeltsch, 1906, pp. 25–26). According to Luther, all works of man—secular as well as religious—are relevant before God and therefore relevant for salvation. This is the crucial point for our topic: Luther includes seemingly secular action into his theology, especially work, thereby setting it out as a religiously crucial part of the believer's life. To work and make a living is not inferior to religious practice. Economic action goes hand in hand with religious action.

For Catholic doctrine, the contemplative, monastic existence was the most desirable lifestyle. Now, in a time of an aspiring bourgeoisie with economic interests, Luther ascribed the industrious, hard-working man religious dignity. Labor is no penalty for a lapse or unworthy activity, but a way of showing respect to God (Frambach, 2010). This explains Luther's extensive theological preoccupation with work and the religious role originating from it (Peukert, 2010, p. 16).

Luther's Interpretations of Work

The complete edition of Luther's works, the *Weimarer Ausgabe* (Edition from Weimar), serves as the historic source from which Luther's stance toward work is described here. The edition was started in 1883, finished in 2009, and contains 127 volumes with more than 80,000 pages, gathering the entirety of Luther's writings. The edition is digitalized, searchable, and available online upon subscription (Chadwyck-Proquest, 2013).

Luther's statements on work are scattered throughout his opus. Therefore, the full text was searched using a semantic collection of words describing work, taking into consideration different spellings. Luther mainly wrote in Middle High German. Orthography and grammatical subtleties differ from Modern High German, but the texts are well understandable for trained speakers. The language can be compared to a strong, written dialect. An example is the well-known passage about man being made for work as birds are made to fly. The quote, taken from the English translation of Luther's *Treatise on Good Works*, reads: "In the sweat of thy face shalt thou eat bread. And … as the birds to flying, so is man born unto labor." Here are the two versions in German:

- Middle High German: *"In dem schweysz deines angesichtes soltu essen dein brot, and […] wie der fogel zum fliegen, szo ist der mensch geborn zur erbeyt."* (Luther, 1888b, pp. 271–272).
- Modern High German: *"Im Schweiße Deines Angesichts sollst Du Dein Brot essen und wie der Vogel zum Fliegen, so ist der Mensch geboren zur Arbeit."*

The term "work" ("Arbeit" in Modern High German) in its various spellings comes up 1,803 times, without temporal or contextual accumulations noticeable. The numbers in parentheses indicate the numbers of passages found in the text: "Arbeiten" (90), "Arbeit" (225), "Arbeyt" (132), "Arbeyten" (60), "Erbeiten" (307), "Erbeit" (620), "Erbeyt" (255), and "Erbeyten" (114). For a first structuring of the passages, secondary literature on Lutheran theology offered points of reference, allowing for the selection of episodes according to their role in the entire work. The passages were then grouped along three (partly overlapping) categories that emerged from the reading:

1. Work as social activity,
2. Work as a law of nature, and
3. Work as self-realization.

In light of the extensive amount of text and the lack of English translations for some of Luther's lesser known writings, the chapter at hand presents one longer, representative quotation for each category. Further references are summarized. The original references are quoted separately in the bibliography for further research and processing.

Work as Social Activity

Luther interprets work as a godly intended social relation. This assessment is theologically substantiated as charity (*caritas*), one of the central expressions of Luther's theology. Every action motivated by belief aims at this brotherly love. The following excerpt, taken from the "Address to the Christian Nobility" (1520), summarizes the social aspects of work. Note that "work" is substituted in the excerpt by the expressions "office," "calling," and "function":

> We see, then, that just as those that we call spiritual, or priests, bishops, or popes, do not differ from other Christians in any other or higher degree but in that they are to be concerned with the word of God and the sacraments— that being their work and office—in the same way the temporal authorities hold the sword and the rod in their hands to punish the wicked and to protect the good. A cobbler, a smith, a peasant, every man, has the office and function of his calling, and yet all alike are consecrated priests and bishops, and every man should by his office or function be useful and beneficial to the rest, so that various kinds of work may all be united for the furtherance of body and soul, just as the members of the body all serve one another. (Luther, 1888a, p. 409; Luther, 1917, translated)

Luther describes society as a body to whose health every single member contributes with his or her work. Every man in every job is a priest, fulfilling his work as a God-given duty. Aggregated, individual work leads to social coherence. Luther interprets work as practiced caritas based on the division of labor: Work is service for the fellow man (Luther 1906, p. 472; Luther, 1925, p. 38). It is the vehicle by which the individual both constitutes independence and contributes to society. Work exceeds the possibilities of the individual, leading to a collective contribution (Luther, 1888a, p. 409, 1925, p. 611). This interpretation constitutes an obligation to work. Who does not work declines to help a fellow man, harming society in two ways: First, by not contributing and second by costing, because the person who does not work usually cannot be liable for him- or herself. As work has the nimbus of the social, not to work becomes antisocial (Luther, 1906, p. 495; 1913b, p. 88; 1914, pp. 383–384; 1929, p. 321).

Work as a "Law of Nature"

Luther considers every kind of work as equal and equally necessary to grace the divine mercy given to man. All differences—esteem, monetary, and regarding the object of work—are constructed by humans and have no impact on the religious value of work. It is the expression of a Godly principle, directed toward the common good. Every work is equally socially and theologically relevant (Luther, 1891, p. 336). By working, humans imitate the creating God, establishing a contact with the divine (Luther, 1899, pp. 367–369; 1913a, p. 436). Work is also probation to accept the God-given task of active, productive participation in society under God. Working hard is a goal for the education of children, to be practiced and internalized at a young age (Luther, 1910, p. 149).

When work is conceptualized as '"profession" or "calling," it is framed in a way that the object of work matters for the individual's place in society (cf. Geser, 2009). Luther interprets the theological function of work on a more fundamental level: The mere activity of work as a divine assignment and material task to human's existence on earth. The following excerpt clarifies this stance. It is taken from the sermon "A Treatise on Good Works," an interpretation of the Ten Commandments (1520):

> But some say: "Yes, rely upon that, take no thought, and see whether a roasted chicken will fly into your mouth!" I do not say that a man shall not labor and seek a living; but he shall not worry, not be greedy, not despair, thinking that he will not have enough; for in Adam we are all condemned to labor, when God says to him, Genesis iii, "In the sweat of thy face shalt thou eat bread." And Job v, "As the birds to flying, so is man born unto labor." Now the birds fly without worry and greed, and so we also should labor without worry and greed; but if you do worry and are greedy, wishing that the roasted chicken fly into your mouth: worry and be greedy, and see whether you will thereby fulfill God's Commandment and be saved! (Luther, 1888b, 271f; Luther, 2008, translated)

Work has a naturalistic implicitness; it is part of an *ordre naturel*. It belongs to humans "as the birds to flying." Regardless of the type, work contributes to a superordinate instance legitimized by divine grace. Those who work do not have to worry, as God will take care of them—as long as the motivation to work is not greed. To negate this natural state by being idle is an open affront to the structuring nature of work and considered counterproductive for social well-being.

Work as Self-Realization

Luther's idea of man is divided into two central aspects: an inner person, his or her thoughts and opinions, and an outer person, the body and deeds visible on the outside. For the reformer, it is the life task of a Christian to bring these two persons in line. Work helps with this integration (Luther, 1897b, p. 21). It bridges the tension between the inner person with his expectations and the outer person hindered by the inertness and idleness of the body. Work connects the inner capabilities, expectations, and moral concepts to the outside world (1897b, pp. 30–33). And it induces a structure for the working individual. Work overcomes the idleness of the body and applies a rhythm between work and leisure (Luther, 1888b, pp. 247–249.). Subsistence is only one, maybe even the lesser aspect of work. It is supposed to be meaningful, useful, and worthwhile. It reflects the worker's personality and fulfills his or her inner expectations of what is good. Work empowers the inner person to do good works by bringing in line mind and body. Work serves the working individual (Luther, 1883, p. 243).

Idleness, on the other hand, is an open affront to this structuring nature of work. Luther elaborates on this aspect in one of his best-known writings, "On the Freedom of a Christian" (1520):

> Thus it comes that from the requirements of his own body a man cannot take his ease, but is compelled on its account to do many good works, that he may bring it into subjection. Yet these works are not the means of his justification before God, he does them out of disinterested love to the service of God; looking to no other end than to do what is well-pleasing to Him whom he desires to obey dutifully in all things. On this principle every man may easily instruct himself in what measure, and with what distinctions, he ought to chasten his own body. He will fast, watch, and labour, just as much as he sees to suffice for keeping down the wantonness and concupiscence of the body. (Luther, 1897b, pp. 30–31; Luther, 2014, translated).

Idleness is strongly connected to sin and blasphemy and counterbalances individual well-being and the superordinate commonwealth. The rejection of work is therefore to be battled (Luther, 1888a, p. 451; 1897a, pp. 654–655).

In the next section we will see, how these three aspects of Luther's interpretation of work relate the production of meaning within the organization.

INDIVIDUAL PRODUCTION OF MEANING: RELIGIOUS AND ORGANIZATIONAL

For Luther, work is key to the human condition. He considers it not only a mere outcome of a *human resource*, but a blend of individual functions. Both for the individual and the organization this interpretation can improve the quality of work—via the ascription of "meaning." To apply Luther's idea to an organizational context, we first have to distinguish the production of meaning in the two systems of reference: religion and the organization.

Religion here is considered a cultural phenomenon with the capability of delivering interpretations of reality, thereby contributing to individual production of meaning. Religion reduces contingency—the fact that life-experiences are open-ended and indeterminate, that the alternatives are endless and uncertainty is the rule. Religion provides a concept to cope with this contingency by connecting the individual to a narrative that is beyond him- or herself. Religion provides a structure and an objective within the chaotic world and produces meaning within the seemingly meaningless (Lübbe, 1986, p. 227). It is marked by a high degree of collective, authoritatively prescribed commitment and backed by elaborate beliefs. It offers a structure for interpreting reality. The interpretations are not confined to the religious sphere, but spill over to other spheres like the economic sphere, such as, by religiously regulating business action (like regulating interest-rated) or promoting a certain attitude toward work ("working as a service for God"). These spherical transgressions produce positive or negative incentives for individual economic action by "fostering traits such as work ethic, honesty (and hence trust), thrift, charity, hospitality to strangers and so on" (McCleary & Barro, 2006, pp. 50–51). Religion strengthens interpretational structures by casting them into belief. It is this individual belief that has the capacity to reinforce or constrain certain actions. External features of religion—such as institutional forms or institutional faith—are relevant in this perspective only so far, as they influence this belief.

This understanding of religion as an individual, interpretational, contingency-reducing structure overlaps with the "secular" production of meaning within the organization. Meaning is closely connected to sense-making, comparable with the function of religion above, as "turning circumstances into a situation that is comprehended explicitly in words and that serves as a springboard into action" (Weick, Sutcliffe, & Obstfeld, 2005, p. 409). In this process, "meaning" is more than just "understanding" the sensemaking. Exceeding the common understanding of meaning in the sensemaking-literature (Maitlis & Christianson, 2014, p. 109), we understand it as the guiding principles behind the sensemaking that arrange action according to what is considered "meaningful," embedding individual action into a bigger picture. Meaning gives action stability and a perspective toward the future (Weick et al., 2005, p. 410) and functions as an interpretation within sensemaking that connects cognitive experience with superordinate concepts.

Unlike the sphere of religion, this "secular" meaning and its production are not restricted to confessional belonging, serving as an individual resource irrespective of religious denomination or believes. "Meaning of work" therefore is defined as an individual orientation gained from work, exceeding work's technical dimension of production and subsistence.

Within any given organizational context, this meaning of work overarches the sensemaking-process and embeds individual economic action into a broader perspective, "beyond what's good for business" (Basu & Palazzo, 2008, p. 129). With work acting as a common denominator on anthropological grounds, religious and organizational productions of meaning play together well, without the theological strings attached.

With this understanding we can now turn to Luther's interpretations of work and see how they work for the production of secular meaning.

Luther as a Source for Meaning in Contemporary Organizations

The analysis of Luther's commensurability for producing meaning within today's organization, takes into account only the social, not the theological functions the reformer ascribes to work. The culturally diverse and multireligious nature of modern-day workplaces (cf. Hartel, Klarsfeld, Ngunjiri, & Syed, 2015) makes the "secularized" version of Luther more applicable: The social functions are independent of cultural diversity, presenting us with the social core of the reformer's thought. Without the theological strings, we transfer Luther's notions of meaningful work to today's organizations and their production of meaning.

We aim at developing meaning and sensemaking with work in different regards: In Luther's interpretations we find corresponding statements on three levels that are not confined to theological concepts. By connecting them to nonreligious economic foundations, the concepts become feasible for nonconfessional applications:

- *Social Meaning*:   Luther describes work as a service to the fellow man that pleases god. We find a secular version of this interpretation in work-psychology, where work is ascribed a socially structuring, forming, mobilizing and community-creating effect—all of which are considered to have a positive impact on social cohesion:

  > First, employment imposes a time structure on the waking day; second, employment implies regularly shared experiences and contacts with people outside the nuclear family; third, employment links individuals to goals and purposes that transcend their own; fourth, employment defines aspects of personal status and identity; and finally, employment enforces activity. (Jahoda, 1981, p. 188)

  From an organizational perspective, embedding the individual work activity into a larger, social horizon has a positive impact on the attitude toward work. By ascribing a common and social "good" to individual work action, it creates *social meaning* by placing it into a larger social context (cf. Basu & Palazzo, 2008, 129);

- *Economic Meaning*:   Luther describes work as a naturalistic, positive process innate to mankind, regardless of the specific type of work. If everyone consistently does his or her duty, common good will come of this collective effort. This is in line with classical economic thought, where national wealth is first and foremost connected to aggregated individual production:

> The annual labour of every nation is the fund which originally supplies it with all the necessaries and conveniencies of life which it annually consumes, and which consist always either in the immediate produce of that labour, or in what is purchased with that produce from other nations. (Smith & Wight, 1776/2007, p. XXXIX)

By pursuing my own work, I can better my own and societies' economic condition. Charging work this way results in giving the individual contribution an *economic meaning* that exceeds the individual. Working means doing good on a national-economic level: The worker with his work becomes part of the mighty *invisible hand*. Within a work-environment based on the division of labor, the naturalistic approach to work makes possible to focus not on the content of a specific work (that you might not fully understand) but on a larger and sensible context. The small individual contribution adds to a larger structure (cf. Basu & Palazzo, 2008, p. 129).

- *Personal Meaning*:   Work according to Luther functions as a tool for personal structuring and mental cleanliness, harmonizing the individual and bringing together his inner and outer self. Reference to God is secondary for this function: Work has the ability to overcome the sluggish body for personal gain. To not work, due to idleness or unemployment, therefore is not only problematic as it affects the aforementioned *social* and *economic* production of meaning. It has a negative impact on the individual itself. This assessment is echoed in modern unemployment research: "[The] unemployed lost their sense of time, they felt isolated, purposeless and on the scrap heap, without identity and self-esteem, and bored" (Jahoda & Rush, 1980, p. 13). To not work therefore from an organizational perspective can be considered as *destroying meaning*.

Luther's functions of work, even without any otherworldly reference, exceed both the subject of work and the working individual. By connecting individual work to social, economic and personal gain, it reduces the individual's burden of contingency, contributes to sense making and ultimately to the production of meaning, making it a role model for the faith-work-nexus in a culturally diverse context.

Conclusions on the Generalizability of Luther's Concept of Work

Lutheran theology, when understood as described above in a nonconfessional way and focused on its social aspects, can serve as a source for individual production of meaning in a modern work-environment. This allows for two conclusions:

Luther's notions of work are not contingent upon a religious context, not even a religious individual. Rather, they contain general guidelines on how work exceeds it's mere technical functions toward the production of meaning. Luther makes work an anthropological cornerstone of the *human condition*. We thus can address religiously diverse workplaces that could benefit from the notions of work derived from the reformer.

Even within a seemingly secular work-environment, religious reasoning has a place. This finding is in line with well-known economist Schumpeter's evaluation that "the capitalist order not only rests on props made of extracapitalist material but also derives its energy from extracapitalist patterns of behavior" (Schumpeter, 2003, pp. 161–162) Schumpeter recognizes economy's need for diverse presuppositions and emphasizes the behavioral patterns that go along with this "extracapitalist material." Luther's understanding of work is a substantiation of this "material." By analyzing it, we gain a more complete picture of the modern economy and its multifactorial composition.

Luther's concept of work as part of the human condition embeds the individual in his social environment, fosters cooperation and productive economic activity. Besides the manifest functions of work, these are major factors for producing meaning—or, if disturbed, for reducing it. The quintessence of Luther's legacy regarding work: Work is more than just a human resource—it is a benevolent service for oneself and others, irrespective of confession or belief.

NOTE

1.   This paper builds on the PhD thesis of one of the authors on Luther's notion of work (Zapf, 2014), being the starting point for the following discussion of meaningfulness in organizations.

REFERENCES

Anderson, G. M. (1988). Mr. Smith and the preachers: The economics of religion in the wealth of nations. *Journal of Political Economy, 96*(5), 1066–1088. doi:10.2307/1837247

Azzi, C., & Ehrenberg, R. (1975). Household allocation of time and church attendance. *The Journal of Political Economy, 83*(1), 27–56.

Basu, K., & Palazzo, G. (2008). Corporate social responsibility: A process model of sensemaking. *Academy of Management Review, 33*(1), 122–136.

Chadwyck-Proquest. (2013). Luthers werke im WWW. Weimarer ausgabe. [Web page] Retrieved from http://www.luther.chadwyck.co.uk

Frambach, H. (2010). Work and ethics in the economic thought of reformation. In J. Backhaus (Ed.), *The reformation as a pre-condition for modern capitalism* (pp. 75–92). Berlin, Germany: Lit.

Geser, H. (2009). Work values and Christian religiosity. *Journal of Religion and Society, 11*, 1–36.

Hartel, C., Klarsfeld, A., Ngunjiri, F., & Syed, J. (2015). Religious diversity in the workplace: Conflict, harmony and performance. *Proceedings of the Academy of Management Annual Meeting, 2015*, 14105.

Iannaccone, L. (1997). Rational choice: Framework for the scientific study of religion. In L. A. Young (Ed.), *Rational choice theory and religion: Summary and assessment* (pp. 25–44). New York, NY: Routledge.

Iannaccone, L. (1998). Introduction to the economics of religion. *Journal of Economic Literature, 36*(3), 1465–1495.

Jahoda, M. (1981). Work, employment, and unemployment: Values, theories, and approaches in social research. *American Psychologist, 36*(2), 184.

Jahoda, M., & Rush, H. (1980). *SPRU Occasional Paper Series: Vol. 12. Work, employment and unemployment: An overview of ideas and research results in the social science literature.* Sussex, England: Science Policy Research Unit, University of Sussex.

Lübbe, C. (1986). *Religion nach der Aufklärung.* Graz, Austria: Styria.

Luther, M. (1883). Eynn sermon von dem ablasz unnd gnade durch den wirdigenn doctornn martinum luther augustiner tzu wittenbergk [A sermon about indulgence and grace by Martin Luther from Wittenberg]. In D. Knaake (Ed.), *D. Martin Luthers Werke: Vol. 6. Schriften, 1. Band, schriften 1512/18* (pp. 243–246). Weimar, Germany: H. Böhlau. (Original work published 1517)

Luther, M. (1888a). An den christlichen adel deutscher nation von des christlichen standes besserung [Address to the Christian nobility]. In D. Knaake (Ed.), *D. Martin Luthers Werke: Vol. 6. Schriften, 6. Band 1519/20* (pp. 404–469). Weimar, Germany: H- Böhlau. (Original work published 1520)

Luther, M. (1888b). Von den guten werckenn [On good works]. In D. Knaake (Ed.), *D. Martin Luthers Werke: Vol. 6. Schriften, 6. Band 1519/20* (pp. 202–276). Weimar, Germany: H. Böhlau. (Original work published 1520)

Luther, M. (1891). Epistel sanct petri gepredigt und ausgelegt [Interpreting and preaching St. Peter's Epistel]. In E. Pietsch (Ed.), *D. Martin Luthers Werke: Vol. 15. Schriften, 12. Band, reihenpredigt über 1. Petrus 1522; predigten 1522/23; schriften 1523* (pp. 293–313). Weimar, Germany: H. Böhlau. (Original work published 1523)

Luther, M. (1897a). Ob kriegsleutte auch ynn seligem stande seyn kuenden [On the question if warriors can be from the blessed station]. In E. Walther (Ed.), *D. Martin Luthers Werke: Vol. 6. Schriften, 19. Band, schriften 1526* (pp. 616–662). Weimar, Germany: H. Böhlau. (Original work published 1526)

Luther, M. (1897b). Von der freyheyt eynisz christen menschen [On the freedom of a Christian]. In E. Pietsch (Ed.), *D. Martin Luthers Werke: Vol. 7. Schriften, 7. Band, schriften 1520/21* (pp. 19–38). Weimar, Germany: H. Böhlau. (Original work published 1520)

Luther, M. (1899). Martinus luther allen lieben freunden ynn christo zu rigen und ynn liffland [From Martin Luther to his dear Christian friends in Riga and Latvia]. In E. Pietsch (Ed.), *D. Martin Luthers Werke: Vol. 15. Schriften, 15. Band, predigten und schriften 1524* (pp. 360–378). Weimar, Germany: H. Böhlau. (Original work published 1524)

Luther, M. (1906). Das fünffte, sechste und siebend capitel S. Matthei gepredigt und ausgelegt [Preaching and interpreting Matthew 5, 6 and 7]. In E. Pietsch (Ed.), *D. Martin Luthers Werke: Vol. 32. Schriften, 32. Band, predigten 1530; reihenpredigten über matthäus 5 –7 1530/32* (pp. 299–544). Weimar, Germany: H. Böhlau. (Original work published 1532)

Luther, M. (1910). Das vierde gepot [The Fourth Commandment]. In K. Drescher (Ed.), *D. Martin Luthers Werke: Vol. 30. Schriften, 30. I. Band, katechismuspredigten 1528; großer und kleiner katechismus 1529* (pp. 146–157). Weimar, Germany: H. Böhlau. (Original work published 1529)

Luther, M. (1913a). Einweyhung eines newen hauses zum predigampt goettlichs worts erbawet jm churfürstlichen schloss zu torgaw [Inauguration of a new church in the castle of Torgau]. In K. Drescher & M. Buchwald (Eds.), *D. Martin Luthers Werke: Vol. 49. Schriften, 49. Band 1540/45* (pp. 588–615). Weimar, Germany: H. Böhlau. (Original work published 1544)

Luther, M. (1913b). Es sagen nu, die den HERRN furchten, das seine guete weret ewiglich [Let those who fear the Lord say, 'His loving kindness endures forever']. In K. Drescher (Ed.), *D. Martin Luthers Werke: Vol. 6. Schriften, 31. I. Band, psalmenauslegungen 1529/32* (pp. 87–92). Weimar, Germany: H. Böhlau. (Original work published 1532)

Luther, M. (1914). An die pfarrherren, wider den wucher zu predigen, vermahnung [To the preachers: A warning, to preach against usury]. In K. Drescher & M. Buchwald (Eds.), *D. Martin Luthers Werke: Vol. 49. Schriften, 51. Band, predigten 1545/46; auslegung des 23. Und 101. Psalms 1534/36; schriften 1540/41; sprichwörter-sammlung* (pp. 331–424). Weimar, Germany: H. Böhlau. (Original work published 1540)

Luther, M. (1917). Address to the Christian nobility of the German nation respecting the reformation of the Christian estate. In C. Eliot (Ed.), *The Harvard classics* (Vol. 36, pp. 276–357). New York, NY: P. F. Collier & Son.

Luther, M. (1925). Das euangelium am ersten sontag des advents [matth. 21, 1 –9] matthei .Xxi [The Gospel on the first Sunday of Advent]. In K. Drescher & A. Bebermeyer (Eds.), *D. Martin Luthers Werke: Vol. 10. Schriften, 10. I. 2. Band, adventspostille 1522; roths sommerpostille 1526* (pp. 21–62). Weimar, Germany: H. Böhlau. (Original work published 1522)

Luther, M. (1929). [CCCLXXXIX] am XIX. Sontag nach trinitatis, epistel [On the XIX. Sunday after Trinitatis]. In A. Bebermeyer (Ed.), *D. Martin Luthers Werke: Vol. 6. Schriften, 22. Band, crucigers sommerpostille (forts.) 1544* (pp. 310–322). Weimar, Germany: H. Böhlau. (Original work published 1544)

Luther, M. (2008). A treatise on good works. *Project gutenberg* [Web page]. Retrieved from http://www.gutenberg.org/files/418/418-h/418-h.htm

Luther, M. (2014). On the freedom of a Christian. Fordham university—Internet history sourcebooks. Text from Henry Wace and C. A. Buchheim, first principles of the Reformation, London: John Murray, 1883 [Web page]. Retrieved from Http://legacy.fordham.edu/halsall/mod/luther-freedomchristian.asp

Lübbe, C. (1986). *Religion nach der Aufklärung.* Graz, Austria: Styria.

Maitlis, S., & Christianson, M. (2014). Sensemaking in organizations: Taking stock and moving forward. *The Academy of Management Annals, 8*(1), 57–125.

McCleary, R., & Barro, R. (2003). Religion and economic growth across countries. *American Sociological Review, 68*, 760–781.

McCleary, R., & Barro, R. (2006). Religion and economy. *The Journal of Economic Perspectives, 20*(2), 49–72.

Peukert. H. (2010). Martin Luther: A first modern economist. In J. Backhaus (Ed.), *The reformation as a pre-condition for modern capitalism* (pp. 13–63). Berlin, Germany: LIT.

Pirenne. H. (1986). *Sozial- und wirtschaftsgeschichte europas im mittelalter.* Tübingen, Germany: Francke.

Schumpeter, J.A. (2003). *Capitalism, socialism and democracy.* New York, NY: Routledge. (Original work published 1943)

Seele, P. (2009). „Gelt ist auff erden der irdisch got" - Überlegungen zu einer Religionsökonomie des Geldes [Money as the mundane God – Observations regarding Ecnomics of Religion and money]. *Theologische Zeitschrift* 04/65. 346–365.

Seele, P. (2010). Interest and discipline. In Russian Christian Academy for the Humanities (Ed.), *Calvin and the modern world* (pp. 91–103). St. Petersburg, Russia: RCAH.

Seele, P., Gatti, L., & Lohse, A. (2014). Whose economics of religion? *Journal of Religion in Europe, 7*, 51–79.

Smith, A., & Wight, J. (2007). *An inquiry into the nature and causes of the wealth of nations.* Petersfield, England: Harriman House. (Original work published 1776)

Troeltsch, E. (1906). Die bedeutung des protestantismus für die entstehung der modernen welt. Vortrag, gehalten auf der IX. Versammlung deutscher historiker zu stuttgart am 21. April 1906 [The meaning of Protestantism for the development of the modern world. Presentation on the IX. Summit of German historians in Stuttgart]. *Historische Zeitschrift, 97*(1), 1–66.

Weber, M. (2001). *Protestant ethic and the spirit of capitalism.* New York, NY: Routledge. (Original work published 1930)

Weick, K., Sutcliffe, K., & Obstfeld, D. (2005). Organizing and the process of sensemaking. *Organization Science, 16*(4), 409–421. doi:10.1287/orsc.1050.0133

Wood, D. (2002). *Medieval economic thought.* Cambridge, England: Cambridge University Press.

Zapf, L. (2014). *Die religiöse arbeit der marktwirtschaft: Ein religionsökonomischer vergleich*. Baden-Baden, Germany: Nomos.
Zapf, L. (2015). Martin Luther, wealth and labor: The market economy's links to prosperity gospel. In M. Heuser (Ed.), *Pastures of plenty: Tracing religio-scapes of prosperity gospel in Africa and beyond* (pp. 279–292). Frankfurt, Germany: Peter Lang.

PART II

ORGANIZATION

CHAPTER 7

DECENT WORK, MEANINGFUL WORK, AND DEVELOPMENTAL WORK

Three Key Ethical Concepts From Catholic Social Teaching

Domènec Melé
IESE Business School

INTRODUCTION

Work is a key element of business enterprise. There is no business without work and organizing work efficiently is a crucial aspect in managing business. However, work also entails important ethical and social dimensions, which have been considered by scholars, international organizations, and moral voices. Among these latter the Catholic Church, who has a long tradition in the social aspects of work and its ethical dimension (Gaburro & Cressotti, 1998; Pontifical Council for Justice and Peace, 2004, Chap. 6). This tradition dates back to the 19th century, when Pope Leo XIII (1891) addressed the condition of workers and other problems, known as the "Social Question," and arising from the backdrop of the Industrial Revo-

Faith and Work: Christian Perspectives, Research, and Insights Into the Movement
pp. 117–130

lution and strong liberal capitalism. Catholic social teaching (CST) has been continued by his successors in the papacy and bishops worldwide and is now a consolidated body of doctrine. The philosophical and theological understanding of work and the ethics of work was specifically considered by Pope John Paul II in his encyclical letter *Laborem exercens* (1981). Connecting with the Social Question, John Paul II stated that "human work is a key, probably the essential key, to the whole social question, if we try to see that question really from the point of view of man's good" (John Paul II, 1981, n. 3). The connection of work with the good of the person is precisely the essence of the ethics of work, if we accept that ethics refers to what contributes to being a good human being.

It is not our purpose to develop here, in the limited space of a chapter, a detailed analysis of Catholic social teachings on the ethics of work. Our aim is rather to present three concepts which can summarize most of these teachings; those of decent work, meaningful work and developmental work.

DECENT WORK

"Decent work," a term used by the International Labour Organization (ILO) since early 21st century,

> to sum up the aspirations of people in their working lives. It involves opportunities for work that is productive and delivers a fair income, security in the workplace and social protection for families, better prospects for personal development and social integration, freedom for people to express their concerns, organize and participate in the decisions that affect their lives and equality of opportunity and treatment for all women and men.[1]

These are old ethical and social demands; the novelty of "decent work" is that is a comprehensive concept and strategically worthy, and a holistic human rights approach (MacNaughton & Frey, 2011).

According to Rodgers, Lee, Swepston, and Daele (2009, pp. 223–224), Mr. Juan Somavia, director-general of the ILO, saw decent work as a strategic way of framing ILO objectives in that the term encompassed the needs of workers and developing countries without alienating employers and industrialized nations. Actually, decent work is a central aspect in the current ILO agenda, with special emphasis in four pillars—employment creation, social protection, rights at work, and social dialogue. These four pillars of the decent work agenda have become *integral elements* of the new 2030 UN Agenda for Sustainable Development.[2]

Catholic social teaching, since its very origins, has included many of the matters included within the notion of decent work, including compensation, working conditions, job security, and labor rights. Pope Leo XIII defended a living wage, dignity in working conditions, and several labor rights including the rights to fair labor contracts, and to form and join trade unions (Leo XIII, 1891). Pope John Paul II devoted the fourth chapter of *Laborem Excercens* to the "rights of workers" and examined these in the broad context of human rights as a whole: "The *human rights that flow from work* are part of the broader context of those fundamental rights of the person" (John Paul II, 1981, n. 16, emphasis in the original here and hereafter).

Regarding the worker's compensation, John Paul II affirms: "in the context of the present there is no more important way for securing a just relationship between the worker and the employer than that constituted by remuneration for work" (John Paul II, 1981, n. 19). More specifically he adds this criterion: "Just remuneration for the work of an adult who is responsible for a family means remuneration which will suffice for estab-lishing and properly maintaining a family and for providing security for its future." He envisages the possibility of a *family wage* sufficient for the needs of the family or through *other social measures* such as family allow-ances or grants to mothers devoting themselves exclusively to their fami-lies. Remuneration includes wages and various *social benefits,* which intend "to ensure the life and health of workers and their families" and "the right to a pension and to insurance for old age and in case of accidents at work" (John Paul II, 1981, n. 19).

Regarding working conditions, John Paul II pointing out that "the whole labor process must be organized and adapted in such a way as to respect the requirements of the person and his or her forms of life, above all life in the home, taking into account the individual's age and sex" (1981, n. 19). Among the labor rights he mentions are the right of associ-ation (unions) (1981, n. 20), the right to weekly rest, including Sunday, reasonable working hours and vacations (1981, n. 19).

Safety and job security is also mentioned: "Among these rights [of the workers] there should never be overlooked the right to a working environ-ment and to manufacturing processes which are not harmful to the work-ers' physical health or to their moral integrity" (John Paul II, 1981, n. 16) He insisted that careful attention must be paid to the physical and psy-chological working conditions of disabled people—as for all workers—to their just remuneration, to the possibility of their promotion, and to the elimination of various obstacles (John Paul II, 1981, n. 21).

Pope John Paul II explicitly highlighted the concept of decent work during the "Jubilee of workers" (2000). Addressing a crowd of workers, he appealed for "a global coalition in favor of 'decent work.'" His successor, Benedict XVI, recalled this in his social encyclical-letter *Caritas in Veritate* (love in truth) and developed the meaning of decent work. According to

Benedict XVI, in short, decent work "means work that expresses the essential dignity of every man and woman in the context of their particular society" (2009, n. 63). To be more specific, he pointed out a number of characteristics included in the concept of decent work. Namely, he stated that decent work is that, which

> is freely chosen, effectively associating workers, both men and women, with the development of their community; work that enables the worker to be respected and free from any form of discrimination; work that makes it possible for families to meet their needs and provide schooling for their children, without the children themselves being forced into labor; work that permits the workers to organize themselves freely, and to make their voices heard; work that leaves enough room for rediscovering one's roots at a personal, familial and spiritual level; work that guarantees those who have retired a decent standard of living. (Benedict XVI, 2009, n. 63).

The Catholic Church is not alone in defending matters included in the concept of decent work. In the 20th century, along with many theoretical developments, labor rights have been progressively recognized and proclaimed by various international organizations and increasingly guaranteed by individual states.

The International Covenant on Economic, Social, and Cultural Rights, a multilateral treaty adopted by the United Nations General Assembly December 16, 1966, deals with several aspects of decent work. Namely, in its Article 7 it recognizes the right of everyone to "just and favorable" working conditions, including fair wages, with equal pay for equal work, sufficient to provide a decent living for workers and their dependents; safe working conditions; equal opportunity in the workplace; and sufficient rest and leisure, including limited working hours and regular, paid holidays.

Now human rights in the workplace is also present in academic literature and in industrial practice in many countries (Byre, 1988; Gross, 2012). However, this is not the case anywhere and the so-called "sweatshops" remain in some developing countries, in factories where people work long hours with low pay, in uncomfortable and even unsafe or dangerous conditions. This has been severely criticized (Arnold & Bowie, 2003; Arnold & Hartman, 2005; Radin & Calkins, 2006), although others (e.g., Zwolinski, 2007) defend the freedom of workers to accept these conditions and as a better alternative facing unemployment and are against interference in the conditions of sweatshop labor by third parties such as governments or consumer boycott groups. Nevertheless, these two objections ignore the injustice of abusing of the situation of need in which workers are involved and imposing them inhuman working conditions. In addition, as Chau (2016) points out, the potential gains of avoiding sweatshops include an increase in decent work employment, workers' capability to be productive at work and to be vertically mobile, a proworker shift in distribution, and an improvement in overall efficiency.

The sweatshops problem was already envisioned by Leo XIII more than a century ago. He was in favor of the workers and the employer make free agreements; nevertheless, he made clear that

> there underlies a dictate of natural justice more imperious and ancient than any bargain between man and man.... If through necessity or fear of a worse evil the workman accept harder conditions because an employer or contractor will afford him no better, he is made the victim of force and injustice. (Leo XIII, 1891, n. 45).

One might wonder if there is a difference regarding decent work in CST and in other approaches. There are not too many different specific contents, but there is a clear difference is the foundation. While international covenants and some movements are based on consensus, CST provides an ethical foundation based on the dignity of human work and the innate human rights associated with this dignity. Apart from philosophical reasons, the Church finds the deep roots of human dignity in the creation of the human being "in the image of God" (Bible, Genesis 1:27), in the Incarnation of Jesus Christ and his Redemption of all humankind –giving a human nature a great dignity– and, above all, in the human person's call to communion with God (Vatican Council II, *Gaudium et Spes*, Chap. 1).

MEANINGFUL WORK

The notion of "meaningful work" has often been related to motives as to why one enjoys one's own work. Initially, the idea of meaningful work arose in contrast with mechanistic approaches, common at the beginning of management, focused exclusively on maximizing productivity through an efficient organization of work. In the 1970 the idea of meaningful work emerged. Terkel, for instance, wrote: "Working is about the search for daily meaning as well as daily bread, for recognition as well as cash, for astonishment rather than torpor; in short, for a sort of life rather than a Monday through Friday sort of dying" (1975, p. 1).

Recent management literature has also focused on meaningful work in a broad sense and interest in this concept has increased considerably, bringing about a wide variety in conceptual and empirical research. Today meaningful work is a concept dealt with in areas related to transformational leadership, organizational culture, and employee engagement, as well as human behavior in organizations, business ethics, and organizational studies.

Conceptual approaches on meaningful work focus on substantive meaningful work, while empirical studies basically analyze what type of work is perceived as meaningful by workers and what influence meaningful work has on performance. Among the former, Bowie (1998) has proposed a Kantian substantive meaningful work, Beadle and Knight (2012), another based on Aristotle and Tablan (2015) explores meaningful work from Catholic social teaching. Empirical studies show that having meaningful work is essential for the well-being of workers and their performance, and consequently providing them with meaningful work should be a requirement for business establishments. As one might expect, meaningful work from this subjective perspective has different significance for different people or groups of people. For instance, empirical research on meaningful work among blue-, pink-, and white-collar occupations found that unity with others and developing the inner self were regarded as equally important for white-, blue-, and pink-collar workers, while white-collar workers placed more importance on expressing full potential and serving others than blue-collar workers (Lips-Wiersma, Wright, & Dik, 2016).

CST points out that "the general situation of man in the modern world, studied, and analyzed in its various aspects of geography, culture and civilization, calls for the discovery of the *new meanings of human work*." (John Paul II 1981, n. 2). CST itself presents a set of meanings of work, and so contributes to substantive meaningful work, which can become motives for subjective meaningful work. Among them the following:

(a) *Work as necessity for life or to live.*   The necessity of work to earn a living is probably a widely-shared meaning of work. Leo XIII present this meaning with special reference to laborers. He stated that work is necessary because "without the result of labor a man cannot live, and self-preservation is a law of nature, which it is wrong to disobey" (Leo XIII, 1891, n. 44). Obviously, the necessity of work to live is not reduced to earning a living. Giving work a wide sense of definition, not one limited to employment, work is an existential aspect of life. Manual labor was reserved to slaves in the Ancient Greece and Rome, but other people devoted a great part of their life to other activities, which can be recognized as work: philosophical refection, politics, army, et cetera. Work is indeed "a fundamental dimension of human existence" (John Paul II, 1981, n. 4), and even people who do not need to work to live practice some work.

(b) *Work as a personal activity that gives a human resealing to production.*   Leo XIII presented this second meaning. Work is personal, he said, "inasmuch as the force which acts is bound up with the personality and is the exclusive property of him who acts, and, further, was given to him for his advantage" (1891, n. 44). This meaning has been particularly emphasized by subsequent CST. Thus, the Vatican Council II states: "labor, whether it is engaged in independently or hired by someone else, comes immediately from the person, who as it were stamps the things of nature with his seal and subdues them to his will" (*Gaudium et Spes*, n. 67). In a certain sense, the worker humanizes matter through his or her work. Perceiving the personal sense of the product of one's work is source of meaning. "I made it" can be said by a little child regarding an elemental drawing, and by an adult looking at the result of her work. This personal character of work entails a deep meaning: "Human labor which is expended in the production and exchange of goods or in the performance of economic services is superior to the other elements of economic life, for the latter have only the nature of tools" (*Gaudium et Spes*, n. 67). The personal aspect of work has been enriched by John Paul II (1981, nn. 5-10) with the notion of "subjective meaning" of work and its pre-eminence over the "objective meaning" (see below).

(c) *Works as creativity and entrepreneurial spirit.*   This is a consequence of the personal character of work. Creativity and innovation –the essence of entrepreneurial spirit– accompany work, to a greater or lesser degree, especially if work is not prevented by external constraints (regulation, proceeding, orders, etc.). The style of attending to customers in a shop could serve as an example, since it entails certain creativity due to the personality and character of the person who deals with clients. CST stresses the role of disciplined and creative human work and, as an essential part of that work, "initiative and entrepreneurial ability" (John Paul II, 1991, n. 32).

(d) *Work as a calling.*   CST takes the view that work is a calling or vocation. Every person is endowed with talents and they try to put them into action working for good causes. The theological perspective presents the vocational sense of human work reflecting from the narrations of the creation. In the first chapter of Genesis appears the calling to work in the divine mandate of "subdue the earth" (Genesis 1:28). More explicitly, in Chapter 2 of Genesis there is "The Lord God took the man and put him in the Garden of Eden to till and keep it" (Genesis 2:15). This sense could have been forgotten over time due to a greater emphasis on the painful side of work after the original sin and the Lord's words: "by the sweat of your face you shall eat bread" (Genesis 3:19). But this vision is a biased interpretation of the Scripture. The original meaning of work as innate vocation of the human being remains after the original fall (John Paul II 1981, n. 9, see also n. 4). Thus seeing work not as a punishment but as a calling introduces a positive meaning for working.

(e) *Work as a means of personal development.* In brief, through work people can grow as human beings. John Paul II is very explicit: "Work is a good thing for man—a good thing for his humanity—because through work man not only transforms nature, adapting it to his own needs, but he also achieves fulfilment as a human being and indeed, in a sense, becomes 'more a human being'" (1981, n. 9). This meaning is another important source of meaningful work and a crucial content, to which we will go back in the next section.

(f) *Work as service.* Work entails service for the usefulness of products or immediate results of work, for the know-how developed through work which may be applicable for future work. Indirectly, work is a means of serving one's own family and perhaps the needs of other people. CST stresses this meaning by recognizing that through labor a person ordinarily supports oneself and his or her family, serves others and can exercise genuine charity (*Gaudium et Spes*, n. 67). These services make a contribution to the common good.

(g) *Work as a moral duty.* Every man has the duty of working faithfully (*Gaudium et Spes*, n. 67). John Paul II provides two arguments for this duty (1981, n. 16). The first is that the human being must work, both because the Creator has commanded it and because of his own humanity. The second is that work is required in order to be maintained and developed. Man must work out of regard for others, especially his own family, but also for the society he belongs to, the country of which he is a child, and the whole human family of which he is a member. This universal sense of belonging comes from the consideration that each individual is heir to the work of generations and at the same time a sharer in building the future of those who will come after one in the succession of history. "All this—John Paul II concludes—constitutes the moral obligation of work, understood in its wide sense" (1981, n. 16).

(h) *Work as a means of establishing human relations and for uniting people.* By working persons join their fellow people (*Gaudium et Spes*, n. 67), and this creates relationships. John Paul II goes beyond this by stating that "it is characteristic of work that it first and foremost unites people" (John Paul II, 1981, n. 20). On this fact is based the possibility of building communities based on work. "In this consists its social power [of work]: the power to build a community" (John Paul II, 1981, n. 20). This is also the case of the business firm, in which different forms of work concur (Naughton, 2006): "both those who work and those who manage the means of produc-

tion or who own them must in some way be united in this community" (John Paul II, 1981, n. 20).

(i) *Work as a transcendent and spiritual activity.*   "The individual human
being may be given the meaning which it has in the eyes of God
and by means of which work enters into the salvation" (John Paul II,
n. 24). Around this, Christian faith has developed a rich spirituality.
Work is seen as a sharing in the activity of the Creator, and the
worker as "a partner in the work of bringing divine creation to per-
fection" (*Guadium et Spes*, n. 67; cf. John Paul II, n. 25). A Christian
tries to follow the footsteps of Jesus Christ, who conferred an emi-
nent dignity with his labor at Nazareth (John Paul II, n. 26), and in
offering labor to God Christians are associated with the redemptive
work of Jesus Christ (*Gaudium et Spes*, n. 67; John Paul II, n. 27).
Work can be a means of sanctification and a way of animating
earthly realities with the Spirit of Christ (*Catechism of Catholic
Church*, n. 2426).

All of these meanings, in one sense or another, have an ethical content.
At least, if we accept that the first stage of being ethical is seeking what is
really good. These meanings show that work is a good for the person: "in
spite of all this toil-perhaps, in a sense, because of it-work is a good thing
for man" (John Paul II, 1981, n. 6). Thus, discovering these meanings not
only leads to meaningful work but also to knowing the aspects in which
work contributes to doing good and being good.

In the human quest for meaning, explored by psychiatrist Victor
Frankl (2004), work should occupy a central position inasmuch as most
adults spend the majority of their waking hours at work, which often
serves as a primary source of purpose, belongingness, and identity
(Michaelson, Pratt, Grant, & Dunn, 2014). As Yeoman (2014) argues,
meaningful work is of first importance because it is a fundamental
human need which all persons require in order to satisfy their inescap-
able interests in freedom, autonomy, and dignity and that society—and
business ought—to be arranged to allow as many people as possible to
experience their work as meaningful through the development of the
relevant capabilities. From a managerial perspective, fostering meaningful work is both a responsibility and a good management practice. In
addition, meaningful work can yield benefits for organizations and lead
to positive work outcomes such as satisfied, engaged, and committed
employees, individual and organizational fulfilment, productivity, retention, and loyalty (Geldenhuys, Łaba, & Venter, 2014) and a significant
source of motivation (Kolstrup, 2012).

DEVELOPMENTAL WORK

Developmental work refers to how the worker can develop him or herself through his or her work. The philosophical base is discovering the inner effects of working on the worker and how he or she can develop him or herself through the work.

The notion of developmental work goes back to Aristotle, although he did not treatise specifically on it. However, he realized that there are some activities whose effects remain within the agent, such as seeing or thinking, while other activities have external production. The former—pure action (*praxis*, in Aristotelian terminology)—is immanent to the agent, while the latter—production (*poiesis*)—is transitive, since is embodied in an object. Aristotle gives primacy to *praxis* over *poiesis*, since in his view, "life is action and not production" (*Politics*, I, iv, 1254a7). One can also affirm that *praxis*—the action itself—is more important than *poiesis*—production—because while the latter is external to the agent, the former remains internal and can contribute to the flourishing of the worker (or his or her degradation as a human being).

Although it is possible an action without production, "production" entails "action" or, to be more precise, all *poiesis* is inscribed in a *praxis*. The reason is that production includes intentionality, not only regarding what and how produce, but also why to produce. In other words, human production has an immanent effect in the agent due to the purpose that one works for. In producing, we realize what we are making and why, and this shapes the agent's life, since life is action.

In a parallel manner, John Paul II coined the expression "subjective meaning of work," referring to the person who works, and based on the fact that the human being is the subject of work, in contrast with the "objective meaning of work" (John Paul II, 1981, nn. 5-6), understood as the sum of activities, resources, instruments and technologies used to produce things. Since the person is the subject of work, John Paul II argues in favor of the "pre-eminence of the subjective meaning of work over the objective one" (John Paul II, 1981, n. 6)

From a related perspective, working brings about not only external effects, but also effects in the worker. Working entails physical and psychological effects (tiredness, anguish, satisfaction, etc.) and learning. This learning includes acquisition of practical know-how or productive experience, with the corresponding development of skills, and also moral habits (virtues or vices) related with the intentionality of work and the awareness of the service or damage caused to others with the work performed. Virtues are the essence of human flourishing, and are acquired when one works with justice, honesty and a sense of service, and in general when practicing virtues. In this context, industriousness, the specific virtue of work, has full sense, inasmuch as virtue is something whereby man becomes good as man (cf. Aquinas, 1981, I-II, q. 40, a. 1, c.; I-II, q. 34, a. 2, ad 1; cf. John Paul II 1981, n. 9). Thus, productive work contributes to the professional and human development of the worker or, to his or her degradation if the work is not well-performed or not oriented to the moral good.

This double aspect of learning by action was considered by Aristotle (1980), who stated that "men become builders by building" and "just by doing just acts" (*Nicomachean Ethics*, II, 1, 1103a 2-4). Similarly, CST emphasizes developmental work, taking into account this learning. Human activity, "just as it proceeds from man, so it is ordered toward man. For when a man works he not only alters things and society, he develops himself as well. He learns much, he cultivates his resources, he goes outside of himself and beyond himself" (*Gaudium et spes*, n. 35). Echoing these words, John Paul II adds: "Work is a good thing for man— a good thing for his humanity—because through work man not only transforms nature, adapting it to his own needs, but he also achieves fulfilment as a human being and indeed, in a sense, becomes 'more a human being" (1981, n. 9).

Developmental work depends primarily on the will of the worker, but the organization can favor or not such development in designing the job, giving participation and fostering initiative, creativity, and responsibility. Actually, the Church applauds reaction against the "degradation of man as the subject of work" of workers engaged in narrowly specialized, monotonous, and depersonalized work in industrial plants, when the machine tends to dominate man (John Paul II, 1981, n. 8). In positive terms, it proposes the priority of labor over the process of production as an ethical principle (John Paul II, 1981, n. 12). In this process labor is always a primary efficient cause, while the process and all means of production remain a mere instrument or instrumental cause. Thus, "we must emphasize— wrote John Paul II—and give prominence to the primacy of man in the production process, the primacy of man over things" (1981, n. 12).

CONCLUSION

Work and the human being are closely related and so are these three concept we have try to sketch here. Decent work is derived from the subject of work—the person and his or her dignity. Meaningful work also refers to the human being: "Human activity, to be sure, takes its significance from its relationship to man" (*Gaudium et Spes*, n. 35) Developmental work has its foundation in that the human being is called to a continuous process of development and work is crucial aspect of the human vocation. "We were created with a vocation to work.... Work is a necessity, part of the meaning of life on this earth, a path to growth, human development and personal fulfilment" (Francis, 2014, n. 128).

The connection of work with the good of the person is precisely the essence of the ethics of work and these concepts are ethical in essence inasmuch as they refer to the good of the person; they are a source of ethical requirements in dealing with workers. Regarding the worker, they entail, first, becoming conscious of the dignity of the work, of any work regardless of its economic value and social evaluation. Second, being aware of the human and personal development one can achieve through work and the calling to do so. Third, being aware of the rich meaning of work which motivates one to work with industriousness to employ one's talents to the service of others and to work with a deeply spiritual sense.

Decent work, developmental work, and meaningful work have ethical normative implications for organizations—as well as economic implications which we do not deal with them here. In essence, they entail recognizing work as human activity, which requires managing workers and the organization of work ethically. The development of the three classes of work, although in an exploratory way, will hopefully provide useful insights for organizations.

Decent work requires a fair remuneration, humane working conditions, and respect for human rights. Meaningful work also has to be managed properly, fostering that workers can seek meaningful work or, at least, not impeding meaningful work to others, including the practice of spirituality at the workplace. Developmental work entails favoring human and personal development at the work place and, above all, avoiding these situations in which whereby "dead matter comes forth from the factory ennobled, while men there are corrupted and degraded" (Pius XI, 1931, n. 135; cf. John Paul II, 1981, n. 9).

Developmental work, as well as meaningful work, invites us to rethink organizational topics such as job design, incentive systems, control and trust, participation, initiative, and empowerment.

NOTES

1. http://www.ilo.org/global/topics/decent-work/lang--en/index.htm. Retrieved November 29, 2016.
2. http://www.ilo.org/global/topics/decent-work/lang--en/index.htm. Retrieved November 29, 2016.

REFERENCES

Aristotle. (1980) *The Nicomachean ethics.* Oxford, England: Oxford University Press. (Original work published 1925)
Aristotle. (1981). *The politics* (T. A. Sinclair, Trans.) London, England: Penguin.

Arnold, D. G., & Bowie, N. E. (2003). Sweatshops and respect for persons. *Business' Ethics Quarterly, 13*(2), 221–242.

Arnold, D. G., & Hartman, L. P. (2005). Beyond sweatshops: Positive deviancy and global labour practices. *Business Ethics: A European Review, 14*(3), 206–222.

Aquinas, T. (1981). *Summa theologiae*. London, England: Burns Oates and Washbourne. (Original work published 1273)

Beadle, R., & Knight, K. (2012). Virtue and meaningful work. *Business Ethics Quarterly, 22*(2), 433–450.

Benedict XVI. (2009), *Encyclical-letter 'Caritas in veritate.'* Retrieved from vatican.va

Bowie, N. E. (1998). A Kantian theory of meaningful work. *Journal of Business Ethics, 17*(8/10), 1083–1092.

Byre, A. D. (1988), *Human rights at the workplace: A handbook for industrial relations practitioners*. London, England: Policy Studies Institute.

Catechism of the Catholic Church. (2003), 2nd ed. London, England: Random House. Retrieved from at vatucan.va

Chau, N. H. (2016). On sweatshop jobs and decent work. *Journal of Development Economics, 121,* 120–134.

Farncis. (2014). Ecyclical-letter 'Laudato si'. Retrieved from vatican.va

Frankl, V. E. (2004). Man's search for meaning: An introduction to logotherapy. London, England: Random House/Rider.

Gaburro, G., & Cressotti, G. (1998). Work as such—The social teaching of the Church on human work. *International Journal of Social Economics, 25*(11/12), 1618–1639.

Geldenhuys, M., Łaba, K., & Venter, C. M. (2014). Meaningful work, work engagement and organisational commitment. *SAJIP: South African Journal of Industrial Psychology, 40*(1), 1–10.

Gross, J. A. (2010). *A shameful business: The case for human rights in the American workplace*. New York, NY: Cornell University Press.

John Paul II. (1981). Encyclical-letter 'Laborem exercerns.' Retrieved from vatican.va

John Paul II. (1991). Encyclical-letter 'Centesimus annus.' Retrieved from vatican.va

John Paul II. (2000). Address to jubilee of workers, greeting after Mass, May 1st. Retrieved from Vatican.va

Leo XIII. (1891). Encyclical-letter 'Rerum Novarum.' Retrieved from vatican.va

Lips-Wiersma, M., Wright, S., & Dik, B. (2016). Meaningful work: Differences among blue-, pink-, and white-collar occupations. *Career Development International, 21*(5), 534–551.

MacNaughton, G., & Frey, D. F. (2011). Decent work for all: A holistic human rights approach. *American University International Law Review, 26*(2), 441–483.

Michaelson, M., Pratt, M., Grant, A., & Dunn, C. P. (2014). Meaningful work: Connecting business ethics and organization studies. *Journal of Business Ethics, 121*(1), 77–90.

Naughton, M. J. (2006). The corporation as a community of work: Understanding the firm within the Catholic social tradition. *Ave Maria Law Review, 4,* 33–75.

Pontifical Council for Justice and Peace. (2004). *Compendium of the social doctrine of the church*. Vatican: Libreria Editrice Vaticana. Retrieved from vatican.va

Pius XI. (1931). Encyclical-letter 'Quadragesimo anno.' Retrieved from vatican.va

Radin, T., & Calkins, M. (2006). The struggle against sweatshops: Moving toward responsible global business. *Journal of Business Ethics, 66*(2), 261–72.

Rodgers, G., Lee, E., Swepston, L., & Daele, J. V. (2009). *The International Labour Organization and the quest for social justice, 1919–2009.* Geneva, Switzerland: International Labour Organization.

Tablan, F. (2015). Catholic social teachings: Toward a meaningful work. *Journal of Business Ethics, 128*(2), 291–303.

Terkel, S. (1975). *Working.* London, England: Wildwood House.

Vatican Council II. (1965). *Pastoral Constitution 'Gaudium et spes.'* Retrieved from vatican.va

Yeoman, R. (2014), Conceptualising meaningful work as a fundamental human need. *Journal of Business Ethics, 125*(2), 235–251.

Zwolinski, M. (2007). Sweatshops, choice, and exploitation. *Business Ethics Quarterly, 17*(4), 689–727.

CHAPTER 8

CARING FOR EMPLOYEES

Corporate Chaplains
as a Model of Faith at Work

David W. Miller
Princeton University Faith and Work Initiative

Faith W. Ngunjiri
Concordia University

James Dennis LoRusso
Princeton University Faith and Work Initiative

When was the last time someone from human relations (HR) visited you because your son was in police custody, the emergency room, or struggling with substance abuse issues, which prevented you from being fully present at work? Welcome to the world of workplace chaplains who do just that and more, regardless of one's faith tradition.

Although chaplains have been integral players in the religious landscape for centuries, corporate (or workplace) chaplaincy has emerged in recent decades as a growing and creative method whereby businesses or not-for-profit organizations hire religious clergy to serve the emotional, psychosocial, and spiritual needs of employees directly in their place of

Faith and Work: Christian Perspectives, Research, and Insights Into the Movement
pp. 131–150
Copyright © 2018 by Information Age Publishing
All rights of reproduction in any form reserved.

work (Miller, Ngunjiri, & LoRusso, 2016). Our research into workplace chaplaincy over the last several years, has found that executive leadership typically implemented corporate chaplaincy programs to extend holistic care to their employees, particularly where span of control and other organizational dynamics might otherwise prevent managers from offering personal support and assistance to employees who face life's daily challenges. While seldom the goal, our research finds that corporate chaplaincy programs often bring many business benefits, including higher employee engagement, loyalty, and profitability. Generally speaking, workplace chaplains are largely comprised of ordained clergy from Protestant and Catholic traditions, in contrast to military and hospital chaplaincy programs, who have wider representation from the world's major religious traditions. According to our research, the majority of companies that implement a chaplaincy program are led by a Christian chief executive officer, and the main chaplaincy providers—third-party firms who provide chaplains to client organizations—are almost exclusively Christian.[1] While CEOs, senior human relations executives, chaplaincy providers, and the chaplains themselves all stress they are to serve all employees, regardless of religious tradition, the phenomenon has a distinctly Christian presence.[2] Perhaps this is not surprising, given that, depending on which poll one follows, 70%–75% of the United States population is Christian (Newport, 2015; Pew Research Center, n.d.), but as we will discuss later in the chapter, this also reflects the fact that chaplaincy has until recently a largely Christian phenomenon. Consequently, exploring the attitudes of these senior leaders toward workplace chaplaincy deepens our collective knowledge about how Christians—of all types and levels—are striving to integrate their faith and work. Through our research into corporate chaplaincy, our aim is to answer the question: what does workplace chaplaincy reveal about Christian faith in the workplace more broadly?

After briefly discussing the history of workplace chaplaincy, we will consider how it manifests itself day to day on the ground, in companies where workplace chaplains may be found. We do this in light of several years' research and study of businesses who embrace workplace chaplaincy, those who deliver, and those who receive these services. Our broader research examines eight organizations from different parts of the United States and combines both qualitative analysis of survey data as well as qualitative, in-depth interviews to explicate how individuals experience, engage, and evaluate these workplace chaplaincy programs.

Our contribution to this book seeks to pursue a more targeted inquiry: *In what ways do Christian business leaders envisage these chaplaincy programs as manifestations of how they seek to integrate their own faith at work, broadly construed? And what does this reveal about the personal faith of these leaders? What opportunities and challenges do these programs pose for business leaders and others seeking to live out their faith on the job?*

In this discussion, we rely on qualitative data from interviews with the senior executive leadership of the eight organizations we studied. These organizations ranged in size from a Fortune 50 company with more than 120,000 employees, to small- and medium-sized enterprises, including one not-for-profit Christian organization (see Table 8.1). We solicited organizations to participate in this research based on prior professional and associational relationships between members of the research team and members of the leadership of those firms. The interviews were semi-structured, meaning that we used prompts to spark conversation but allowed the interaction between researcher and subject to evolve beyond the initial list of questions. The length of interviews varied between 10 minutes to over an hour with an average of approximately 20 minutes. We interviewed CEOs, presidents, and other senior executives responsible for or in some way involved in the hiring and implementation of these chaplaincy services to find out why they did it, and their experiences positive or negative.

Our analysis of these executive responses is organized around two broad themes: (1) *the relationship between various manifestations of personal faith and work* (2) *how chaplaincy serves as one example of this faith and work integration*. Executives offer a wide range of answers to the former, with some viewing their faith as having the ability to shape personal behavior whereas others declared their faith inseparable from larger organizational identity and goals. For the latter, while some see chaplaincy as an out-

Table 8.1.   Participant Organizations

Company	Industry	Number of Employees	Number of Chaplains
A&J Specialty Services	Property restoration & emergency response	25	1
Cardone Industries	Autoparts (re)manufacturing	~3,000	
Coyle Carpet One	Carpeting and flooring	35	1
Herr Foods	Snack foods	1,000-2,000	20-25
Intervarsity Christian Fellowship	Christian nonprofit	120	2
PacMoore	Contract food manufacturing waste management	45	1
Pelliteri Waste Systems	Waste management	45	1
Tyson Foods	Food processing	>115,000	125

growth of their personal faith, according to other business leaders we studied, chaplaincy transcends their own Christian beliefs and instead is a way to establish a work environment welcoming of all faiths. In general, however, leaders with whom we spoke agreed that *workplace chaplaincy represented an extension of their personal faith*.

A BRIEF HISTORY OF CHAPLAINCY IN THE WORKPLACE

Today's iteration of workplace, or corporate chaplaincy programs, can be understood as the outcome of two broad historical developments. First, it arose in the last decades of the twentieth century as one part of the much broader social movement to integrate *faith* and *work*. Scholars describe this movement variously as workplace spirituality (Lambert, 2009; Neal & Biberman, 2003) corporate religion (Hicks, 2002), and spirituality at work to capture the phenomenon. However, as Miller (2007) argues, terms like *religion* and *spirituality* are frequently perceived as oppositional and contentious terms. Instead, he suggests *faith* as a more elastic term, allowing "for the inclusion of the various interpretations of both spirituality and religion" (p. 18). In this chapter, we therefore use *faith and work* to describe general attention and efforts by individuals and organizations to promote the integration of religion, faith, or spirituality into workplace cultures.

While a part of the faith and work movement, workplace chaplaincy is also intimately tied to the institutional history of chaplaincy as it emerged out of Western Europe. The word "chaplain" evolved from the Medieval French term for clergyman, *chapelein*, which itself stemmed from the earlier Latin term referring to the "custodian of St. Martin's cloak" (*cappellanus*). According to Sullivan (2014), these so-called *capellani* worked within the ranks of Charlemagne's early medieval Frankish military and were responsible for the maintenance relics and the veneration of Christian Saints associated with warfare (Sullivan, 2014). As medieval monarchical regimes gave way to modern nation-states, chaplains continued to play an integral role in Western military institutions, providing spiritual care for and tending to the morale of soldiers.

In the English language, "chaplain" has typically referred to members of the clergy who perform religious services outside the walls of a church, and over the centuries, chaplaincy has extended far beyond the confines of its initial role within the military and its traditional association with Christianity to embrace other contexts and religious persuasions. this tradition continues to this day. For instance, the U.S. military has had chaplains since 1775, originally just Christians, in order to protect solders right to freedom of worship (Zieger, n.d.). They appointed the first Jewish chaplain during the American Civil War, and opened its chaplaincy corps to Muslims in 1993 to accommodate the greater cultural and religious diversity of the armed forces. The presence of workplace chaplains can be felt in the evolution of several other modern institutions such as prisons and hospitals. Moreover, recent scholarship suggests that over the 20th century, chaplaincy in the United States has become increasingly professionalized and has moved away from doctrinal, evangelistic activities. Today, as Cadge (2012) illustrates, chaplaincy work exhibits a more ecumenical, therapeutic style of pastoral care that downplays the specifics of belief for either the chaplain or their clientele. Rather, they serve as reservoirs of emotional support for the terminally ill hospice resident, the remorseful convicted felon, or the war-weary soldier far from her home. While this might suggest that chaplains are becoming less religious and more secular, Sullivan (2014) argues that chaplaincy has become one of the rare institutions where the state is not only protecting religion but also, actively supporting its activities within presumably secular institutions. Whether such arguments are true, it is nonetheless important to recognize that the popular image of the chaplain as Christian and active primarily in the military proves misleading.

Many might expect to see chaplaincy services in the military, in hospitals, or in prisons, places where pain, suffering, and spiritual need is obvious. Seeing chaplains in the workplace might seem like a new and unusual phenomenon, and yet, the modern workplace has its own forms of pain, suffering, and spiritual needs. Indeed, chaplains have been active in workplaces since the dawn of modern business. Historian Daniel O'Connor has tracked how the British East India Company hired chaplains for its employees as the corporation rapidly expanded its operations in South Asia (O'Connor, 2013). This relationship between religious faith and the marketplace continued as the Industrial Revolution transformed the organization of work in nineteenth century Western Europe and North America. A number of business owners established so-called "company towns" in places like Pullman, Illinois (Pullman Palace Car, Co.) or Hershey, Pennsylvania (The Hershey Company) where employers constructed entire communities, designed recreational public spaces, and operated stores to provide for the needs of employees and their families. In many cases, these industrial towns also featured company-owned churches where ministers were employed by the company to serve as religious leaders to the community.

Despite the decline of company towns in the early 20th century, faith nonetheless remained an important concern for business owners and working people in industrialized societies. By the mid-20th century, chaplaincy was emerging as a strategy for religious institutions to engage organizational life. Through the British Industrial Mission, the Church of

England introduced industrial chaplains to serve as arbiters of class struggle between labor and capital, between employees and their employers.
During these same years, French *worker-priests* took positions as ordinary
employees within companies to revitalize the seemingly imperiled relationship between the Catholic Church and working people (Dale, 2001;
Miller, 2007; Plummer, 1996; Seales, 2012)

Consequently, workplace chaplaincy differs from its historical antecedents in many ways. On one hand, because they are hired as employees or
agents (i.e., independent contractors) of the company to serve formally as
chaplains, corporate chaplains more closely resemble the ministers of
company towns who received compensation for their activities than they
do the British industrial chaplains, who typically worked for the Anglican
church, or the French worker-priests hired not as chaplains or religious
leaders but as laborers. Moreover, unlike earlier versions of industrial
chaplains, contemporary workplace chaplains do not aim primarily at
preaching the Christian gospel among workers on the factory floor.
Indeed, as in the military, professional guidelines generally prohibit
corporate chaplains from advocating a particular religious worldview or
proselytizing unless explicitly invited by workers to share. Furthermore,
whereas 20th century industrial chaplains typically sided with labor, and
company town ministers were often accused of doing the "bidding" of
management, corporate chaplains aspire to neutrality. They seek to provide individual counseling and support for any employee regardless of
title or position, and to be an honest broker, beholden neither to traditional categories of labor or management.

Chad Seales, a professor of religious studies at the University of Texas
Austin, suggests that corporate chaplains have largely jettisoned their
Protestant heritage and have adopted a broader language focused generi-
cally on the "spiritual needs" of an increasingly diverse workforce in the
21st century. Seales argues that "corporate chaplains rebranded the pastoral care of their industrial antecedents, translating its confessional par-
ticularities of protestant religiosity into noncommittal generalities of
secularity" (Seales, 2012, p. 196). As the National Institute of Business
and Industrial Chaplains notes, chaplaincy "is an interdenominational,
ecumenical counseling ministry to people in business and industry,
responding to individual and family needs, as well as work-life concerns,
such as job stress and career."[3] Chaplains, then, see themselves as providing care and showing compassion to all employees, including those who
do not affiliate with any religion.

All in all, workplace chaplaincy in the 21st century represents the con-
fluence of a range of historical and contemporary influences. It is neither
merely the progeny of earlier forms of chaplaincy in the workplace or
strictly a product of paternalism on the part of management and business

owners. Instead, corporate chaplaincy is a response to the specific challenges and expectations facing individuals, organizations, and societies peculiar to the late 20th and early 21st century workplace.

THE RELATIONSHIP BETWEEN CHRISTIAN FAITH AND WORK

Before discussing how workplace chaplaincy represents a particularly *Christian* example of bringing faith into work, we should first consider what *faith and work* means to the business owner or the senior executive who identifies as a Christian. The leadership of the companies in our study defined the idea of a Christian business in numerous ways and offered a varied picture of the relationship of personal faith to work. Some executives we studied understood the goals of faith and business as fully aligned, and drew directly on biblical teachings as guiding principles to help run their business. Whereas others viewed them as more distinct and primarily about the intentions and motivations with which one carried out one's work. And other leaders emphasized the outcomes of integrating faith and work. In one way or another, however, all of these executives agreed on one thing: how they run their business enterprises is an extension of the personal Christian faith.

Faith as Practice, Not Theology

Because the Christian business leaders we studied consider business as an extension or manifestation of their faith, they tend to articulate faith and work in practical terms, rather than abstract theological terms. They are less concerned with exploring the finer points of theology or doctrine regarding work than they are in translating their understanding of Christian faith, as a whole, into worldly action. In other words, faith and work, for these senior leaders, is not primarily about understanding Luther's ideas on "vocation" or how their business may or may fit into a Kuyperian vision of a Christian society. Indeed, most business leaders are not theologically yet they intuitively seem to know or desire to carve out a legitimate space for their individual faith at work rather than it being left at home. As one executive stated, "being a good Christian businessman means being a Christian 24-7, and not just on Sundays or anything like that." It is about overcoming what many in the faith and work movement have called the "Sunday–Monday gap" (Nash & McLennan, 2001; Miller, 2007) that assumes a strict separation between the professional and religious dimensions of life.

The business leaders we studied described the practical relationship between faith and work in different and sometimes competing ways. First, some understood their personal faith inextricably tied to the goals of the business, frequently using passages from Christian scripture to explain their approach to business. For example, in our interview with Kent Rawhouser, CEO of A&J Specialty Services, he referred to Micah 6:8—"And what does the Lord require of you? To act justly and to love mercy, and to walk humbly with your God" (New International Version)—in order to explain how faith informs his business:

> To act justly, that means to be fair. You know, to do what's right in every situation, whether it's paying your taxes or it's paying an employee, or how you invoice. To show mercy, you know, there's times when, as much as I think something might be right, it might not be the proper way to apply it.... And then to walk humbly with your God, there's ups and downs, there's successes, there's all those different things, but you still need to be humble in how you act.

This individual, the owner of a small property restoration business, sees the Bible as not only a guide for his individual behavior but as an important resource for ethical business practices. One chief executive created a name for his Biblically based business philosophy. Tom Pellitteri of Pellitteri Waste Systems, described "Creation Care" as a "Biblical approach to everything we do. The Bible, God's Word," he continued, "is the most important thing. And I think in my family's life, we put that first and foremost. And certainly, being good stewards is very important to us."

Christian Business as Mission

For some, their personal faith served as a guide to developing business strategies and conduct. Yet other business owners appeared to position their personal faith as distinct from the operating and running of the business. For them, faith is present within but separate from the organization. As one CEO stated of his Christian business, "the opportunity is that we, every day, get an opportunity to be a witness for Christ. This [the business], this is our mission, this is our ministry." The workplace is not only *shaped by* the personal faith of executive; the workplace represents *a context* within which ministry or "witnessing for Christ" can occur. Similarly, for Bill Moore, president of PacMoore Solutions, business activities provide the infrastructure along which the company may pursue its "Kingdom Purpose."[4] This Kingdom Purpose, however, remains something unique from the business purpose, as Moore stated in our discussion with him,

I don't ever want my people, anybody that works for me to ever think that I would use faith, spirituality, Christ, God in any way to manipulate the results of the company. That's absolutely, you know, it's like selling the Gospel. You know, Paul said, we don't do that. That's why we work and then we preach the gospel because we're not gonna sell it, we're not gonna profit from this.

Moore's remarks suggest that too much overlap between faith and business activities risks corrupting the former. The marketplace might provide the networks and relationships through which the Gospel may be preached but it also threatens to enlist faith as another marketing tactic (i.e., selling).

The Faith-Friendly Approach

Just as PacMoore declares a Kingdom Purpose, Tyson Foods is also intentional in describing the role of faith and work. The company's chairman, John Tyson, envisions the workplace as a space in which the appropriate expression of everyone's faith, regardless of tradition, should be permitted and welcomed. The company core values expressly note that they "strive to honor God in all we do" and that they "strive to be a faith-friendly company,"[5] where faith is more broadly conceived. Both Moore and Tyson identify as Christians, but Tyson Foods aspires to be "faith-friendly" rather than strictly Christian or "faith-based" (Miller, 2007; Miller & Ewest, 2013). Tyson himself recalls in our interview with him,

Somewhere it was laid upon me, the good Lord said you got this company called Tyson Foods, maybe if we created an environment for all faiths to have a discussion, maybe that's where you should do it, instead of making the proverbial mission trip to countries around the world where people are doing great mission work.

Although Tyson ultimately attributes his vision to his Christian faith, its role in the business is neither one of preaching in Moore's sense nor strictly one of informing business activities. Rather, Tyson's understanding of the faith-business relationship mirrors the faith-friendly approach of the firm. The workplace functions here as a safe place where religiously diverse individuals may come together and openly engage one another.

Faith as Ethical Guide and Measure

The Christian business leaders we studied also expect different things from the integration of faith and work in their businesses. For some, the role of faith is to guide intentions. Having faith changes how one thinks and acts in the business. "I'm also a Christian," says Mike Coyle, owner of Coyle Carpeting, "and believe it's my role to, you know, help where I can in that fashion." Tom Pelliteri, too, credits his Christian faith with transforming his motivations as a business owner. He admits, "since I became a Christian I was more concerned over my employees' welfare. And so, at that time (after becoming a Christian) I saw the need for my employees to have good benefits." Both Coyle and Pelliteri, emphasize the change that faith reportedly foments within themselves, rather than in others or in the organization. Indeed, as Kent Rawhouser stated in a previous quote, "there's ups and downs, there's successes, there's all those different things." Bringing faith to work is not about achieving financial success for these executives; it is about accepting a particular ethical framework for personal and professional decisions.

Still, other leaders suggest that simply having faith is not enough to transform the individual. One's faith must be followed by deliberate action. Kevin Crampton, the CEO of auto-parts remanufacturer Cardone Industries, says that he does not "like plaques on the wall," referring to James 1:22, "but be ye doers of the word, and not hearers only, deceiving your own selves" (King James Version). Crampton explains to us his practical theology:

> When you're a doer of the Word, a lot of great things will happen. One, you're truly being a Servant Leader. You're being like Jesus. Two, everybody from every faith, from every part of the World likes to be served and likes people that are focused on doing.

Actions, as much as belief, matter to Crampton.

While all of these individuals articulate faith as self-transformative, Bill Moore's idea of "business as mission" emphasizes the changes that faith at work should have on others. "Are we changing lives?" he asks, and "are people coming to know Christ? Are people being disciples? Are they on a different trajectory? Are they in service? Where are they leading, spiritually, others? We want to measure that stuff." For Moore, one's intentions, motivations, and values are far less important than results, and PacMoore therefore is interested in measuring the effectiveness of faith on the various constituents of the business.

Business as an Extension of Personal Faith

Of course, these different positions on the role of Christian faith in business are neither comprehensive nor mutually exclusive. Most of the business leaders with whom we spoke oscillated between these various accents at different times and depending the topic of conversation. Yet, all of them discuss faith as something deeply personal. Moreover, they understand their businesses, whether faith-*based* or faith-*friendly* (Miller & Ewest, 2015), as extensions of this private faith. Just as Kent Rawhouser can be a "witness for Christ" though his business, another executive can describe his "faith's journey," as a call to religious pluralism:

> I have more of a love of God than I ever had, but more importantly to me, more of a love of people that don't believe the way I do. And that makes me the happiest. I don't share that everywhere, but that's kind of where I am, you know. I grew up I a very narrow view. Now I have, you know, Hindu people that work for me, Muslim people that work for me, and I love them crazy just the way they are.

Such sentiments seem to echo the Biblical injunction in Matthew 22:39 to "love your neighbor as yourself," but they also illustrate the diversity of views to which senior business leaders appeal in order to define the idea of faith and work integration.

CHAPLAINCY AS A MANIFESTATION OF FAITH AND WORK

The business leaders we studied all understood their enterprises as an opportunity to exercise faith in and through their work. Despite having different accents, as noted above, they all agreed that workplace chaplaincy is an important tool through which this integration between their personal faith and their work is achieved. We observed a couple of different ways in which they expressed this notion of faith/work integration. First, workplace chaplaincy serves as an extension and affirmation of one's personal faith, while it also provides the moral foundation for sound business practices.

Chaplaincy as an Extension of Personal Faith

Kevin Crampton of Cardone, perhaps, most succinctly linked chaplaincy to personal faith, stating that he "grew up from a background that we were focused on 'Live Your Faith.'" "And so," he continues, "I think the chaplaincy is really an extension of that. For us, when you're in a big organization, we can't do all this individually." Here, Crampton suggests that chaplaincy represents a surrogate for an executive's faith, when the company's size and scope may prohibit him or her from reaching every employee directly.

Similarly, Bill Moore sees the chaplaincy as an expression of his Christian faith in his organization. "I've got to have some people to get this love of Christ thing, and these guys [the chaplains] get that and that's what makes you love people, your love for the Lord." Further, Moore also perceived chaplaincy as a way for him to touch his employees, an extension of himself as one who cares about his employees and overcome the personal distance that a growing firm has between management and employees:

> You got 250 employees and you don't know all of their names. And I was in one of the growth modes where I had lost touch with people and it really bothered me. I didn't even have a second plant; I still had one plant. But it was big enough where there were people walking around and I didn't know their names; I didn't know how they got there. It really bothered me. And so, I'm like, you know, we have to touch these people. They have to know we love them.

While Moore and Crampton experience the chaplains as way of reflecting the leaders love of their people by supporting the workforce impersonal ways they can no longer do, Tom Pellitteri and others see the chaplaincy as evidence of the company's Christian identity. When orienting new employees, Tom claimed:

> I tell them that we are a Christian family owned business and what that means. And I try to relate to them that we're not asking anybody to follow suit ... and then we go in and talk to them a little bit about the benefit program, and why we have those types of things, and the chaplaincy program.

JM Herr, the CEO of Herr Foods, articulated a similar justification for the chaplaincy program that his firm introduced.

> I liked the concept [of chaplaincy] from the beginning just because I felt like it's a way for us to be more intentional about our faith ... one of the things that appeals to me about the program is that if a person is searching, this would make it easier for them to become a Christian and to have a conversion experience if there was somebody there that was engaging them.

Herr felt that chaplaincy provided an opportunity for those who were seeking to have someone that converse with them and perhaps lead to a conversion. In a society where "church attendance is falling," he understands chaplaincy as "a substitute in a way for people going to church." Executives like Herr and Pellitteri demonstrate that chaplaincy can be an effective way of translating the idea of Christian business into actionable policies.

Chaplaincy as Good Business Practice

It might seem obvious that Christian business executives would perceive workplace chaplaincy as a way to bolster the "Christian-ness" of a
company, nonetheless many of their responses indicate a more complicated relationship between chaplaincy, personal religious identity, and the
business. For some executives, chaplaincy is not only an extension of personal faith but just good business practice in today's religiously diverse
workforce. In fact, even though Kevin Crampton of Cardone may identify
as a Christian, the chaplains are foremost employees. He refers to them as
"key contributors to the business" who are "trying to contribute to the bottom line." While Cardone considers itself a Christian business, "at the end
of the day," Kevin exclaims, "we're a business. And if we don't' make
money, we don't survive." Thus, it makes sense to have chaplaincy only
insofar as it meets particular business needs and at Cardone, this means
that the chaplains are situated as part of Human Resources and perform
"specific assignments." Of these tasks, one of the most important, according to Crampton, is caring for the "wide array of people from different
faith backgrounds" comprising the workforce.

> Even if you're Muslim or Jewish, and you see an environment where people
> are loving and caring for you, and willing to go the extra mile, it's kind of
> better to be in that environment than some environments that don't have
> that.

Therefore, despite the Christian identity of the firm, chaplaincy is successful at Cardone because it endeavors to overcome the challenges of a
religiously pluralistic workforce that can threaten to affect productivity
and profitability.

J.M. Herr argues that being a "professing Christian" is only "step one."
Rather,

> It really needs to be manifested in how you treat people. And I don't think
> that it's necessarily always consistent. In other words, I think that you could
> easily find companies that are owned by Christians that don't treat employ-
> ees any better, or maybe not as good as other companies whose owners
> aren't professing Christians.... So the chaplaincy program would be a way of
> defining a Christian company by caring about spiritual things for your
> employees, as well as other nonspiritual ways of caring for them.

Herr suggests that religious identity is a partial ingredient of the Christian business but ultimately this must be coupled with ethically sound
practices that care for the needs of the organization's constituents. Simi-

larly, Mike Coyle stresses that chaplaincy is simply a good management strategy, regardless of one's religious identity.

> Christian or not Christian, I just thought that [the chaplains] are the right people for this job. And, you know, if it should happen where somebody finds their faith, you know, that's good. But that's not, you know, the reason for, that's not the only reason for it.

Coyle characterizes religiosity as incidental to the primary goal of caring for the employees. He sees the chaplains as a way of helping "people who are disconnected" from upper management to feel valued. For Coyle, this is about much more than his identity as a Christian. "Even if I weren't a Christian," he admits, "I think I should be doing that."

Like Coyle, Bill Moore sees a distinction between one's Christian identity and one's ethics and performance on the job. "Just because a guy's a born-again believer does not necessarily give him a hall pass or that he's a kind of good fit for your organization and he's growing in his work ethic," warns Moore. Instead, he remains more concerned with how individuals conduct themselves than their purported faith, which sheds light on why Moore wanted his chaplains to minimize overt religious language and to "lead with need" rather than "leading with Christ." This, he says, allows people to "use the love, the [chaplaincy] service, and they divest themselves of that service" without having to feel pressured to adopt a particular religious identity.

All in all, the relationship between faith, business, and chaplaincy manifests in multiple ways in multiple contexts. While senior leaders who implement and oversee these programs may understand workplace chaplaincy as an extension of their personal faith, as a way to integrate faith and work, this can mean many different things and take many different forms, as chaplains themselves demonstrate, a topic to which we now turn.

DISCUSSION

By focusing on how business leaders who identify as Christians explain the role of chaplaincy in their organizations, this chapter helps to demonstrate various ways that chaplaincy serves as one manifestation of their own faith at work. We see that chaplaincy can be seen through the eyes of the business leader as a practical expression of personal faith in the workplace. Further, chaplaincy can be perceived as a more corporate expression of the company's Christian identity, for those organizations where such Christian identity is important and explicit. Chaplaincy, for some business leaders, is merely good business practice, as well as an expression of ethics in the workplace. It enables business leaders to demonstrate to their employees that they care about them, not merely as the hands that do the work, but as full human beings with emotional, social, and material needs—needs that, if not met, can impede their performance at work (see Miller & Ngunjiri, 2015). The leaders interviewed held more than one view or perspective of how corporate chaplaincy fits with their own Christian identity, such that one could see it as both ethical practice and expression of personal faith, or as good business practice that is also a way to express their Christian identity.

Qualifications and Autonomy

One implication of envisioning chaplaincy primarily as an extension of the leader's personal faith at work is that it informs the standards by which chaplains are chosen to serve in each business. The Christian business leaders with whom we spoke emphasized different ideas that reflect their individual understandings of Christian faith. According to Mike Coyle, for instance, any kind of theological training is sufficient to qualify one to serve as a chaplain in his company.

> So, the fact that he's a Christian almost is like, this, you know, it's like, do we hire somebody that you know, has got a college degree, or hire somebody that's not got a college degree? Well the fact that they have a college degree might not mean anything, but it means that can complete a job. Somebody who's a pastor, somebody who's completed a theological degree, can get things done because they've had to do that. So just by virtue of him having gone through school to earn his doctorate in theology tells me that he can get a job done.

For executives like Coyle therefore, formal credentials—a theological degree, ordination as a minister—sufficiently qualifies an individual to become a workplace chaplain.

For Bill Moore, on the other hand, simply having some kind of formal religious training is insufficient. He expects the specific theological orientation of each chaplain to align more closely with his own.

> You got to go listen to some of these conversations [that the chaplains are having] because some of these guys have some screwed up theology. And it is your responsibility to know. You need to have enough sense what the Scripture says to be able to identify false doctrine from good doctrine. And false doctrine's bad doctrine, and that can hurt your people. You got to discern that. And that is a pitfall. There's no question about it. And while Marketplace Chaplains [the third-party chaplaincy provider] vets the them, they can't catch everything. They can't see it all.

These remarks suggest that Moore assumes a more active role than Coyle in vetting and managing the particular theological orientation of his chaplaincy services. Seeking this theological consistency naturally places some constraints on the chaplains. The point here is that how each leader understands their personal faith has an impact on the standards, qualifications, and level of autonomy accords to workplace chaplains.

Faith Integration

Miller's "TIP" instrument (The Integration Profile), which maps four primary modes through which individuals and organizations integrate faith and work, provides a useful framework for making sense of these overlapping views. He identifies these four modes or manifestations of faith at work, referred to as the Four Es, as (1) Ethics, (2) Expression, (3) Experience, and (4) Enrichment. An "ethics" orientation understands faith as a guide for behavior and decision making both at the personal and organizational/societal level. We can discern this type, for instance, in Tom Pellitteri's assertion that when he became a Christian, he began to more seriously consider his "employees' welfare" or when Kevin Crampton describes his faith as a way to embody Servant Leadership. According to both of these leaders, personal faith provided them with an ethical infrastructure for the employee-employer relationship.

Those who favor the "expression" type are concerned more with expressing or asserting their particular religious identity, either verbally or nonverbally. Business philosophies like PacMoore's "Kingdom Purpose" or Pellitteri's "Creation Care" overtly link their respective organizations to a Christian identity. In addition, when CEOs describe chaplaincy as a "way for us to be more intentional about our faith," or as "an opportunity to be a witness for Christ," they are stressing how it bolsters and reaffirms the "Christian-ness" of themselves and of the larger organization.

The third type, "experience," refers to those who experience their faith/work integration primarily as a means to find or cultivate meaning and purpose in the workplace. These people experience their work as more than just a job but as a calling, viewing it with spiritual significance. This orientation imagines work and faith less as two separate overlapping domains but as inextricable and serving a godly purpose, evident in Pellitteri's aspiration to employ a "Biblical approach to everything we do." Likewise, Bill Moore embodies this type when he looks to his faith to ask "Are we changing lives?" For him, chaplaincy should ultimately transform the lives of his employees, to imbue them with a Christ-centered purpose.

Finally, "enrichment," the last of Miller's orientations, envisions faith at work as a practical resource for improving oneself and one's peers. Faith represents a repository of practices—such as meditation, prayer, the study of scripture, etc.—from which one can learn and grow. Chaplains, as some executives noted, facilitate a number of activities for employees. Some organize weekly Bible studies, prayer chains, and even activities that foster interreligious dialogue. This type was perhaps best exhibited in John Tyson's remark about chaplaincy as a form of faith and work integration that helps to create "an environment for all faiths to have a discussion." Tyson sees faith as a valuable ingredient that each individual should be emboldened to bring to work, not exclusively as a way to find meaning or to assert one's Christian identity.

The example of John Tyson and Tyson Foods is interesting for two reasons. First, he demonstrates how these four "Es" are discrete but not mutually exclusive ways of manifesting faith in the workplace. Individuals frequently exhibit more than of these styles depending on the context. When Tyson, for instance, asserts that the workplace should be open to all faiths, he nonetheless attributes this to his personal Christian faith, claiming that it was "the good Lord" that encouraged him to take this approach. We can see that Tyson, on one hand, sees personal faith as source for enrichment, while on the other hand he understands the chaplains program as an expression of Christian principles. Similarly, Kevin Crampton can describe how his faith serves as an ethical guide for his individual decisions at work while he also sees chaplaincy as an overt embodiment of Cardone's formal Christian identity.

Second, Tyson draws our attention to the importance of organizational context for understanding Christian faith in the workplace. Unlike the other firms in our research, Tyson Foods is a publicly traded corporation that describes itself as "faith-friendly." Although John Tyson identifies personally as a Christian, his company does not. Therefore, it is no surprise that his personal perspective on faith/work integration differs from those executives working in small or midsize companies that openly identify as Christian. Tyson more clearly distinguishes his personal faith from faith as a general ingredient in the lives of his employees because this reflects the particular organizational culture and structure of Tyson Foods. While Bill Moore explicitly links chaplaincy to PacMoore's Christian "Kingdom Purpose," Tyson imagines workplace chaplaincy in more ecumenical terms. In short, not only is workplace chaplaincy a reflection of the executive's personal faith, but the way that this personal faith is articulated varies from one organizational context to another. Workplace chaplaincy therefore provides a unique opportunity to map out this complex and dynamic relationship between Christian faith and work.

CONCLUDING THOUGHTS

Our focus in this chapter has been looking at workplace chaplaincy through the distinct lens of Christian leaders who have implemented such programs in the organization. We have discovered certain common themes as well as very distinct implementations of corporate chaplaincy. Not surprisingly we also have observed some promising human and business benefits, as well as observed areas of possible challenge and conflict that are worthy of further study. This exploration of corporate chaplaincy, that an increasing number of Christian business leaders our introducing into their organizations, raises as many questions as it answers. One implication that we draw from this chapter that focuses on the Christian experience of workplace chaplaincy is that it is a viable model and approach toward the integration of faith and work for Christians. Further study would help us understand if this would also be accurate for non-Christians. Future studies could also focus more on phenomenological asking questions that are specific to Christian identity and Christian expressions of faith and work, looking perhaps at denominational differences or other markers of diverse Christian expressions. Furthermore, this chapter focuses exclusively on the perspectives of Christian business executives, all of whom are White, well-educated, male, and in positions of organizational authority. Given these variables, future research could expand from this subset to explore how chaplaincy shapes or is shaped by the Christian faith of other crucial stakeholders. For example, how do females, front-line employees, racial minorities, or other historically marginalized groups engage workplace chaplaincy as a means for faith/work integration? Would corporate chaplaincy be effective in white-collar professional settings, as well as blue-collar labor settings? Moreover, how is workplace chaplaincy distinct from, say, other contexts where chaplains are present, such as the military, prisons, or hospice? A comparative approach could reveal what, if anything, is distinctive about Christian faith as it manifests in the workplace.

Further, future studies could utilize new or existing research instruments to study chaplaincy, such as instruments measuring religiosity, or linking particular approaches to leadership with chaplaincy. For example, what is the relationship between servant leadership and chaplaincy in the workplace? What approaches to leadership do business leaders in organizations that have corporate chaplains use? Are those leadership approaches more likely to be ethical, authentic, spiritual, and/or normative as opposed to more transactional styles? We see good potential here for exploring the linkages between corporate chaplaincy and spiritual leadership.

In this chapter, we sought to explore what ways Christian business leaders understand chaplaincy programs one manifestation of how they seek to integrate their own faith at work, what this reveals about the personal faith of these leaders, and what opportunities and challenges do these programs pose for them and others seeking to live out their faith on the job. We observed that implementing a workplace chaplaincy program was often an extension of the CEOs own personal faith, and impacted in diverse ways how the integration of faith and work might manifest itself and be treated in the organization.

The next time you or one of your coworkers is experiencing a substance abuse issue, overwhelming amounts of workplace stress, or problems on the home front, maybe you will consider contacting your own workplace chaplain for comfort, guidance, and if desired, spiritual support. And if your organization does not have one, maybe you will consider trying to change that.

NOTES

1. For example, the two largest corporate chaplaincy providers, Marketplace Ministries, Inc. and Corporate Chaplains of America, are each formally Christian organizations, headed by Christian CEOs, and staff their firms exclusively with Christian chaplains. Consequently, the organizations with whom they do business will also feature only Christian chaplains. It should be noted, however, that although most of these agencies are run and staffed exclusively by Christians and Christian chaplains, the larger agencies feature referral services and connections with chaplains or religious clergy from other traditions, should a company or employee they are serving request a chaplain from their own religious community.

2. In tracking the chaplaincy programs present in over 100 different companies, nonprofits, and organizations, we found the vast majority of these firms (~80%) utilized six different corporate chaplaincy providers. Among these six providers, only one provider—Corporate Care, Inc.—identifies as ecumenical/multifaith. The remaining five providers are explicitly Christian and feature exclusively Christian staffs of chaplains. As stated in the previous note, however, these Christian chaplaincy providers are typically willing and able to refer employees to a chaplain or religious leader from other faith traditions as needed on a case by case basis.

3. See the National Institute of Business and Industrial Chaplains (2011). It is an organization dedicated to serving the needs of workplace chaplains.

4. See "Who We Are," PacMoore Solutions, https://www.pacmoore.com/who-we-are/.

5. See "Core Values," Tyson Foods, http://www.tysonfoods.com/our-story/core-values.

REFERENCES

Cadge, W. (2012). *Paging God: Religion in the halls of medicine*. Chicago, IL: University of Chicago Press.

Dale, D. C. (2001, May/June). Three streams of corporate chaplaincy. *EAPA Exchange*, 11–13.

Hicks, D. A. (2002). Spiritual and religious diversity in the workplace: Implications for leadership. *The Leadership Quarterly, 13*(4), 379–396.

Lambert, L. (2009). *Spirituality, Inc.: Religion in the American workplace*. New York, NY: New York University Press.

Miller, D. W. (2007). *God at work: The history and promise of the faith at work movement*. Oxford, England: Oxford University Press.

Miller, D. W., & Ewest, T. (2013). The Integration Box (TIB): An individual and institutional faith, religion, and spirituality at work assessment tool. In J. Neal (Ed.), *Handbook of faith and spirituality in the workplace* (pp. 403–417). New York, NY: Springer.

Miller, D. W., & Ewest, T. (2015). A new framework for analyzing organizational workplace religion and spirituality. *Journal of Management, Spirituality & Religion, 12*(4), 305–328. doi:10.1080/14766086.2015.1054864

Miller, D. W., & Ngunjiri, F. W. (2015). Leadership views on corporate chaplains: business, sociocultural, and spiritual justifications. *Journal of Management, Spirituality & Religion, 12*(2), 129–155. doi:10.1080/14766086.2014.950318

Miller, D. W., Ngunjiri, F. W., & LoRusso, J. D. (2016, August). *Making sense of sense-making: Workplace chaplains as sources of organizational cohesion*. Paper presented at the Academy of Management annual conference, Anaheim.

Nash, L. L., & McLennan, S. (2001). *Church on Sunday, work on Monday: The challenge of fusing Christian values with business life* (1st ed.). San Francisco, CA: Jossey-Bass.

Neal, J., & Biberman, J. (2003). Introduction: The leading edge in research on spirituality and organizations. *Journal of Organizational Change Management, 16*(4), 363–366.

Newport, F. (2015, December 24). Percentage of Christians in US drifting down, but still high. Retrieved from the Gallup website: http://www.gallup.com/poll/187955/percentage-christians-drifting-down-high.aspx

Pew Research Center. Religious Landscape Study. (n.d.). Retrieved December 22, 2016, from http://www.pewforum.org/religious-landscape-study/

Plummer, D. B. (1996). Chaplaincy: The greatest story never told. *Journal of Pastoral Care, 50*(1), 1–12.

Seales, C. E. (2012). Corporate chaplaincy and the American workplace. *Religion Compass, 6*(3), 195–203.

Sullivan, W. F. (2014). *A ministry of presence: Chaplaincy, spiritual care, and the law*. Chicago, IL: The University of Chicago Press.

Zieger, H. (n.d.). Why does the US Military have chaplains? Retrieved December 28, 2016, from https://publicpolicy.pepperdine.edu/academics/research/policy-review/2009v2/why-does-us-military-have-chaplains.htm

CHAPTER 9

FAITH, FAMILY, AND WORK

A Christian Perspective on Family Businesses

Allan Discua Cruz
The University of Lancaster

Family businesses represent an ideal context in which to examine the integration of Christian faith at work (Discua Cruz, 2013, 2015). There are several reasons why a closer look at a Christian perspective in family businesses is relevant. First, family businesses continue to be the predominant business model worldwide (Howorth, Hamilton, Rose, & Westhead, 2010; International Family Enterprise Research Academy, 2003; "To Have and to Hold," 2015). Family businesses come in many forms, operate in all industries, and represent start-ups as well as millenary firms involved in both local and international trade. Second, the study of family businesses has developed into an interdisciplinary research field (Craig, Moores, Howorth, & Poutziouris, 2009; Melin, Nordqvist, & Sharma, 2014), with increasing calls made to study the influence of faith (Litz, 2013). Finally, the integration of a particular faith, such as Christianity, can shape and significantly inform an organization's culture, practices, and workplace dynamics when it reflects the faith of its founders and his/her family's religious heritage (Miller & Ewest, 2015).

Christianity, when rightly understood and applied, can be a powerful force in business (Higginson, 2012). While some individuals may

Faith and Work: Christian Perspectives, Research, and Insights Into the Movement
pp. 151–167
151

approach the integration of the Christian faith at work as employees, others may attempt to do it as owners or managers. Family businesses that are influenced by the Christian faith have been around for a long time, with some becoming major corporations and beacons in diverse industries (Higginson, 2015; Popp, 2015). Yet, while Christianity has not gone unnoticed in the study of family businesses, its integration depends largely on the attitudes of its leaders, thus it cannot be oversimplified (Discua Cruz, 2013).

This chapter focuses on a Christian perspective in family businesses. First, a discussion of the early relationship between Christianity and the family realm is presented. Then, contemporary conceptualizations and typologies of family businesses are emphasized, before moving on to theoretical perspectives. Finally, a Christian perspective on succession is discussed. Throughout the chapter, reference to the Bible is made to enlighten and support. Challenges, research opportunities, and conclusions are presented at the end.

THE EARLY RELATIONSHIP OF CHRISTIANITY, FAMILY, AND WORK

Family businesses have existed long before the term was introduced. The earliest representation of families in business in the Bible relates to households or "*oikos*" (Faraone, 2008). The households (*oikos*) were "a group of people bound together by close kinship, who live together and make a living together" (Moxnes, 1997, p. 23). Each household showcased often large kin associations, marked by "economic, social, legal, and cultural disparities, such as differences in age, gender, class, and ethnicity" (Elliott, 2003, p. 204). Households engaged in business activities and traded with other households, within towns and later across cities and nations.

Households were the platform for Christianity to be integrated in all aspects of life. Elliott (2003, p. 188) states that

> a key feature of the Christian movement was its household orientation: its mission focused not on individuals but household groups; believers assembled in houses for worship; and the household or family (*oikos*) provided a chief metaphor, for characterizing relations and responsibilities within and among the believing communities.

The household was a context where economic activity was linked with social functions, becoming a place where wealth transfer (land), transmission of trades (e.g., carpentry, masonry), values and beliefs became crucial for its continuity. The New Testament illustrates that Christianity thrived through household codes, becoming the pillars of the Christian communal identity (Elliott, 2003; Elser, 1997). Thus, the *oikos* household became like a foundation stone for Christianity, intertwining everyday work and faith.

Yet such integration was, from its inception, afflicted with conflict. Many of the Bible's individual books relate that households often had mixed structures and beliefs (1 Corinthians 7:12–16). The teachings of Jesus presented countercultural challenges for households. Jesus challenged the inward-looking, exclusive behavior of households, which focused solely on the welfare and care of individuals and/or family members who belonged to that household. Instead, households were challenged to extend the same hospitality, loyalty and kin-like attitude toward an extended Christian family (Elliott, 2003). The Christian message called its followers to embrace individuals outside of the closely-knit kinship circle in individual households, now bound together in a new metaphorical family as brothers and sisters in Christ (Elser, 1997). Furthermore, early Christian households were challenged to create enduring identities. Paul's letter to the Galatians calls on believers to produce "a model of enduring identity while resisting pressures calling for conformity and assimilation of society at the time" (Elser, 1997, p. 144). Such tensions gradually shaped the features of the Christian faith.

The *oikos* was very different to the modern concept of family today (Moxnes, 1997), yet it provides the first glimpse of the earliest form of families in businesses known to mankind, and was a precursor of the universal family business (Dodd & Dyck, 2015). While the household concept was relevant to understand basic social functions in early societies, diverse pressures made it progress from a unit of analysis focused on a large and homogeneous extended kin group to a smaller, specialized, and nuclear group (Hammel, 1984). The rise of private property ownership and committed marriage structures shaped the concept of family around a nuclear unit composed of husband, wife, and children (Netting, Wilk, & Arnould, 1984). Such change, argue Netting and colleagues, allowed researchers to focus attention on direct descendants who engaged in basic social functions (e.g., production and reproduction) as well as ownership transfer of diverse assets over time in order to ensure family survival. The repercussions of such progress influenced the concept of family in the study of family businesses.

CONTEMPORARY CONCEPTUALIZATIONS

Today, the words "*family business*" may be commonly associated with a small firm where closely related family members—parents, offspring, or even extended family—work on its day-to-day management. Around the world, the legal status of a family firm is often associated with a closely held and private company (Howorth, Rose, & Hamilton, 2006). Such private and closely held features were contested by scholars, who heralded that family business features were transitory and could not dominate a firm indefinitely (Chandler, 1977), which affected the development of the family business field (Litz, 1997). Comprehensive studies acknowledge the diversity of family business conceptualizations and loosely define a family business as a business where a family owns enough of the equity to be able to exert control over strategy and is involved in top management positions (Howorth et al., 2010). Such a broad view suggests a significant influence by members of a family through involvement and participation in the way the firm operates. Howorth et al.'s (2010) definition implies a context where family objectives are legitimized and have both an immediate as well as a long-term impact. It implicitly suggests that as family members retain control through ownership and participation in the firm management over time, their faith can be influential in the way the company operates.

The Christian faith can influence family businesses, yet it is often not visible to the public eye (Discua Cruz, 2015). Prior works pose that Christian principles and values shape business leadership because of deeply held personal values that influence an owner-manager's approach to managerial challenges or work practices (Van Buren & Agle, 1998). The influence of a particular religion in a business organization has been previously associated with aspects such as ethical decision making or organizational practices (Chan-Serafin, Brief, & George, 2013; Weaver & Agle, 2002). Yet, while some family business owners/managers may aspire to purposely integrate their Christian faith at work, others may prefer to keep it distant or act more as "secret agents" (Discua Cruz, 2015). The motivation to make changes in an organization may depend on the level of influence an individual has on the different systems and the way an organization allows beliefs to be put to use (Chan-Serafin et al., 2013).

More recently, Mabey, Conroy, Blakeley, and de Marco (2016) have highlighted that Christians can integrate the teachings of Jesus at work through "radical nonconformity." This occurs in two ways: First, taking a risk in personal integrity by demonstrating a willingness to be self-sacrificial. Such approach implies leadership based on Jesus as a role model in leading a family business. Teachings within the Bible show the approach to relate to God and to others through the life, death, and resurrection of Jesus. Calculative and opportunistic ways of behaving when leading or working for a family business are replaced with a new role for love and trust toward others, which allow the transformation of individually centred leadership behavior into a more collective servant-type leadership (Discua Cruz, 2013). Second, Mabey et al. (2016) suggest that individuals (e.g., family business members, who can exert influence in the day-to-day management and long-term development of the firm) could make a difference in the workplace following the example and teaching of Jesus in five ways: Questioning dubious practice rather than staying silent; embracing work as a calling rather than a job; thinking theologically rather than materially; maintaining ethical purpose rather than bowing to market pressure; and being transformed internally rather than regulated externally. From a radical nonconformity perspective, a family business represents a context where values and beliefs rooted in the Christian faith can operate in tandem with management and ownership objectives through time. Yet we can expect variability in the way Christianity is integrated.

THE DIVERSITY OF CHRISTIANITY INTEGRATION IN FAMILY BUSINESSES

Family businesses are not a homogeneous group and therefore should not be oversimplified (Howorth et al., 2010). Variations are found from the overlap of an emotionally based system (family) with an objective and rational system (business) (Dyer, 2003). Today, distinct "types" of family businesses can be conceptually and empirically identified, based on diverse family and business objectives associated with ownership and management (Westhead & Howorth, 2007). Furthermore, there is evidence that businesses that label themselves as "Christian" exhibit levels of variation (Ibrahim & Angelidis, 2005), and that tensions can be expected when attempting to integrate Christianity in business (Nash & McLennan, 2001).

Table 9.1 shows recent typologies of faith integration in organizations. Miller and Ewest's (2015) typology provides room for further empirical study, as no particular faith is highlighted. The typologies suggest that while some firms may be unresponsive to faith expressions or attitudes, others may be reactive and/or proactive in integrating faith into an organization. A faith-based organization is "overtly and clearly grounded in one particular faith (religious or spiritual) tradition ... it reflects the faith convictions of its founder and his or her family's religious heritage" (Miller & Ewest, 2015, p. 317). Such depiction relates strongly to family firms. Discua Cruz (2013), drawing on Niebuhr (1951), homed in on Christianity as a faith and proposed five different ways that family firms balance Christian and cultural values in society. Such typology highlights a continuum between Christ and culture, where Christ "exists rather as the focusing point in the continuous alteration of movements from God to man and man to God" (Niebuhr, 1951, p. 29). The long-term orienta-

Table 9.1.   Christianity and Family Business Typologies

Adapted From	Organization Type	Main View
Miller and Ewest (2015)	Faith avoidance	Family businesses may seek to suppress personal or community expressions of faith, religion, and spirituality at work
	Faith safe	Family businesses that tolerates employee interest in faith at work and does not seek to quell its expression. Top management acts on faith expression in a reactive approach.
	Faith-friendly	Family businesses that address all the complexity, challenges, and potential benefits of multidimensional expressions of faith at work. The family business acts proactively to embrace the employee and institutional value of faith at work
	Faith based	Family businesses that are overtly and clearly grounded in one particular faith (i.e., Christianity) tradition. The family business reflects the faith convictions of its founder and his or her family's religious heritage.
Discua Cruz (2013)	Opposed	Family businesses that should either decline engaging in business practices altogether or conduct business activities only with fellow believers.
	Dualistic	Family businesses that have a clear separation between business practices and Christian principles.
	Catalyst	Family businesses that attempt to develop mechanisms that show Christian values in practices such as succession and governance. Family businesses practices may be shaped to reflect Christian principles.
	Restorative	Family businesses can be transformed through the engagement of Christians to glorify Christ and uphold Christian principles.
	Accommodating	Family businesses are an expression of God's creation and can accommodate practices that align with Christian principles.

tion of family firms and the unpredictability of succession (Howorth et al., 2010), may shift the firm along the continuum over time.

Table 9.1 shows that Christianity may have a transforming rationale for some family businesses. This is most evident in a firm where those leading it place Christianity as a transforming force in business (Higginson, 2012). Seibert (2001) points out that Christianity can be transformational

—that is, working to redeem secular systems—and also countercultural—that is, offering an alternative to prevailing business models in diverse industries. In family firms where a transforming perspective dominates, faith integration may be most concerned with the renewal of the business through a process that brings alignment with Christian principles and values (Discua Cruz, 2013). Family businesses upholding a transformational view will engage in activities with the world, aiming to gradually redeem it through the power of Christ. This may occur deliberately, by engaging in practices that display Christian beliefs and actions in relationship with diverse stakeholders (e.g., placing Scripture extracts in their products/mission/yearly reports, chaplaincy programs, rituals), aiming to transform their organization and the context in which they operate.

Key Theoretical Perspectives and Christianity Integration

While several theoretical lenses help to understand family businesses (Chua, Chrisman, & Steier, 2003), two competing views provide a starting point to discuss the integration of Christianity in a family firm: agency and stewardship theory.

Agency Theory

Agency theory (Eisenhardt, 1989) explains relationships in which organizational leaders' (e.g., principals) and employees' (e.g., agents) interests are at odds with each other and may only be aligned through compensation systems and appropriate monitoring. Agency theory is based on a long-established perspective that employees cannot be expected to zealously watch over the owner's assets as they would watch their own (Smith, 1776). Agency theory reminds us that organizational dynamics may be affected by the self-interest of individuals (Eisenhardt, 1989). In family firms, agency theory helps to understand, in its simplest form, the misaligned objectives in the working relationship between family business owners, acting as principals, and employees (family and nonfamily), acting as agents of principals (Chua, Chrisman, & Sharma, 2003). Agency costs are created when owners have to devise mechanisms to ensure employees follow and fulfill their objectives, thus a misalignment of objectives may often translate into costly monitoring (Eisenhardt, 1989). Conversely, a Christian perspective on agency theory calls for a focus on owners and employees as embedded in a social relationship that mirrors a relationship between God and mankind, and to rethink the relationship between owners and employees when business objectives and aims are set and monitored (Cafferky, 2012).

From a Christian perspective, family business owners (principals) can influence the integration of Christianity in the workplace. Nowadays, most family firms employ a diverse workforce, featuring diverse motivations, faith beliefs, skills. and attitudes (Chan, Lee, & Yeung, 2010). Such workforce heterogeneity can be a source of strength in a firm led by Christian principles (Pollard, 1996). Prior works suggest that a Christian perspective will emphasize a basic confidence in agents, alongside a continuous effort to judge where competencies and weaknesses lie (Johnson, 1957). Agency costs may arise when dealing with motivation, salary compensation, benefits, and ethics (Cohn & Friedman, 2002). Family business owners have a duty to show by example how employees should approach activities entrusted to them and explain consequences if a responsible attitude is neglected (Harris, 2013). An optimal scenario is when moral standards in employer-employee relationships (e.g., welfare and compensation) are based on Bible teachings, which often demand employers to go beyond what is legally expected (Cohn & Friedman, 2002). Family business owners involved in the firm should monitor and correct in patience, gentleness, love, humility, and wisdom but not with harshness (Cafferky, 2012, p. 455). Rather than designing intricate monitoring mechanisms, practices that promote trust in employees, fairness and appropriate review of actions performed are encouraged (Cohn & Friedman, 2002). NG Bailey, a family firm led by Christian principles, suggests that looking after the welfare of its workforce and introducing monitoring mechanisms based on such aspects has created a strong and durable organization (Bailey, 2015).

A Christian perspective also highlights the input of employees as agents. Tensions between employees and family business owners may originate when Christian beliefs are not aligned (Discua Cruz, 2013). Hill (2008) underscores that tensions may arise depending on whether the attitude of employees is based on a submissive or a purist attitude to work. A submissive agent places a strong emphasis on loyalty and obedience to their employers, accommodating mandates which often compromise their Christian values. In contrast, a purist agent would refuse to compromise Christian values in order to accommodate employers. Hill (2008) suggests that variations exist in both models. Furthermore, employees that aim to integrate their Christian faith at work in family businesses "must not slack off and find ways to minimize their productivity" (Cohn & Friedman, 2002, p. 961). When faith misalignment exists, employees, acting as Christian agents, ought not to compromise ethical standards to benefit principals; like Christ they should attempt to love God and their colleagues, expect harassment for upholding their values, avoid retaliation, and seek vindication from God (Hill, 2008). Christian employees in family businesses are encouraged to engage in efficient work that glorifies and testifies for Christ (Cafferky, 2013; Mabey et al., 2016).

From a Christian perspective, agency does not mean complacency; rather, it looks at the relationship between employer and employees as one in which Christian behavior can be modeled with patience and purpose for business. While lower agency costs can be expected when employers and employees share the same faith (Seibert, 2001), a Christian perspective does not deny that agency costs may arise in family businesses, as not everyone in the family firm, as in the early Christian *oikos*, may share the same faith at work.

Stewardship Theory

In contrast to agency theory, which focuses on the misalignment of objectives between owners and employees, a contrasting perspective highlights the relevance of stewards and stewardship in family businesses. Stewardship is broadly defined as "the attitudes and behaviors that place the long-term best interests of a group ahead of personal goals that serve an individual's self-interest" (Hernandez, 2008, p.122). Stewardship theory focuses on individuals acting as stewards in family businesses and helps to understand behaviors when objectives and goals between owners and employees are aligned (Davis et al., 2010). Hernandez (2008) suggests that stewardship behavior is created through social exchanges between family business owners and employees, often extending across generations. Stewardship theory has a strong Biblical foundation and is an appropriate lens through which to theorize about the integration of the Christian faith in family firms (Discua Cruz, 2015).

Stewardship theory, from an economic viewpoint, focuses on items such as "financial assets, physical facilities, products and services, systems, and processes" in order to benefit several generations (McCuddy & Pirie, 2007, p. 962). Yet a Christian perspective of stewardship calls for those working in family businesses to go beyond guarding assets for the sustainability of the firm. First, it demands looking at the family business, and everything in it, from God's perspective (Joshua 24:15; Leviticus 25:23; Psalms 50: 10-12). A Christian perspective of stewardship means that family members in business should not see the family business as theirs but the Lord's (Discua Cruz, 2015). Second, stewardship reflects a "balancing of interests" of responsibility to God and to fellow man (Rossouw, 1994). Various Bible teachings underscore the communal and relational nature of accountability that owners and employees should have for creation (Deuteronomy 10:14; 1 Chronicles 29:1; Psalm 24:1-2; Psalm 95:3-5).

The goal of stewardship, from a Christian perspective, is not only to safeguard existing skills and resources but to put them to use for the benefit of those in the organization. Stewardship goes beyond guardianship when it encourages the application of sound business tools and acumen as well as skills and expertise (1 Peter 4:10; Proverbs 23:4). Liang (2011) suggests that employees, acting as stewards in a family firm, should engage in: (a) serving the owner's best interests in the long term; (b) seeking to maximize the real worth of resources entrusted; (c) saving strategically for a better, albeit uncertain, future; and (d) investing in relationships and building equity as shrewd counsel and trusted executor for the owners. There are illustrations in the Bible of such approaches: in the parable of the talents (Matthew 25:14-30) and the portrayal of ideal steward characters (Genesis, 39; 41; 47). Furthermore, Christian principles charge family business owners to be diligent and wise investors with what has been entrusted to them, both for the family's welfare and for those who work with them (Proverbs 27:23-27). Stewardship, from a Christian perspective, challenges family business owners to invest wisely and to diversify, with the help of God's wisdom and guidance (Discua Cruz, 2015). Stewardship can be entrepreneurial when expanding an existing firm, entering new markets, introducing new products or starting new businesses (Rosa, Howorth, & Discua Cruz, 2014). Christian stewardship in family businesses ultimately involves acting as God would act (Discua Cruz, 2015).

Intergenerational Succession

The creation and development of a family business very often aspires to the goal of intergenerational succession, that is, the transfer of ownership and managerial leadership to family members (Howorth et al., 2010). Succession can be a complex yet potentially fragile process that every family business must eventually face and cope with (Le Breton-Miller, Miller, & Steier, 2004). Thus, it is not uncommon to find that succession in family firms is deeply affected by tensions such as the illness or sudden death of a family business leader (or successor), the reluctance of family members to train potential successors, and the absence of family members who are willing (or capable) to lead the firm (Davis & Harveston, 1998). Succession in family businesses aims to establish family identity, guide decisions, and embed organizational commitment across generations (Duh, Belak, & Milfelner, 2010). Mishandling the succession process may translate into unresolved conflict and potentially the demise of a family firm as such, thus the process is often considered "the ultimate challenge" for family businesses (Fletcher, 2000, p. 157). The meaning of, and approach to, succession in family firms can also be understood from a Christian perspective (Discua Cruz, 2015). The theme of succession is constant throughout the Bible, from the Book of Genesis to Jesus himself following the trade of the head of his Nazareth household and beyond

(Discua Cruz, 2013). Christianity calls for attention to succession in terms of communication, fellowship and legacy.

First, the succession process allows family members to communicate the Christian faith. Compared to other firms, whatever affects the family in business does not finish at the end of a work day. It continues into homes, dinner tables, family trips and even during family games, shaping the culture of the family in business (Discua Cruz, Hamilton, & Jack, 2012). Family leaders that aim to influence future generations communicate their faith through shared activities, rituals and experiences, including praying, Bible reading and discussions around the applicability of Biblical principles (Elliot, 2001). Several studies encourage the process of socialization for Christians leading family businesses (Solomon, 2004). Communicating the Christian faith may also involve communal activities and rituals, sermons, worship, teaching, sharing, and communion, both at home and at work (Redmer, 2007, 2008). It makes sense to communicate the Christian faith early on, when the size and structure of a family firm may make faith integration easier, rather than later in the life cycle of a business (and a family) (Discua Cruz, 2015).

Second, succession is an opportunity for fellowship. The Christian faith was designed to be transmitted through mentorship (Mays & Mason, 2010). Families in business learn to develop their own way of doing business, or business culture, when they spend time together and allow closure to instill shared values and beliefs (Pearson, Carr, & Shaw, 2008). Fellowship is paramount when founders aim to transmit enduring Christian values and a way of thinking that goes beyond mere short-term decision making (Discua Cruz, 2015). Fellowship provides a context to show new generations how the Christian faith can be integrated in business over time—to do business God's way (Peacocke, 2005). Fellowship may allow incumbent and next generation members to apply Biblical wisdom at work together when facing decisions dealing with business risks, challenges and trials. Until new generations experience the applicability of the Christian faith by themselves, it remains mainly the faith of their parents. Fellowship may be nurtured through diverse experiences, which can become part of the shared knowledge and cognition of families across generations—part of a collective family narrative that can be communicated throughout time and have lasting effects.

Finally, there is an increasing concern about the relationship between succession and legacy (Tucker, 2011). Christian family business founders and incumbents in business aspire to leave a legacy (Nash, 1994). Yet, compared with transferring physical and financial assets, a Christian perspective may focus on legacy by family entrepreneurs as "lessons and knowledge that are transmitted from one generation to the next" (Goosen & Stevens, 2013, p. 173). Such lessons may be taught through experiential learning, aiming for the next generation to gain discernment based on Christian principles. Discernment, compared to following gut feelings, calls for a deep understanding of the self and the organization, whilst working for the benefit of others (Traüffer, Bekker, Bocârnea, & Winston, 2010). Furthermore, such legacy may be transmitted over a long period of time, and may be most effective through role modeling (Mays & Mason, 2010). Succeeding generations may be more concerned with watching and learning how incumbent generations react to everyday management issues guided by their Christian faith. The biblical story of a widow, her offspring and a pot of oil provides a powerful illustration (2 Kings 4:1-7). C. Hoare & Co. bank, a family business that has survived more than 200 years, and where a strong Christian legacy continues to influence the way business is conducted amidst economic crises, provides a contemporary example (Higginson, 2015).

Nevertheless, while Christianity may influence the process of succession, there is no guarantee that Christian values aspired to by founders will be continued by subsequent generations (Discua Cruz, 2015). The integration of the Christian faith in the organizational practices of family businesses is ultimately in the hands of those taking over the family business. Yet, failing to create the context to transmit the Christian faith may create confusion and uncertainty for succeeding generations, as previous Christian values and principles may seem to no longer matter and may put the culture fostered by previous (Christian) generations in jeopardy.

Challenges

Appreciating the integration of Christianity in family businesses is not straightforward. Mitroff and Denton (1999) highlight that an organization that aims to integrate a particular faith too strongly runs the risk of creating organizational practices that may discourage the engagement and development of a diverse workforce. Challenges, alongside opportunities, relate mainly to methodological and contextual aspects. First, both qualitative and quantitative studies can contribute to understand the integration of the Christian faith in family business research (Reay & Whetten, 2011; Woodhead, 2009). Furthermore, there are several linkages between Christianity and theoretical perspectives that need further attention (Fang, Randolph, Chrisman, & Barnett, 2013; Jeong, 2010). Studies that use one or various methods alongside comprehensive theoretical frameworks may bring light onto the integration of the Christian faith in family firms (Discua Cruz, 2013). Second, every family business is embedded in a society that is associated with particular sets of values, attitudes, laws, and business practices (Howorth et al., 2010).

Although similarities in Christian beliefs and practices exist, strong contrasts may be found within countries and across borders. Woodhead, Fletcher, Kawanami, and Smith (2002) pose that the center of gravity of Christianity is shifting, particularly toward countries where collectivistic cultural behavior prevails. Further studies in such contexts, as well as comparative efforts, may provide a more nuanced understanding of the integration of faith in family businesses around the world (Gupta & Levenburg, 2010).

Conclusion

Clearly, the integration of Christianity in family businesses cannot be underestimated. This chapter argues that the integration of Christianity can help shape a family business in the way owners and employees approach work. Christianity, when communicated, shared and experienced by members of a family in business, may provide the basis for a lasting and transforming legacy which can transform the businesses they own and control. Yet, the integration of the Christian faith in a family business does not emerge overnight and may require the deliberate action of incumbent and incoming generations.

REFERENCES

Bailey, C. (2015). The Kingdom, the power and the glory. *Faith in Business Quarterly, 17*(2), 13–20.

Cafferky, M. E. (2012). *Management: A faith-based perspective*. Hoboken, NJ: Pearson Education.

Cafferky, M. E. (2013). Toward a biblical theology of efficiency. *Journal of Biblical Integration in Business, 16*(2), 41–60.

Chan, A., Lee, S. K., & Yeung, M. W. (2010). Holistic struggles and judgmental behaviors in the work place: An empirical study of Hong Kong Christians. *Journal of Biblical Integration in Business, 13*, 46–70.

Chandler, A. D. (1977). *The visible hand: Managerial revolution in American business*. Cambridge, MA: Harvard University Press.

Chan-Serafin, S., Brief, A. P., & George, J. M. (2013). Perspective—How does religion matter and why? Religion and the organizational sciences. *Organization Science, 24*(5), 1585–1600.

Chua, J., Chrisman, J. J., & Sharma, P. (2003). Succession and non-succession concerns of family firms and agency relationships with non-family managers. *Family Business Review, 16*(2), 89–107.

Chua, J., Chrisman, J. J., & Steier, L. P. (2003). Extending the theoretical horizons of family business research. *Entrepreneurship Theory and Practice, 27*(4), 331–338.

Cohn, G., & Friedman, H. H. (2002). Improving employer-employee relationships: A Biblical and Talmudic perspective on human resource management. *Management Decision, 40*(10), 955–961.

Craig, J. B., Moores, K., Howorth, C., & Poutziouris, P. (2009). Family business research at a tipping point threshold. *Journal of Management and Organization, 15*(3), 282–293.

Davis, P. S., & Harveston, P. D. (1998). The influence of family on the family business succession process: A multi-generational perspective. *Entrepreneurship: Theory & Practice, 22*(3), 31.

Davis, J. H., Allen, M. R., & Hayes, H. D. (2010). Is blood thicker than water? A study of stewardship perceptions in family business. *Entrepreneurship Theory and Practice, 34*(6), 1093–1116.

Discua Cruz, A. (2013). Christian family businesses: Opportunities for further research. *Journal of Biblical Integration in Business, 16*(2), 7–28.

Discua Cruz, A. (2015). Rethinking family businesses through a Christian perspective. *Faith in Business Quarterly, 17*(1), 23–30.

Discua Cruz, A., Hamilton, E., & Jack, S. L. (2012). Understanding entrepreneurial cultures in family businesses: A study of family entrepreneurial teams in Honduras. *Journal of Family Business Strategy, 3*(3), 147–161.

Dodd, S. D., & Dyck, B. (2015). Agency, stewardship, and the universal-family firm A qualitative historical analysis. *Family Business Review, 28*(4), 312–331.

Duh, M., Belak, J., & Milfelner, B. (2010). Core values, culture and ethical climate as constitutional elements of ethical behaviour: Exploring differences between family and non-family enterprises. *Journal of Business Ethics, 97*(3), 473–489.

Dyer, W. G. (2003). The family: The missing variable in organizational research. *Entrepreneurship Theory and Practice, 27*(4), 401–416.

Eisenhardt, K. (1989). Agency theory: An assessment and review. *Academy of Management Review, 14*(1), 57–74.

Elliot, E. (2001). *Shaping of a Christian family.* Grand Rapids, MI: Fleming H. Revell, Baker Book House Co.

Elliott, J. H. (2003). The Jesus movement was not egalitarian but family-oriented. *Biblical Interpretation, 11*, 173–210.

Elser, P. F. (1997). Family imagery and Christian identity in Gal 5:13 to 6:10. In H. Moxnes (Ed.), *Constructing early Christian families: Family as social reality and metaphor* (pp. 121–149). New York, NY: Taylor & Francis.

Fang, H., Randolph, R. V. de G., Chrisman, J. J., & Barnett, T. (2013). Firm religiosity, bounded stakeholder salience, and stakeholder relationships in family firms. *Journal of Management, Spirituality & Religion, 10*(3), 253–270.

Faraone, C. A. (2008). Household religion in ancient Greece. In J. Bodelessor & S. M. Olyanessor (Eds.), *Household and family religion in antiquity* (pp. 210–228). Hoboken, NJ: Blackwell.

Fletcher, D. (2000). Family and enterprise. In S. Carter & D. Jones-Evans (Eds.), *Enterprise and small business: Principles, practice and policy* (pp. 155–165). Hoboken, NJ: Pearson Education.

Goossen, R. J., & Stevens, R. P. (2013). *Entrepreneurial leadership.* Downers Grove, IL: InterVarsity Press.

Gupta, V., & Levenburg, N. (2010). A thematic analysis of cultural variations in family businesses: The CASE project. *Family Business Review, 23*(2), 155–169.

Hammel, E. A. (1984). On the *** of studying household form and function. In R. M. Netting, R. R. Wilk, & E. J. Arnould (Eds.), *Households: Comparative and historical studies of the domestic group* (pp. 29–43). Berkeley, CA: University of California Press.

Harris, R. H. (2013). *The heart of business: Solomon's wisdom for success in any economy.* Colorado Springs, CO: NavPress.

Hernandez, M. (2008). Promoting stewardship behavior in organizations: A leadership model. *Journal of Business Ethics, 80*(1), 121–128.

Higginson, R. (2012). *Faith, hope & the global economy.* Downers Grove, IL: InterVarsity Press.

Higginson, R. (2015). A bank with a Christian ethos. *Faith in Business Quarterly, 17*(1), 27–28.

Hill, A. (2008). *Just business: Christian ethics for the marketplace* (2nd ed.) Downers Grove, IL: InterVarsity Press.

Howorth, C., Rose, M., & Hamilton, E. (2006). Definitions, diversity and development: Key debates in family business research. In M. Casson, B. Yeung, A. Cassu, & N. Wadeson (Eds.), *Oxford handbook of entrepreneurship* (pp. 225–247). Oxford, England: Oxford University Press.

Howorth, C., Rose, M., Hamilton, E., & Westhead, P. (2010). Family firm diversity and development: An introduction. *International Small Business Journal, 28*(5), 437–451.

Ibrahim, N., & Angelidis, J. (2005). The long-term performance of small businesses: Are there differences between "Christian-based" companies and their secular counterparts? *Journal of Business Ethics, 58*(1), 187–193.

International Family Enterprise Research Academy. (2003). Family businesses dominate: International family enterprise research academy (IFERA). *Family Business Review, 16*(4), 235–241.

Jeong, H. O. (2010). How do religions differ in their impact on individuals' social capital? The case of South Korea. *Nonprofit and Voluntary Sector Quarterly, 39*(1), 142–160.

Johnson, H. L. (1957). Can the businessman apply Christianity? *Harvard Business Review, 5*(September–October), 68–76.

Le Breton-Miller, I., Miller, D., & Steier, L. P. (2004). Toward an integrative model of effective FOB succession. *Entrepreneurship, Theory and Practice, 28*(4), 305–328.

Liang, E. P. (2011). The global financial crisis: Biblical perspectives on corporate finance. *Journal of Biblical Integration in Business, 12*, 48–61.

Litz, R. A. (1997). The family firm's exclusion from business school research: Explaining the void; addressing the opportunity. *Entrepreneurship: Theory and Practice, 21*(3), 55–72.

Litz, R. A. (2013). Leaving the godfather to follow God the father: Successor generation conversion in a mob family. *Journal of Management, Spirituality & Religion, 10*(2), 183–211.

Mabey, C., Conroy, M., Blakeley, K., & de Marco, S. (2016). Having burned the straw man of Christian spiritual leadership, what can we learn from Jesus about leading ethically? *Journal of Business Ethics*, 1–13. https://doi.org/10.1007/s10551-016-3054-5

Mays, K. W., & Mason, S. D. (2010). Richard C. Chewning: Model and mentor of business and faith integration. *Journal of Biblical Integration in Business, 12*, 63–72.

Melin, L., Nordqvist, M., & Sharma, P. (2014). *The SAGE handbook of family business.* London, England: SAGE.

McCuddy, M. K., & Pirie, W. L. (2007). Spirituality, stewardship, and financial decision-making. *Managerial Finance, 33*(12), 957–969.

Miller, D. W., & Ewest, T. (2015). A new framework for analyzing organizational workplace religion and spirituality. *Journal of Management, Spirituality & Religion, 12*(4), 305–328.

Mitroff, I. I. & Denton, E. A. (1999). *A spiritual audit of corporate America.* San Francisco, CA: Jossey-Bass.

Moxnes, H. (Ed.). (1997). What is family? Problems in constructing early Christian families. In *Constructing early Christian families: Family as social reality and metaphor* (pp. 13–41). New York, NY: Taylor & Francis.

Nash, L. (1994). *Believers in business.* Nashville, TN: Thomas Nelson.

Nash, L., & McLennan, S. (2001). *Church on Sunday, work on Monday: The challenge of fusing Christian values with business life.* San Francisco, CA: Jossey- Bass.

Netting, R. M., Wilk, R. R., & Arnould, E. J. (1984). *Households: Comparative and historical studies of the domestic group.* Berkeley, CA: University of California Press.

Niebuhr, R. H. (1951). *Christ and culture.* New York, NY: Harper & Row.

Peacocke, D. (2005). *Doing business God's way.* Santa Rosa, CA: Rebuild.

Pearson, A. W., Carr, J. C., & Shaw, J. C. (2008). Toward a theory of familiness: A social capital perspective. *Entrepreneurship Theory and Practice, 32*(6), 949–969.

Pollard, C. W. (1996). *The soul of the firm.* Grand Rapids, MI: Zondervan.

Popp, A. (2015). *Entrepreneurial families: Business, marriage and life in the early nineteenth century.* London, England: Routledge.

Reay, T., & Whetten, D. A. (2011). What constitutes a theoretical contribution in family business? *Family Business Review, 24*(2), 105–110.

Redmer, T. A. O. (2007). Case study R. W. Beckett Corporation: Corporate culture. *Christian Business Academy Review, 2*(1), 75–82.

Redmer, T. A. O. (2008). Case study: Cardone Industries, Chaplain program. *Christian Business Academy Review, 3*(1), 62–68.

Rosa, P., Howorth, C., & Discua Cruz, A. (2014). Habitual and portfolio entrepreneurship and the family in business. In L. Melin, M. Nordqvist, & P. Sharma (Eds.), *The SAGE handbook of family business* (pp. 364–382). London, England: SAGE.

Rossouw, G. J. (1994). Business ethics: Where have all the Christians gone? *Journal of Business Ethics, 13*(7), 557–570.

Seibert, K. W. (2001). Learning the ropes without getting strangled: The believer and socialization in business. *Journal of Biblical Integration in Business, 6*, 90–108.

Smith, A. (1776). *An inquiry into the nature and causes of wealth of nations.* Oxford, England: Oxford University Press.

Solomon, L. D. (2004). *Evangelical Christian executives: A new model for business corporation*. New Brunswick, NJ: Transaction.

To have and to hold [Special report]. (2015, April 18). *The Economist*, pp. 3–16.

Tucker, J. (2011). Keeping the business in the family and the family in business: "What is the legacy?" *Journal of Family Business Management, 1*(1), 65–73.

Traüffer, H. C., Bekker, C., Bocârnea, M., & Winston, B. E. (2010). Towards an understanding of discernment: A conceptual paper. *Leadership & Organization Development Journal, 31*(2), 176–184.

Van Buren, H. J., III, & Agle, B. R. (1998). Measuring Christian beliefs that affect managerial decision-making: A beginning. *International Journal of Value-Based Management, 11*(2), 159–177.

Weaver, G. R., & Agle, B. R. (2002). Religiosity and ethical behavior in organizations: A symbolic interactionist perspective. *Academy of Management Review, 27*(1), 77–97.

Woodhead, L. (2009). Old, new and emerging paradigms in the sociological study of religion. *Nordic Journal of Religion and Society, 22*(2), 103–121.

Woodhead, L., Fletcher, P., Kawanami, H., & Smith, D. (Eds.). (2002). *Religions in the modern world: Traditions and transformations*. London, England: Routledge.

Westhead, P., & Howorth, C. (2007). "Types" of private family firms: An exploratory conceptual and empirical analysis. *Entrepreneurship & Regional Development, 19*(5), 405–431.

CHAPTER 10

INNOVATIVE WORK AND WORSHIP CONTEXTS AND THEIR ASSOCIATIONS WITH REGULATORY FOCUS MINDSETS AND NASCENT HYBRID ENTREPRENEURSHIP

Mitchell J. Neubert and Kevin D. Dougherty
Baylor University

The question of what explains entrepreneurial behavior has a long history (Weber, 1904–5). In addition to individual experiences and personal characteristics, organizational contexts help explain who engages in entrepreneurial behavior (Frese & Gielnik, 2014). This chapter describes the influence of two prevalent organizational contexts, where people work and where they worship, on a specific type of entrepreneurial behavior, nascent hybrid entrepreneurship. Nascent hybrid entrepreneurs are those who are trying to start a business while simultaneously working for someone else (Burmeister-Lamp, Lévesque, & Schade, 2012; Folta, Delmar, & Wennberg, 2010; Raffiee & Feng, 2014). Because starting businesses and innovation are "two major sources both of economic growth and social

Faith and Work: Christian Perspectives, Research, and Insights Into the Movement
pp. 169–190

well-being" (D. Miller, 2011, p. 877), nascent hybrid entrepreneurship makes an important contribution to vibrant communities.

A limited amount of research addresses factors that influence the nascent phase of the entrepreneurial process which spans from idea generation or opportunity recognition to the actual start of a business (Hopp & Sonderegger, 2015; Khan, Tang, & Joshi, 2014; Klyver & Schenkel, 2013). Even less is known about nascent hybrid entrepreneurs. Nascent entrepreneurial behavior has been explained in part by the personality of the entrepreneur, their competencies, and experiences in their background, but much is left unexplained (Klyver & Schenkel, 2013; Obschonka, Silbereisen, Schmitt-Rodermund, & Stuetzer, 2011; Schmitt-Rodermund, 2004; Wooten, Timmerman, & Folger, 1999). In this chapter we explore how organizational contexts are associated with mindsets that contribute to explaining nascent hybrid entrepreneurship.

The workplace is a potentially powerful social context for influencing an individual's mindset and subsequent behavior (Brockner & Higgins, 2001; Neubert, Kacmar, Carlson, Chonko, & Roberts, 2008). One characteristic of a social context is innovativeness, which is a subdimension of the broader entrepreneurial orientation construct used to assess commercial enterprises and the individuals within these workplaces (Covin, Green, & Slevin, 2006; De Clercq & Rius, 2007; Lumpkin & Dess, 1996; Monsen & Boss, 2009; Morris & Kuratko, 2002). Innovativeness is the expressed commitment of an organization to develop new products and services or enhancements to processes or technology (Covin & Slevin, 1989). Innovative organizations are widely celebrated in American society.

Commercial businesses are not the only context of innovation. Like workplaces, congregations can be characterized by their extent of innovativeness (Pearce, Fritz, & Davis, 2010). Religious congregations, although ubiquitous, are often overlooked as organizational contexts with the capacity for shaping the vocational thinking of entrepreneurs (Dodd & Seaman, 1998; Tracey, 2012). More than 60% of American adults identify with a place of worship, making religious congregations the most prevalent form of voluntary organization in the United States (Chaves, 2004). Congregations provide a sense of meaning and moral order that help define and organize the everyday life of members (Iannaccone, 1990; Wuthnow, 1987).

Where people work and where they worship are two contexts that have the potential to shape mindsets that can lead to nascent hybrid entrepreneurial behavior. Specifically, an individual's regulatory focus mindset is a sociocognitive mechanism representing a specific aspect of thinking that has potential to explain entrepreneurial processes (Brockner, Higgins, & Low, 2004; McMullen & Shepherd, 2002; Wallace, Little, Hill, & Ridge, 2010). Regulatory focus mindsets are recognized as fundamental proximal motivations for behavior (Johnson, Shull, & Wallace, 2011; Kark & Van Dijk, 2007; Lanaj, Chang, & Johnson, 2012). Essentially, one's regulatory focus mindset is directed toward avoiding pain and undesirable outcomes (i.e., prevention focus) or attaining pleasure and desirable outcomes (i.e., promotion focus) (Higgins, 1997, 1998). Although an individual's regulatory focus can be dispositional, it also can be a malleable mindset induced by the characteristics of a social context (Brockner & Higgins, 2001; Wallace, Johnson, & Frazier, 2009). In the pages that follow, we articulate how work and worship contexts shape an individual's malleable regulatory mindset and, in turn, help explain nascent entrepreneurship.

INNOVATIVENESS IN ORGANIZATIONAL CONTEXTS

Entrepreneurial orientation (EO) refers to the behaviors, preferences, practices, and decision-making activities of the leaders of an organization (Covin et al., 2006; Lumpkin & Dess, 1996). EO has been conceptualized in a variety of ways but most include some or all of the following dimensions: innovativeness, proactiveness, risk taking, autonomy, and competitive aggressiveness (Covin & Lumpkin, 2011; Lumpkin & Dess, 2001; Miller, 2011). Although a substantial amount of research aggregates these dimensions into a gestalt construct, inconsistent results suggest that research utilizing individual dimensions is necessary (Hughes & Morgan, 2007; Kreiser, Marino, Kuratko, & Weaver, 2013; Rauch, Wiklund, Lumpkin, & Frese, 2009); indeed, individual dimensions have the potential to offer distinct explanations for entrepreneurial behavior (Lumpkin & Dess, 2001; Miller, 2011).

In workplaces, EO dimensions of an organization have been shown to influence the attitudes and intentions of organizational members (De Clercq & Rius, 2007; Monsen & Boss, 2009). Pearce et al. (2010) also demonstrated the relevance of EO dimensions to congregations. They found that an adapted version of EO, especially innovativeness, related to increased attendance and contributions. Our interest is in innovativeness in workplace and worship contexts. Innovativeness as conceptualized by Covin and Slevin (1989) focuses on the actions of leaders to encourage developing novel products and services or improving existing processes or technology. Innovativeness is demonstrated by organizational leaders through exercising creativity, embracing experimentation, and supporting new practices (Hughes & Morgan, 2007; Pearce et al., 2010).

In organizational contexts, leaders cue learning and influence others' thinking through what leaders' pay attention to and reward, where they allocate resources, how they deal with challenges and make decisions, and the messages they communicate (Bandura, 1986). The prevailing perceptions of the organizational context as shaped by leaders and perceived by its members can evoke a subconscious process of adaptation in which people align their thinking to become more congruent with the characteristics of their context (James, James, & Ashe, 1990; Piperopoulos & Dimov, 2015; Wallace & Chen, 2006).

Although regulatory mindsets can be dispositional, at any given point in time, people may engage in self-regulation with a promotion focus or a prevention focus influenced, in part, by cues from the contexts in which they live and work (Crowe & Higgins, 1997; Kark & Van Dijk, 2007). A promotion focus is evoked by an emphasis on ideals, growth, or achieving gains, while a prevention focus is evoked by an emphasis on duties, security, or avoiding losses (Higgins, 1997, 1998; Shah, Higgins, & Friedman, 1998). Regulatory focus can be induced by the characteristics of a context through priming, framing, or role modeling (Liberman, Idson, Camacho, & Higgins, 1999; Neubert et al., 2008).

In workplaces, leaders play a prominent role in shaping the regulatory mindsets that determine what employees attend to and how they think about their work (Brocker & Higgins, 2001). A leader who emphasizes growth and improvement is likely to engender a promotion focus in employees, while a leader who emphasizes following established procedures is likely to engender a prevention focus in employees (Neubert et al., 2008). Innovativeness modeled by leaders can be a salient social cue and a source of social learning regarding behavioral expectations for employees (Bandura, 1986; Brettel & Rottenberger, 2013; Scott & Bruce, 1994). Through this process of social learning and adaptation, innovativeness is likely to encourage a promotion mindset of pursuing ideals, growth, and taking risks, while at the same time discourage a prevention mindset of fulfilling duties, maintaining the status quo, and avoiding risk (Brockner & Higgins, 2001).

Hypothesis 1: Workplace innovativeness will be positively associated with an individual's promotion focus mindset.

Hypothesis 2: Workplace innovativeness will be negatively associated with an individual's prevention focus mindset.

Most of the research related to innovativeness has occurred in work organizations, but leaders within religious organizations also can model innovativeness (Pearce et al., 2010). The history of American religion reflects the benefits that come with innovative organizations and leaders. In colonial America, Baptist and Methodist sects introduced novel practices and programs that spurred rapid expansion; among these innovations were itinerant ministers, camp meetings, and prayers meetings (Finke & Stark, 2005). Entrepreneurial religious leaders emerged from the masses and their messages resonated with common people (Hatch, 1989). Rather than the learned experts of established denominations, the clergy of upstart sects brought high enthusiasm with a low price tag; many worked as bivocational pastors, which kept overhead costs low for congregations (Finke & Stark, 2005).

Research on contemporary religious trends likewise highlights the importance of innovation. Mosaic is an Evangelical church in Los Angeles celebrated for its ethnic diversity. The transition of this small, White, Southern Baptist congregation into a multiethnic megachurch is a story of innovation. In his ethnography of Mosaic, sociologist Gerardo Martí (2005) makes the case that "ongoing innovation is a fundamental feature of this congregation" (p. 4). Active experimentation defines the church and its minister Erwin McManus (Martí, 2005). The ability to change is a key correlate to congregational success. Survey data from over 30,000 congregations across 15 years reveal that openness to change and innovative worship music are related to increased spiritual vitality and attendance growth (Roozen, 2011, 2016). Religious leaders play a pivotal role in these innovations. Celebrity clergy such as T.D. Jakes and Rick Warren, each of whom lead congregations of over 20,000 adherents, display a unique capacity for providing religion in ways that resonate with contemporary audiences (Lee & Sinitiere, 2009). However, no matter the size of a congregation, clergy are primary purveyors of a congregation's religious culture (Carroll, 2006).

Congregational innovation takes numerous forms including changes or enhancements that occur both within the organization's practices (e.g., increasing racial diversity or changing expressions of sacred rituals) and in the organizations' efforts to reach out to the larger community (e.g., civic volunteering or political mobilization) (see Emerson & Woo, 2006, Lichterman, 2005). In this context, congregational leaders have a profound influence on their members through what is emphasized from the pulpit, in programs, and through leaders' personal example (Miller, 2002; Pearce et al., 2010). This influence extends to shaping members' work attitudes and behaviors (Park, Griebel, Neubert, & Dougherty, 2014). Therefore, innovativeness modeled by leaders within a congregation may cross over to encourage a promotion mindset in work matters, while discouraging a prevention mindset.

Hypothesis 3:   Congregation innovativeness will be positively associated with an individual's promotion focus mindset.

Hypothesis 4:   Congregation innovativeness will be negatively associated with an individual's prevention focus mindset.

REGULATORY FOCUS MINDSETS AND ENTREPRENEURSHIP

Regulatory mindsets are associated with a range of positive behaviors within the workplace such as creativity, innovation, task performance, safety, citizenship behaviors, and commitment (Gorman et al., 2012; Lanja, Chang, & Johnson, 2012). However, much less is known about how regulatory foci influence entrepreneurial behavior. Initial research indicates that among existing entrepreneurs, promotion focus is positively associated with success in dynamic industries while prevention focus is negatively related to success (Hmieleski & Baron, 2008). Likewise, in an experiment involving entrepreneurs, a promotion focus mindset was associated with the number of opportunities identified and their novelty; prevention focus was not associated with either variable (Tumasjan & Braun, 2012).

Hybrid entrepreneurs are more similar to nonentrepreneurs than fully self-employed entrepreneurs in having high levels of risk aversion and low levels of core self-evaluations related to esteem, efficacy, emotional stability, and locus of control (Raffiee & Feng, 2014). Additional influences on the decision to be a hybrid entrepreneur compared to being a fully self-employed entrepreneur or working for others are likely to be unique as well (Folta et al., 2010). No research to date directly explores how regulatory focus might distinguish who among currently employed individuals is likely to concurrently try to start a new business. However, there is research illuminating how regulatory foci may influence entrepreneurial behavior. A study of simulated decisions found that those assuming the role of hybrid entrepreneurs and facing increasing levels of risk spent more time on their side business if they had a promotion focus and less time if they had a prevention focus (Burmeister-Lamp et al., 2012). Altogether, this points to the relevance of an individual's regulatory focus to nascent hybrid entrepreneurial behavior.

Entrepreneurial action is predicated on identifying that an opportunity exists and then evaluating the opportunity for oneself (Grégoire, Barr, & Shepherd, 2010; McMullen & Shepherd, 2006). Brockner et al. (2004) proposed that regulatory foci might operate differentially across phases of the entrepreneurial process. A promotion focus mindset emphasizing aspirations, growth, and gains is generally more advantageous to recognizing and conceiving of opportunities for entrepreneurial endeavors (Brockner et al., 2004). A promotion mindset further translates into creative and innovative behavior (McMullen, Shepherd, & Patzelt, 2009; Neubert et al., 2008; Wu, McMullen, Neubert, & Yi, 2008). Those with a promotion focus mindset show attention to new possibilities and aptitude for generating novel solutions that are central to nascent entrepreneurial behavior (Brockner et al., 2004; Liberman et al., 1999).

In contrast to a promotion focus mindset, a prevention focus mindset is duty-bound, security seeking, and conservative (Higgins, 1997, 1998). A promotion focus mindset tends to be manifest in attitudinal and behavioral responses that are action-oriented, while a prevention focus tends to be vigilant and cautious (McMullen, Shepherd, & Zahra, 2007). A prevention focus is unlikely to generate novel ideas or to inspire perseverance for novel and uncertain tasks (Markman & Baron, 2003). A prevention focus mindset lends itself well to the task of determining the feasibility of opportunities, not seeking out opportunities (Brockner et al., 2004). In this process of due diligence, a prevention focus can result in screening out opportunities or hindering further entrepreneurial action (Brockner et al., 2004).

As such, we expect that promotion focus will be positively related to trying to start a business, whereas prevention focus will be negatively related to trying to start a business.

Hypothesis 5: An individual's promotion focus mindset will be positively associated with trying to start a new venture.

Hypothesis 6: An individual's prevention focus mindset will be negatively associated with trying to start a new venture.

Figure 10.1 depicts our six hypotheses in a conceptual model.

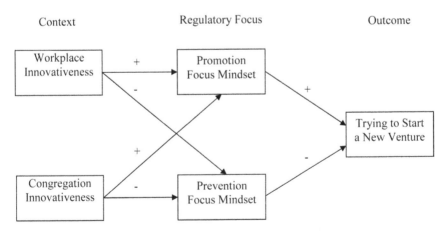

Figure 10.1.   Conceptual model of organizational context, regulatory focus, and entrepreneurial outcome.

METHOD

Sample

We tested our hypotheses with a sample of 1,022 full-time working, American adults. Participants were drawn from a probability based web panel developed by Knowledge Networks. Web panels are an increasingly popular and useful method of data collection (Callegaro et al., 2014). Knowledge Networks assembled their panel through random-digit dialing and address-based sampling. The panel covers 97% of U.S. households, including those with unlisted telephone numbers and those lacking Internet access. Unlike opt-in panels, individuals cannot volunteer to be a member of this panel. Screening questions narrowed the sample to full-time workers age 18 or older in for-profit firms. Knowledge Networks administered our surveys at two time periods 3 weeks apart in November 2010. Respondents had to complete both surveys to earn rewards from Knowledge Networks. The independent and dependent variables used to test our model were collected at different times. This time lag helps minimize consistency motifs and demand characteristics, thereby, reducing common method bias (Podsakoff, MacKenzie, & Lee, 2003). Because of our interest in a current organizational context, we narrowed our analytical sample to respondents who worked for someone else and who identified with a place of worship. This reduced our sample size to 803 respondents.

Time 1 Measures

All Time 1 measures in this study are based on a 5-point Likert scale where 1 = *strongly disagree* and 5 = *strongly agree*. We averaged items within the scales to create composite measures. High scores equate to high levels of the construct of interest.

Workplace Innovativeness.   Covin and Slevin (1989) initially conceptualized EO as consisting of nine items that measure innovativeness, risk-taking, and proactiveness. We identified the innovativeness dimension of EO as most theoretically relevant to assess the internal operations of both workplaces and places of worship. Examining the EO items associated with place of work and congregation separately, we isolated a unitary factor of innovativeness consisting of two items for each organizational context. The two items to measure workplace innovativeness were "In general, the leaders where I work favor a strong emphasis on research and technological innovations" and "In the last 5 years, my organization has introduced many new product lines or services." In the current sample, the Cronbach's alpha for this scale was .61.

Congregation Innovativeness.   We used the same two items to construct an innovativeness scale for a respondent's congregation. Following Pearce et al. (2010), we adjusted the wording of the items slightly to be applicable to a congregation: "In general, the leaders where I worship favor a strong emphasis on ministry and worship style innovation" and "In the last 5 years, my place of worship has tried many new ministry outreach endeavors or new worship service styles." The Cronbach's alpha for this scale was .75.

Regulatory Focus Mindsets.   Our mediating variables are the promotion dimension and prevention dimension of Neubert et al.'s (2008) Work Regulatory Focus scale. The scale measures regulatory focus mindsets as conceptualized in a work environment. The promotion focus subscale and the prevention focus subscale each consist of nine items. The Cronbach's alpha for the promotion focus subscale was .86. The Cronbach's alpha for the prevention focus subscale was .90.

Time 2 Measures

Nascent Entrepreneurial Behavior.   To identify nascent entrepreneurs, we asked: "Are you currently trying to start a business or organization including any kind of self-employment?" Response options were coded as 1 = yes and 0 = no. A follow-up question asked whether the new venture was for-profit or not-for-profit. All of the nascent entrepreneurs in our sample were trying to start for-profit businesses.

Controls.   We controlled for a host of demographic and religious characteristics. Standard demographic variables were gender (1 = female, 0 = male), age (in years), race (1 = non-White, 0 = White), education (1 = no formal education to 14 = professional or doctorate degree), income (1 = household income of less than $5,000 to 19 = household income of $175,000 or more), and region (Northeast, Midwest, West, with South as the omitted reference category). In addition to income, we controlled for other known influences on nascent entrepreneurship, such as having a working spouse (1 = spouse or partner employed full-time, 0 = no full-time working spouse/partner) and previous start-up experience (1 = previously started a business or organization, 0 = no previous start-up experience) (Davidsson & Honig, 2003; Khan et al., 2014). Because the significance of a workplace to an individual may hinge on their position in the workplace, we controlled for occupation. The survey asked, "What is your occupation?" Response options were "white collar—professional, managerial, owner;" "white collar—sales, clerical;" "blue collar—

craftsman/foreman;" "blue collar—semiskilled, unskilled;" "service worker;" and "other." We created a dichotomous variable for professional/managerial/owner (coded as 1, with all other occupations coded as 0). A final control variable in our analysis was religious tradition. Congregations reside within larger religious traditions defined by theology, history, and culture (Steensland et al., 2000). Following the coding scheme of Dougherty, Johnson, and Polson (2007), we used survey questions on religion, denomination, and congregation name to construct five religious tradition categories: Evangelical Protestant, Black Protestant, Mainline Protestant, Catholic, or Other. Respondents without a religious affiliation were excluded from our study.

RESULTS

Table 10.1 reports descriptive statistics for the variables in our study and correlation coefficients for the three dependent variables. Associations not included in our hypotheses but worth mentioning were that Mainline Protestants were negatively correlated with a promotion focus. Catholics were negatively associated with trying to start a new venture. Those in the sample with previous start-up experience were more likely to engage in nascent entrepreneurial behavior. Further, men were more likely than women to be trying to start a new venture. Age was negatively associated with a promotion focus and positively associated with a prevention focus. Non-Whites were more likely than Whites in the sample to be trying to start a new venture. Finally, respondents in the western United States were significantly associated with trying to start a new venture.

Hypothesis Testing

Our hypotheses proposed that perceptions of the workplace and congregation as innovative would be associated with an individual's regulatory focus mindset and, in turn, regulatory focus mindsets (promotion and prevention) would be associated with entrepreneurial behavior but in contrasting ways. We tested these predictions using path analysis (Schumacker & Lomax, 2004), which reduced our sample to 638 respondents who provided information for all the variables in our analyses.

We estimated our conceptual model with Mplus 7.11 using robust weighted least squares estimation (weighted least square means and variance adjusted, WLSMV). The ability to handle binary dependent (endogenous) variables is a strength of Mplus (Muthén & Muthén, 2010). WLSMV is the estimation technique recommended for such models

**Table 10.1. Descriptive Statistics
and Correlations With Dependent Variables**

Variable	Mean	S.D.	Promotion Mindset	Prevention Mindset	Trying to Start a New Venture
			Correlations (r)		
Promotion focus mindset	3.252	.647	—	—	—
Prevention focus mindset	4.009	.619	.287**	—	—
Trying to start a new venture	.059	.235	.147**	.032	—
Workplace innovativeness	3.163	.902	.310**	.132**	.061
Congregation innovativeness	3.027	.837	.155**	.084*	.086*
Female	.458	.499	−.113**	.097*	−.102**
Age	44.265	12.532	−.297**	.084*	−.059
Non-White	.210	.408	.108**	−.015	.105**
Education	10.867	1.755	.023	−.065	−.002
Income	12.628	3.426	−.041	−.060	−.051
Working spouse	.387	.487	−.002	−.027	−.035
Professional/manager/owner	.444	.497	.102**	.005	−.009
Previously started a business/ organization	.125	.331	.022	−.045	.195**
Evangelical Protestant	.293	.455	.010	.0003	.003
Black Protestant	.056	.230	.062	.007	.054
Mainline Protestant	.201	.402	−.070*	.054	.020
Catholic	.272	.446	−.009	−.005	−.082*
Other religious tradition	.126	.332	.059	−.007	.034
Northeast	.181	.385	−.018	.015	−.021
Midwest	.237	.402	−.027	−.031	−.014
West	.181	.385	−.021	−.007	.076*
South	.402	.491	.054	.020	−.031

Note: N = 803. *p < .05. **p < .01.

(Asparouhov & Muthén, 2010). The innovativeness scales for workplace and congregation were exogenous variables in the model. Endogenous variables were promotion focus and prevention focus mindsets and trying to start a new venture. In addition, we controlled for gender, age, race, education, income, working spouse, occupation, previous start-up experience, religious tradition, and region. Based on the correlation matrix and

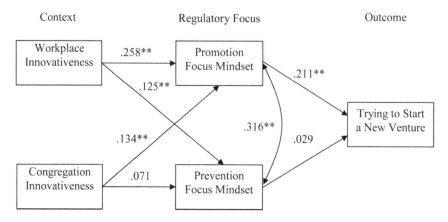

Note: Standardized coefficients reported. Control variables not shown. See Table 10.2 for full results. *p < .05. **p < .01.

Figure 10.2.   Estimated model of organizational context, regulatory focus, and entrepreneurial outcome.

preliminary analysis, we made one adjustment to improve model fit. We allowed the two regulatory focus mindsets to correlate. With this modification, the estimated model achieved good model fit. Chi-square was not significant (χ^2 = 1.998, df = 2, p = 0.368); Comparative Fit Index (CFI = 1.00) and Tucker-Lewis Index (TLI = 1.00) were above .95; and the root mean square error of approximation (RMSEA=.000) was below .05.

Standardized path coefficients associated with the hypotheses are presented in Figure 10.2. Controlling for demographic variables and religious tradition, workplace innovativeness and congregation innovativeness positively related to a promotion focus mindset, thus supporting Hypotheses 1 and 3. The relationship between organizational innovativeness and prevention focus did not match our expectations. Hypotheses 2 and 4 predicted negative relationships for the two innovativeness scales and prevention focus. Neither hypothesis was supported. Instead, workplace innovativeness was positively related to a prevention focus mindset and the path coefficient for congregation innovativeness was not statistically significant. Likewise, we found mixed results for the association of regulatory focus mindsets with our measure of nascent entrepreneurial behavior. Hypothesis 5, which predicted that promotion focus mindset would be positively associated with trying to start a new venture, was supported. On the other hand, prevention focus mindset was not significantly related to trying to start a new venture. Hence, hypothesis 6 was not supported.

Table 10.2.   Unstandardized Path Coefficients (and Standard Errors) for Focal Variables and Controls

Variables	Promotion Mindset	Prevention Mindset	Trying to Start a New Venture
Independent Variables			
Workplace innovativeness	.181**	.086**	—
	(.022)	(.025)	
Congregation innovativeness	.101**	.053	—
	(.026)	(.030)	
Mediators			
Promotion focus mindset	—	—	.381**
			(.105)
Prevention focus mindset	—	—	.053
			(.104)
Control Variables			
Female	−.119*	.096	−.435*
	(.047)	(.051)	(.218)
Age	−.012**	.005*	−.004
	(.002)	(.002)	(.010)
Non-White	.084	−.040	.508*
	(.062)	(.062)	(.246)
Education	.001	−.025	.058
	(.017)	(.018)	(.127)
Income	−.007	−.008	−.017
	(.008)	(.009)	(.038)
Working spouse	.018	−.018	−.085
	(.049)	(.053)	(.234)
Professional/manager/owner	.133*	.052	−.151
	(.055)	(0.58)	(.622)
Previously started a business/ organization	.054	−.087	.890**
	(.075)	(.077)	(.233)
Evangelical Protestant[a]	−.077	.017	.120
	(.058)	(.064)	(.284)
Black Protestant[a]	.072	−.040	.040
	(.135)	(.122)	(.416)
Mainline Protestant[a]	−.081	.072	.441
	(.066)	(.071)	(.300)
Other religious tradition[a]	.002	−.005	.299
	(.087)	(.087)	(.387)
Northeast[b]	.021	.105	.018
	(.069)	(.073)	(.299)
Midwest[b]	−.032	−.029	−.057
	(.059)	(.061)	(.319)
West[b]	.003	.076	.393
	(.066)	(.072)	(.248)

Notes: $N = 668$. Fit Statistics: Chi-Square $= 1.998$, $df = 2$, $p = .368$; CFI $= 1.00$, TIL $= 1.00$; RMSEA $= .000$. [a]Contrast category is Catholic. [b]Contrast category is South. *$p < .05$. **$p < .01$.

Table 10.2 provides results from the full model, including unstandardized coefficients for all control variables. Women were less likely than men to have a promotion focus mindset or be engaged in starting a new venture. Older respondents were less promotion focused, but more prevention focused. Non-Whites were more likely to be trying to start a new venture than Whites in our sample. Respondents in professional, managerial, or owner positions exhibited more of a promotion focus mindset. Predictably, previous start-up experience was strongly related to trying to start a new venture. None of the religious tradition or region variables were significant.

Test of Selection Effect

The associations between innovativeness and regulatory foci may be the result of social role modeling and adaptation effects as proposed, or the associations may be a selection effect, whereby people chose to work and worship in organizations that reflect their regulatory mindsets. We have data that can partially address the issue of selection effects in relation to congregational choice. Our research team conducted interviews with 156 working adults in eight congregations. The places of worship included two Catholic parishes in the Western United States, two Evangelical Protestant churches in the Midwest, two Mainline Protestant churches in the Northeast, and two Black Protestant churches in the South. In each place of worship, we interviewed business owners and those who worked full-time for someone else. The sample of interviewees was 55% men and 45% women. Forty-four percent were business owners.

The interview posed several questions about why an individual attended the place of worship. Two research assistants independently coded the selection question. The level of agreement in their coding exceeded 75% with Kappa-statistics for interrater reliability above .60. The most common explanation given for choosing a place of worship was relational ties, such as family, friends, or coworkers in the congregation. These findings match national survey results which show family and friends as important correlates to why individuals choose a congregation (Putnam & Campbell, 2010). Location was another common explanation. Innovativeness or entrepreneurial orientation was not a prevalent theme for why individuals chose a congregation.

DISCUSSION

One in four entrepreneurs start a business while employed by someone else (Burmeister-Lamp et al., 2012), yet we know little about what contributes to nascent hybrid entrepreneurship. This research addresses a gap in the entrepreneurship literature related to factors explaining entrepreneurs who are trying to start a business while working for someone else (Burmeister-Lamp et al., 2012; Raffiee & Feng, 2014). Our findings support our assertions that organizational contexts have an influence on the regulatory focus mindsets of individuals (Brockner & Higgins, 2001; Grégoire, Corbett, & McMullen, 2011). A promotion focus mindset, in particular, is positively related to trying to start a new venture. The significant relationships held even after controlling for gender, age, race, education, income, working spouse, occupation, previous start-up experience, religious tradition, and region. This is likely an unforeseen and unintended consequence of the influence organizations and their leaders have on employees, especially if it leads to employees eventually exiting the company. Future research should explore when regulatory foci may be associated with behavior that is harmful to the organization. For example, Gino and Margolis (2011) recently found in initial laboratory experiments that risk-seeking behavior associated with a promotion focus mindset can contribute to unethical behavior.

The discovery that the innovativeness of a congregation is significantly associated with a work-oriented promotion focus mindset may be surprising to management scholars who tend to dismiss the relevance of religious life to work (King, 2008; Tracey, 2012). Despite individuals spending relatively fewer hours associating with their congregation as compared to their workplace, places of worship do more than promote religious meanings and practices; they also are an important site for the transmission of motivation for social services, civic and political engagement, and artistic activity (Chaves, 2004; Putnam & Campbell, 2010; Wuthnow & Evans, 2002). Our findings imply that congregation innovativeness spills over to influence a work-oriented promotion focus mindset and, in turn, entrepreneurial behavior outside of one's congregation.

From a sociological perspective, the crossover of congregational experiences to work behavior is a notable contribution. There is some evidence that congregations and their leaders influence the lives of worshipers in other ways, but it is limited. For example, clergy help foster motivation among religious people to engage in collective action outside the doors of their congregation (e.g., Brewer, Kersh, & Peterson, 2003; Lichterman, 2008; Warren, 2001). Consistent with the modeling theory undergirding our hypotheses, Oman and Thoresen (2003) assert that spiritual authorities can act as role models in shaping the mindset and behaviors of adherents of a religion. Moreover, beliefs about the integration of faith and work promoted within a congregation are associated with work attitudes and behaviors (Park et al., 2014). Our findings further demonstrate that places of worship are related to work related promotion focus and entrepreneurial behavior, thus providing evidence of meaningful crossover effects for places of worship. Future research should explore this and other links between religious participation and entrepreneurial behavior, which to this point have received limited attention in the entrepreneurship literature but hold promise given their historical associations (Dodd & Gotsis, 2007).

Contrary to our hypotheses, a prevention mindset was not negatively associated with innovative organizational contexts. Prevention focus was positively associated with innovativeness in workplaces, while there was no relationship with innovativeness in congregations in our path model. It may be that in innovative workplaces a prevention focus is valued and reinforced among employees given the need to manage risk and discern the costs as well as benefits of possible innovations (Brockner et al., 2004); whereas, in innovative congregations less attention to financial viability may limit the development and reinforcement of a prevention mindset. Furthermore, our findings do not support a negative association of prevention focus with trying to start a business. However, this finding may be limited to nascent hybrid entrepreneurs. In research related to risk aversion, which is associated with a prevention focus, hybrid entrepreneurs are similar to nonentrepreneurs in having higher levels of risk aversion than fully self-employed entrepreneurs (Raffiee & Feng, 2014). Given our research compares nascent hybrid entrepreneurs with nonentrepreneurs, Raffiee and Feng's (2014) findings may help explain why prevention focus was not a significant factor in drawing distinctions between employees who are trying to start a business and those who are not. Future research on regulatory mindsets in entrepreneurship should explore under what conditions the development of a prevention mindset is likely to occur and address in more detail how regulatory mindsets influence stages of the entrepreneurial process as well as types of entrepreneurs.

This study has limitations that suggest caution in interpreting the findings. First, despite collecting data at two time periods, the cross-sectional nature of our data is insufficient to confirm causality. To test for the possibility of a selection effect, in which entrepreneurial individuals self-select into innovative congregations, we present a post hoc analysis of interview data. Personal ties rather than innovativeness emerged as the dominant reason for choosing a congregation. Consequently, we believe a selection effect is less plausible than our hypothesized relationships. Second, we included only one modest scale to measure the nature of organizations in which respondents' work and worship. The innovativeness of a workplace or place of worship is only one dimension of an organization and cannot capture the complexity of an organization or fully depict the means by which an organization and its leaders affect members' regulatory focus mindsets. Future research should include additional dimensions of EO (Miller, 2011) as well as other yet to be developed characteristics of organizations that might influence entrepreneurial behavior (Covin & Lumpkin, 2011). This likely will require qualitative approaches to uncover the complexities of the context and explain the unique perspective of participants (Marshall & Rossman, 2006).

Overall, this study contributes to the growing research that helps explain why people try to start businesses (Klyver & Schenkel, 2013; Obschonka et al., 2011; Schmitt-Rodermund, 2004). Our data indicate that organizational contexts do matter in shaping the mindsets or ways of thinking that contribute to nascent entrepreneurial behavior. In doing so it also affirms an important role for regulatory focus mindsets in explaining entrepreneurship (Brockner et al., 2004; Burmeister-Lamp et al., 2012). We find that workplace innovativeness and congregation innovativeness are associated with a promotion focus mindset, and, in turn, a promotion focus mindset is positively related to nascent entrepreneurship. This research extends our understanding of the types of organizational influences that might influence members' regulatory mindsets and expands our understanding of why some new ventures come into being.

ACKNOWLEDGMENT

This chapter is based on research supported by the National Science Foundation under Grant #0925907. Any opinions, findings, and conclusions or recommendations expressed in this chapter are those of the authors and do not necessarily reflect the views of the National Science Foundation.

REFERENCES

Asparouhov, T., & B. Muthén (2010). Weighted least squares estimation with missing data. Retrieved from http://www.statmodel.com/download/GstrucMissingRevision.pdf

Bandura, A. (1986). *Social foundations of thought and action: A social cognitive theory.* Englewood Cliffs, NJ: Prentice Hall.

Brettel, M., & Rottenberger, J. (2013). Examining the link between entrepreneurial orientation and learning processes in small and medium-sized enterprises. *Journal of Small Business Management, 51*(4), 471–490.

Brewer, M., Kersh, R., & Petersen, R. E. (2003). Assessing conventional wisdom about religion and politics: A preliminary view from the pews. *Journal for the Scientific Study of Religion, 42*(1), 125–136.

Brockner, J., & Higgins, E. T. (2001). Regulatory focus theory: Implications for the study of emotions at work *Organizational Behavior and Human Decision Processes, 86*(1), 35–66.

Brockner, J., Higgins, E. T., & Low, M. B. (2004). Regulatory focus theory and the entrepreneurial process. *Journal of Business Venturing, 19*(2), 203–220.

Burmeister-Lamp, K., Lévesque, M., & Schade, C. (2012). Are entrepreneurs influenced by risk attitude, regulatory focus or both? An experiment on entrepreneurs' time allocation. *Journal of Business Venturing, 27*(4), 456–476.

Callegaro, M., Baker, R., Bethlehem, J., Göritz, A. S., Krosnick, J. A., & Lavrakas, P. J. (Eds.). (2014). *Online panel research: A data quality perspective*. Chichester, England: Wiley.

Carroll, J. W. (2006). *God's potters: Pastoral leadership and the shaping of congregations*. Grand Rapids, MI: William B. Eerdmans.

Chaves, M. (2004). *Congregations in America*. Cambridge, MA: Harvard University Press.

Covin, J. G., Green, K. M., & Slevin, D. P. (2006). Strategic process effects on the entrepreneurial orientation sales growth rate relationship. *Entrepreneurship Theory and Practice, 30*(1), 57–81.

Covin, J. G., & Lumpkin, G. T. (2011). Entrepreneurial orientation theory and research: Reflections on a needed construct. *Entrepreneurship Theory and Practice, 35*(5), 855–872.

Covin, J., & Slevin, D. (1989). Strategic management of small firms in hostile and benign environments. *Strategic Management Journal, 10*(1), 75–87.

Crowe, E., & Higgins, E. T. (1997). Regulatory focus and strategic inclinations: Promotion and prevention in decision-making. *Organizational Behavior and Human Decision Processes, 69*(2), 117–132.

Davidsson, P., & Honig, B. (2003). The role of social and human capital among nascent entrepreneurs. *Journal of Business Venturing, 18*(3), 301–331.

De Clercq, D., & Rius, I. (2007). Organizational commitment in Mexican small and medium-sized firms: The role of work status, organizational climate, and entrepreneurial orientation. *Journal of Small Business Management, 45*(4), 467–490.

Dodd, S. D., & Gotsis, G. (2007). An examination of the inter-relationships between entrepreneurship and religion. *Journal of Entrepreneurship and Innovation, 8*(2), 93–104.

Dodd, S. D., & Seaman, P. T. (1998). Religion and enterprise: An introductory exploration. *Entrepreneurship Theory and Practice, 23*(1), 71–86.

Dougherty, K. D., Johnson, B. R., & Polson, E. C. (2007). Recovering the lost: Remeasuring U.S. religious affiliation. *Journal for the Scientific Study of Religion, 46*(4), 483–499.

Emerson, M. O., & Woo, R. (2006). *People of the dream: Multiracial congregations in the United States*. Princeton, NJ: Princeton University Press.

Finke, R., & Stark, R. (2005). *The church of America, 1776–2005: Winners and losers in our religious economy*. New Brunswick, NJ: Rutgers University Press.

Folta, T. B., Delmar, F., & Wennberg, K. (2010). Hybrid entrepreneurship. *Management Science, 56*(2), 253–269.

Frese, M., & Gielnik, M. M. (2014). The psychology of entrepreneurship. *Annual Review of Organizational Psychology and Organizational Behavior, 1*(1), 413–438.

Gorman, C. A., Meriac, J. P., Overstreet, B. L., Apodaca, S., McIntyre, A. L., Park, P., & Godbey, J. N. (2012). A meta-analysis of the regulatory focus nomological network: Work-related antecedents and consequences. *Journal of Vocational Behavior, 80*(1), 160–172.

Gino, F., & Margolis, J. D. (2011). Bringing ethics into focus: How regulatory focus and risk preferences influence unethical behavior. *Organizational Behavior and Human Decision Processes, 115*(2), 145–156.

Grégoire, D. A., Barr, P. S., & Shepherd, D. A. (2010). Cognitive processes of opportunity recognition: The role of structural alignment. *Organization Science, 21*(2), 413–431.

Grégoire, D. A., Corbett, A. C., & McMullen, J. S. (2011). The cognitive perspective in entrepreneurship: An agenda for future research. *Journal of Management Studies, 48*(6), 1443–1477.

Hatch, N. O. (1989). *The democratization of American Christianity.* New Haven, CT: Yale University Press.

Higgins, E. T. (1997). Beyond pleasure and pain. *American Psychologist, 52*(12), 1280–1300.

Higgins, E. T. (1998). Promotion and prevention regulatory focus as a motivational principle. *Advances in Experimental Social Psychology, 30*, 1–41.

Hmieleski, K. M., & Baron, R. A. (2008). Regulatory focus and new venture performance: A study of entrepreneurial opportunity exploitation under conditions of risk versus uncertainty. *Strategic Entrepreneurship Journal, 2*(4), 285–299.

Hopp, C., & Sonderegger, R. (2015). Understanding the dynamics of nascent entrepreneurship—Prestart-up experience, intentions, and entrepreneurial success. *Journal of Small Business Management, 53*(4), 1076–1096.

Hughes, M., & Morgan, R. E. (2007). Deconstructing the relationship between entrepreneurial orientation and business performance at the embryonic stage of firm growth. *Industrial Marketing Management, 36*(5), 651–661.

Iannaccone, L. R. (1990). Religious practice: A human capital approach. *Journal for the Scientific Study of Religion, 29*(3), 297–314.

James, L. R., James, L. A., & Ashe, D. (1990). The meaning of organizations: The role of cognition and values. In B. Schneider (Ed.), *Organizational climate and culture* (pp. 40–84). San Francisco, CA: Jossey-Bass.

Johnson, P. D., Shull, A., & Wallace, J. (2011). Regulatory focus as a mediator in goal orientation and performance relationships. *Journal of Organizational Behavior, 32*(5), 751–766.

Kark, R., & Van Dijk, D. (2007). Motivation to lead, motivation to follow: The role of the self-regulatory focus in leadership processes. *Academy of Management Review, 32*(2), 500–528.

Khan, S. A., Tang, J., & Joshi, K. (2014). Disengagement of nascent entrepreneurs from the start-up process. *Journal of Small Business Management, 52*(1), 39–58.

King, J. E., Jr. (2008). Dismissing the obvious: Will mainstream management research ever take religion seriously? *Journal of Management Inquiry, 17*(3), 214–224.

Klyver, K., & Schenkel, M. T. (2013). From resource access to use: Exploring the impact of resource combinations on nascent entrepreneurship. *Journal of Small Business Management, 51*(4), 539–556.

Kreiser, P. M., Marino, L. D., Kuratko, D. F., & Weaver, K. M. (2013). Disaggregating entrepreneurial orientation: The non-linear impact of innovativeness, proactiveness and risk-taking on SME performance. *Small Business Economics, 40*(2), 273–291.

Lanaj, K., Chang, C., & Johnson, R. E. (2012). Regulatory focus and work-related outcomes: A review and meta-analysis. *Psychological Bulletin, 138*(5), 998–1034.

Lee, S., & Sinitiere, P. L. (2009). *Holy mavericks: Evangelical innovators and the spiritual marketplace*. New York, NY: New York University Press.

Liberman, N., Idson, L. C., Camacho, C. J., & Higgins, E. T. (1999). Promotion and prevention choices between stability and change. *Journal of Personality and Social Psychology, 77*(6), 1135–1145.

Lichterman, P. (2005). *Elusive togetherness: Church groups trying to bridge America's divisions*. Princeton, NJ: Princeton University Press.

Lichterman, P. (2008). Religion and the construction of civic identity. *American Sociological Review, 73*(1), 83–104.

Lumpkin, G. T., & Dess, G. G. (1996). Clarifying the entrepreneurial orientation construct and linking it to performance. *Academy of Management Review, 21*(1), 135–172.

Lumpkin, G. T., & Dess, G. G. (2001). Linking two dimensions of entrepreneurial orientation to firm performance: The moderating role of environment and industry life cycle. *Journal of Business Venturing, 16*(5), 429–451.

Markman, G. D., & Barron, R. A. (2003). Person–entrepreneurship fit: Why some people are more successful as entrepreneurs than others. *Human Resource Management Review, 13*(2), 281–301.

Marshall, C., & Rossman, G. B. (2006). *Designing qualitative research*. London, England: SAGE.

Martí, G. (2005). *A mosaic of believers: Diversity and innovation in a multiethnic church*. Bloomington, IN: Indiana University Press.

McMullen, J. S., & Shepherd, D. A. (2002). Action bias and opportunity recognition: An empirical examination of entrepreneurial attitude as regulatory focus. In *Frontiers of entrepreneurship research: Proceedings of the Babson College Entrepreneurship Research Conference*. Wellesley, MA: Babson College.

McMullen, J. S., & Shepherd, D. A. (2006). Entrepreneurial action and the role of uncertainty in the theory of the entrepreneur. *Academy of Management Review, 31*(1), 132–152.

McMullen, J. S., Shepherd, D. A., & Patzelt, H. (2009). Managerial (in)attention to competitive threats. *Journal of Management Studies, 46*(2), 157–181.

McMullen, J. S., Shepherd, D. A., & Zarhra, S. (2007). Regulatory focus and executives intentions to commit their firms to entrepreneurial action. *Frontiers of entrepreneurial research: Proceedings of the Babson College Entrepreneurial Research Conference*. Bloomington, IN: Indiana University.

Miller, D. (2011). Miller (1983) revisited: A reflection on EO research and some suggestions for the future. *Entrepreneurship Theory and Practice, 35*(5), 699–716.

Miller, K. D. (2002). Competitive strategies of religious organizations. *Strategic Management Journal, 23*(5), 435–456.

Monsen, E., & R. W. Boss (2009). The impact of strategic entrepreneurship inside the organization: Examining job stress and employee retention. *Journal of Entrepreneurship Theory and Practice, 33*(1), 71–104.

Morris, M. H., & Kuratko, D. F. (2002). *Corporate entrepreneurship*. Fort Worth, TX: Harcourt College.

Muthén, L. K., & Muthén, B. O. (2010). *Mplus user's guide* (6th ed.). Los Angeles, CA: Author.

Neubert, M. J., Kacmar, K. M., Carlson, D. S., Chonko, L. B., & Roberts, J. A. (2008). Regulatory focus as a mediator of the influence of initiating structure and servant leadership on employee behavior. *Journal of Applied Psychology, 93*(6), 1220–1233.

Obschonka, M., Silbereisen, R. K., Schmitt-Rodermund, E., & Stuetzer, M. (2011). Nascent entrepreneurship and the developing individual: Early entrepreneurial competence in adolescence and venture creation success during the career. *Journal of Vocational Behavior, 79*(1), 121–133.

Oman, D., & Thoresen, C. E. (2003). Spiritual modeling: A key to spiritual and religious growth? *The International Journal for the Psychology of Religion, 13*(3), 149–165.

Park, J., Griebel, J., Neubert, M. J., & Dougherty, K. D. (2014). Workplace-Bridging religious capital: Connecting congregations to work outcomes. *Sociology of Religion, 75*(2), 309–331.

Pearce, J. A., II, Fritz, D. A., & Davis, P. S. (2010). Entrepreneurial orientation and the performance of religious congregations as predicted by rational choice theory. *Journal of Entrepreneurship Theory and Practice, 34*(1), 219–248.

Piperopoulos, P., & Dimov, D. (2015). Burst bubbles or build steam? Entrepreneurship education, entrepreneurial self-efficacy, and entrepreneurial intentions. *Journal of Small Business Management, 53*(4), 970–985.

Podsakoff, P., MacKenzie, S., & J. Lee (2003). Common method biases in behavioral research: A critical review of the literature and recommended remedies. *Journal of Applied Psychology, 88*(5), 879–903.

Putnam, R. D., & Campbell, D. E. (2010). *American grace: How religion divides and unites us*. New York, NY: Simon & Schuster.

Raffiee, J., & Feng, J. (2014). Should I quit my day job? A hybrid path to entrepreneurship. *Academy of Management Journal, 57*(4), 936–963.

Rauch, A., Wiklund, J., Lumpkin, G. T., & Frese, M. (2009). Entrepreneurial orientation and business performance: An assessment of past research and suggestions for the future. *Entrepreneurship Theory and Practice, 33*(3), 761–787.

Roozen, D. A. (2011). *A decade of change in American congregations 2000–2010*. Hartford, CT: Hartford Institute for Religion Research.

Roozen, D. A. (2016). *American congregations 2015: Thriving and surviving*. Hartford, CT: Hartford Institute for Religion Research.

Schmitt-Rodermund, E. (2004). Pathways to successful entrepreneurship: Parenting, personality, early entrepreneurial competence, and interests. *Journal of Vocational Behavior, 65*(3), 498–518.

Schumacker, R. E., and Lomax, R. G. (2004). *A beginner's guide to structural equation modeling* (2nd ed.). Mahwah, NJ: Erlbaum.

Scott, S. G., & Bruce, R. A. (1994). Determinants of innovative behavior: A path model of individual innovation in the workplace. *Academy of Management Journal, 37*(3), 580–607.

Shah, J., Higgins, T., & Friedman, R. (1998). Performance incentives and means: How regulatory focus influences goal attainment. *Journal of Personality and Social Psychology, 74*(2), 285–293.

Steensland, B., Park, J. Z., Regnerus, M. D., Robinson, L. D., Wilcox, W. B., & Woodberry, R. D. (2000). The measure of American religion: Toward improving the state of the art. *Social Forces, 79*(1), 291–318.

Tracey, P. (2012). Religion and organization: A critical review of current trends and future directions. *Academy of Management Annals, 6*(1), 87–134.

Tumasjan, A., & R. Braun (2012). In the eye of the beholder: How regulatory focus and self-efficacy interact in influencing opportunity recognition. *Journal of Business Venturing, 27*(6), 622–636.

Wallace, J. C., & Chen, G. (2006). A multilevel integration of personality, climate, self-regulation, and performance. *Personnel Psychology, 59*(3), 529–557.

Wallace, J. C., Johnson, P. D., & Frazier, M. (2009). An examination of the factorial, construct, and predictive validity and utility of the regulatory focus at work scale. *Journal of Organizational Behavior, 30*(6), 805–831.

Wallace, J. C., Little, L. M., Hill, A. D., & Ridge, J. W. (2010). CEO regulatory foci, environmental dynamism, and small firm performance. *Journal of Small Business Management, 48*(4), 580–604.

Warren, M. R. (2001). *Dry bones rattling: Community building to revitalize democracy.* Princeton, NJ: Princeton University Press.

Weber, M. [1904–5] (1992). *The Protestant ethic and the spirit of capitalism* (T. Parsons, Trans.). London: Routledge.

Wooten, K. C., Timmerman, T. A., & Folger, R. (1999). The use of personality and the five-factor model to predict new business ventures: From outplacement to start-up. *Journal of Vocational Behavior, 54*(1), 82–101.

Wu, C., McMullen, J., Neubert, M. J., & Yi, X. (2008). The influence of leader regulatory focus on employee creativity. *Journal of Business Venturing, 23*(5), 587–601.

Wuthnow, R. (1987). *Meaning and moral order: Explorations in cultural analysis.* Berkeley, CA: University of California Press.

Wuthnow, R., & Evans, J. H. (2002). *The quiet hand of God: Faith-based activism and the public role of Mainline Protestantism.* Berkeley, CA: University of California Press.

PART III

SOCIETY

CHAPTER 11

ETHIOPIAN ORTHODOX CHRISTIANITY

Exploratory Implications for the Diaspora in the United States

Tamrat Gashaw
Wartburg College

Timothy Ewest
Houston Baptist University

In the fourth century Christian missionaries from Egypt and Syria introduced Christianity to Ethiopia, establishing the Ethiopian Orthodox Tewahedo[1] Church (EOTC), thus making it one of the oldest Christian sects in the world (Melaku, 2010). And, while the EOTC is recognized as being a genuine historical expression of traditional Christianity, the EOTC practices and corresponding religious calendar differ from Protestants and Catholics. While the American workplace has secularized Christianity by aligning Christian holidays with national (workplace) days off (Alexis, 2015) and correspondingly will face challenges from various religions with differing practices and worship calendars (Cash & Gray, 2000; Greenwald, 2012), in the case of the EOTC accommodation is challenged

Faith and Work: Christian Perspectives, Research, and Insights Into the Movement
pp. 193–210
Copyright © 2018 by Information Age Publishing

by a fellow Christian sect. Specifically, the diaspora of EOTC in the United States counters the established narrative in which a Christian nation is challenged with accommodating only other great religious traditions (Wuthnow, 2005).

The purpose of this chapter is to stress the importance of religious accommodation in the American workplace by providing the EOTC as a counternarrative to the widely accepted narrative of an American "Christian" workplace. The governing and accepted narrative describes an American workplace where it has secularized Christianity and must accommodate other religious faith traditions (Alexis, 2015), and where Christians may tend to feel they deserve a special status (Hicks, 2003).

To this end, this chapter will provide an introduction to the beliefs and practices of EOTC to aid in determining distinctions and similarities between Protestantism, Catholicism, and the EOTC. The chapter will also determine levels of religiosity in Ethiopian society as a means to better determine the respective impacts EOTC immigrants will have on the American workforce. Religiosity has been demonstrated to have a multi-faceted role in both discrimination and self-esteem (Hassan, Rousseau, & Moreau, 2013) and thus, the chapter will explore religious practices and trends of the larger population of Orthodox Christians within the United States providing a comparison to immigration patterns of the EOTC. Finally, implications for the American workforce will be explored including implications for human rights. Specific attention will be given to how the practice of fasting with their corresponding feast days affect expectations as does the expectations of inclusivity based on the historical practiced inclusivity of the EOTC within Ethiopia.

BELIEFS OF THE EOTC

EOTC has *five* main doctrines (i.e., pillars or mysteries of faith) which theologically align with the historical Christian faith as espoused by Protestant and Catholic tenets of faith (Jenkins, 2011). These five doctrines are the (1) *Trinity*, that God is one in being, and three in person. The (2) *Incarnation*, is the teaching that a person of the Holy Trinity, God the Son, was incarnated from the Virgin Mary. (3) *Baptism*, is the invisible grace of childhood by a second birth from the Holy Spirit. (4) *Holy Communion*, is the bread and wine offered during Liturgy which changes into the true body and blood of Jesus Christ. Finally, the 5) *Resurrection*, is when Jesus Christ comes in glory surrounded by angels for judgment, every person shall be resurrected from the dead—the righteous for an everlasting peace and the sinners for judgment and condemnation (John 5: 28–29). These pillars are called mysteries (Persoon, 2010), because the EOTC believes that one cannot completely understand these mysteries by human intelligence, but only through faith (Desta, 2012; Hable Sellassie & Tamerat, 1970; Wainwright, 2006).

In the EOTC, there are also *seven* sacraments from which adherents believe they receive the invisible grace of the Holy Spirit. The seven sacraments are: Baptism, confirmation, Holy Communion, priesthood, confession (repentance), matrimony, and Unction of the Sick. According to the church's teaching, the first three sacraments are essential and all Orthodox Christians should partake of for salvation. The last one is administered to those with disability or sickness. The sacraments of baptism, confirmation, matrimony and priesthood are administered only once to a person. The sacraments of Holy Communion and confession are spiritual rites that every Christian should partake of throughout his/her spiritual life (Desta, 2012; Melaku, 2010). These beliefs, while nuanced from Protestant and Catholic beliefs, are considered to be part of the historical Christian faith tradition (Jenkins, 2011; Wainwright, 2006).

FAITH PRACTICES OF THE EOTC

For the EOTC there are expectations regarding prayer and fasting which are distinct in practice from Protestants and Catholics. For example, prayer for the religiously faithful in the EOTC should occur seven times each day: Upon arising from bed in the morning, at the third hour, at the sixth hour, at the ninth hour, an evening prayer, the prayer before sleep and lastly the midnight prayer (Hable Sellassie & Tamerat, 1970).

However, other practices are dictated by Ethiopia's unique ancient calendar. The Ethiopian Calendar has 365 days per year, based on the Book of Enoch (Milik, 1976) which mentions the completion of the year in 364 days (Enoch 28:11). The Ethiopian calendar, much like Coptic calendar has a total of 13 months, 12 months with equal 30 days each and an intercalary month at the end of the year of 5 or 6 days if the year is a leap year (Desta, 2012; Molla, 2002). The Ethiopian Calendar has asynchronous rhythms with the Gregorian calendar which is used by Protestants and Catholics to set their religious holidays and correspondingly workplace calendar for days off (Boylston, 2013). So, for example all of the nine major Christian holidays observed in the EOTC occur on differing days than Protestant and Catholic holidays. See Table 11.1.

Fasting, represents one distinction for the religiously faithful EOTC, requiring a significant lifestyle commitment. There are seven official fasting periods for Ethiopian Christians. *Fetha Negest*, one of the EOTC churches teaching document, defines fasting as the following:

Table 11.1. Major Holidays for Ethiopian Orthodox Church

Holy Day	Date*
The Incarnation	January 6
The Birth of Christ	January 7
Epiphany	January 19
Hosanna (Palm Sunday)	April 9
Crucifixion	April 14
Easter	April 16
The Ascension	May 25
Pentecost	June 4
The Feast of Mount Tabor	August 19

Note: *Example based on 2017 calendar.

Fasting is abstinence from food, and is observed by man and woman at certain times determined by law, to attain forgiveness of sins and much reward, obeying thus the one who fixed the law. Fasting (also) serves to weaken the force of concupiscence so that (the body) may obey the rational soul. (Strauss, 2009, p. 43)

The feast days, are tied directly to fasting and are an integral component to the ETOC religiously devotee's practice. There are approximately 250 fast days in the year, although not all of these are compulsory for the religiously devote within the EOTC. The EOTC adherent typically fast about 180 days in the year (Hable Sellassie & Tamerat, 1970). The importance of feast days, and the fasting that accompany them, are extended into the EOTC's symbolic nature of food which is derived from and informs individual adherent's theory of nature, the world and man (Knutsson & Selinus, 1970).

Research demonstrates that fasting as a religious practice for the individual in the EOTC has a significant impact on health, since religious practices for the religiously devote presume and contribute to lifestyle choices (Basu-Zharku, 2011). This is so widely embraced and practiced that the frequency and participation in fasting impacts the nutritional impacts on children in the EOTC (Knutsson & Selinus, 1970). Moreover, for the EOTC in Ethiopia and America, beliefs regarding fasting and the determination of food choices contribute to convictions on how the individual is to live the life of faith in a non-Orthodox society and larger moral issues regarding church teaching (Knutsson & Selinus, 1970). See Table 11.2 for various fast days and length of fasting (Larebo, 1988).

While the beliefs within EOTC resonate with historic Christianity (Amundsen & Mandahl, 1995; Wainwright, 2006), there are distinctions

Table 11.2.   Official Fasting Periods for Ethiopian Christians

Fast Days	*Length of Fast*
All Wednesdays and Fridays	Except for the 50 days after Easter
The Lenten fast	55 days
The Nineveh fast	3 days
The Vigils of Christmas and Epiphany	Varies
The Fast of the Apostles	Minimum of 14 days/maximum of 44 days
Fast of the Prophets	43 days
Fast of the Assumption	15 days in August

regarding theological emphasis on accepted universal Christian tenets (e.g., The prominence of the Virgin Mary, over and against Protestantism), as well as emphasis on fast days and frequency and rapidity of prayer times. These differences are theological but are also indigenous and not indigenized within the country of Ethiopia for the EOTC adherents (Shenk, 1988).

RELIGIOSITY OF THE ORTHODOX IN ETHIOPIA

The present data of population in Ethiopia by religion was reported by the Central Statistical Agency of Ethiopia and was based on the 2007 national census data (Macro, 2008). The data demonstrates that 44% are Orthodox Christians, 19% are Protestants, and 1% are Catholics. Islam comprises 34% of the population and the remaining 4% are those who follow traditional and other faiths. A key point from the data is that 64% of the Ethiopian (indigenous) population is self-identifying with Christianity. See Table 11.3.

What is of note, is even with the predominate adherence to Christianity in Ethiopia, the relationship between Christians and Muslims within the country have been both conflictual and consensual, but ultimately has found harmonies in humanistic synergies (Ahmed, 2006). So, while the

Table 11.3.   Population by Region in 2007

Item	*Total*	*Orthodox*	*Protestant*	*Catholic*	*Islam*	*Traditional*	*Other*
Population	73,750,932	32,082,182	13,661,588	532,187	25,037,646	1,956,647	470,682
Share (%)	100	44	19	1	34	3	1

Source: Central Statistical Agency of Ethiopia (n.d.).

Table 11.4.   Public Holidays in Ethiopia in 2017

Date	Weekday	Holiday Name	Type of Holy Day
January 7	Saturday	Ethiopian Christmas Day	Christian holy day
January 7	Thursday	Epiphany	Christian holy day
March 2	Thursday	Adwa Victory Day	Nonreligious
April 14	Friday	Ethiopian Good Friday	Christian holy day
April 14	Sunday	Ethiopian Easter Sunday	Christian holy day
May 1	Monday	International Labor Day	Nonreligious
May 5	Friday	Freedom Day	Nonreligious
May 28	Sunday	Derg's (Millitary Junta) Downfall Day	Nonreligious
June 26	Monday	Eid-al-Fitr	Muslim holy day
September 2	Saturday	Eid al-Adha	Muslim holy day
September 2	Monday	Ethiopian New Year	Nonreligious
September 27	Wednesday	Meskel (Holy Cross)	Christian holy day
December 1	Friday	The Prophet's Birthday	Muslim holy day

EOTC in Ethiopia is the dominate faith, it respects and honors the other majority faith tradition, Islam, with state sanctioned holidays (see Table 11.4). Ethiopia has intentionally introduced policies which recognize the country's long-standing religious diversity, so all faith groups can contribute to the formation of communities, while endeavoring to keep the Ethiopian government distinctly separate from religious faith (Haustein & Østebø, 2011).

While religious self-identification does not necessitate levels of religiosity, which determines levels of religious adherence, it does allow for an understanding of large expression of faith and values (Holdcroft, 2006). The World Values Word's Value Survey (2014) conducted in 2007, while not allowing for a specific approximation of religious adherence of those within the EOTC, does provide an explorative and summative overview of levels of religiosity within that country. Degrees of religiosity have been determined by frequency of attendance at religious services, frequency of prayer, and personal importance placed on religion (Nonnemaker, McNeely, & Blum, 2003). See Tables 11.5–11.8.

When these levels of religiosity are compared to the religious in the United States there are some things of note. Prayer and meditation were approximately the same for Ethiopians (87.9%) and those in the United States at the same time (80.4%). The frequency of church attendance for Ethiopians either attending religious services more than once a week or one time a week was 77%, while in the United States for the same time it was 34.5%, although this does not specifically address feast/fast days.

Table 11.5.   Religious Service Attendance

Apart from weddings and funerals,
about how often do attend religious services?

Frequency	Percentage Total
More than once a week	37.3
One a week	39.9
One a month	9.7
Only holy days	4.1
Once a year	0.3
Less often	6.1
Never	2.6
N	1,500

Table 11.6.

Regardless of whether you attend religious services or not, would you say you are:	
A religious person	76.7
Not a religious person	17.5
A convinced atheist	0.3
No answer	4.7
Don't know	0.7
N	1,500

Table 11.7.

Do you take moments for prayer, meditation, or contemplation?	
Yes	87.9
No	4.9
No answer	5.9
Don't know	1.2
N	1,500

Table 11.8.   Importance of God

How important is God in your life?
Please use the scale to indicate.

Not at all	1.3
2	0.2
3	0.3
4	0.2
5	1.4
6	1.6
7	5.0
8	9.2
9	13.5
Very important	65.5
No answer	1.5
Don't know	0.3
N	1,500

Note: 10 = very important; 1 = not at all important.

Table 11.9

	Ethiopia	United States
Do you take time for prayer, meditation, or contemplation?		
Yes	87.9	80.4
No	4.9	15.3
No answer	5.9	0.8
Don't know	1.2	2.0
	N = 1,500	N = 1,249

Table 11.10.   Importance of God

	Ethiopia	United States
How important is God in your life? Please use the scale to indicate.		
Not at all	1.3	5.1
2	0.2	1.4
3	0.3	2.2
4	0.2	2.3
5	1.4	5.6
6	1.6	5.3
7	5.0	4.5
8	9.2	6.6
9	13.5	7.3
Very important	65.5	55.3
No answer	1.5	1.4
Don't know	0.3	0.8
	N = 1,500	N = 1,195

Note: 10 = *very important*; 1 = *not at all important.*

When considering how important religion is to the individual, Ethiopians report religion as very important, or rated their faith as a 9 on a scale of 10, at 79%, with the United States at that same time having 62%. See Table 11.9–11.12.

Almost twice as many Ethiopians obligate themselves to church attendance, including holy days, as do those in the United States. This exploratory evidence suggests that any diaspora in the United States of EOTC Christians, may require special days off or have special religious holiday needs, since they work on an asynchronous calendar, especially given the fact that they demonstrate high levels of religiosity. Moreover, given the inclusiveness of the Ethiopian religious polity with differing faiths (Muslim), those who adhere to the EOTC may expect similar inclusivity within the United States.

Table 11.11.

Frequency	Ethiopia Percentage Total	United States Percentage Total
Apart from weddings and funerals, about how often do attend religious services?		
More than once a week	37.3	11.3
One a week	39.9	23.2
One a month	9.7	12.3
Only holy days	4.1	8.5
Once a year	0.3	4.4
Less often	6.1	11.5
Never	2.6	24.5
	$N = 1,500$	$N = 1,249$

Table 11.12

	Ethiopia	United States
Regardless of whether you attend religious services or not, would you say you are:		
A religious person	76.7	69.0
Not a religious person	17.5	27.9
A convinced atheist	0.3	3.4
No answer	4.7	3.5
Don't know	0.7	0.7
	$N = 1,500$	$N = 1,249$

TRENDS OF EOTC DIASPORA TO THE UNITED STATES

According to Engedayehu (2014), despite some division, the EOTC has expanded considerably during the last 2 decades throughout the globe, including the United States. When one considers immigration patters from 1970–2015, 36.8 million people obtained lawful permanent resident status (Immigration, U.S., Enforcement's, & Audit, 2011). Immigrants from Europe, Asia, and American continent contribute 12.89%, 34.30%, and 45.36%, respectively. Africa's share is 5.19% out of the total 36.8 million people immigrated to the United States and Ethiopia's contribution is only 0.61%. However, Ethiopia's share out of the total African immigrants to the United States is 11% which is the second African nation following Egypt. See Table 11.13.

Engedayehu (2014) documented the EOTC diaspora over the past two decades in the midst of turbulence and division. In the United States, the trend and religious adherence of Orthodox Christianity from 2007 to 2014 by immigrants has increased by 2%, while there has been a decline of orthodox Christianity from 7% to 4% by second generation of immigrants.

Table 11.13.   Persons Obtaining Lawful Permanent Resident Status by Region and Selected Country of Last Residence

Region and Country of Last Residence	1970 to 1979	1980 to 1989	1990 to 1999	2000 to 2009	2010
Total	4,248,203	6,244,379	9,775,398	10,299,430	1,042,625
Europe	826,327	669,694	1,349,219	1,349,609	95,429
Asia	1,406,526	2,391,356	2,859,899	3,470,835	410,209
America	1,903,636	2,694,504	5,137,142	4,441,529	426,981
Canada and Newfoundland	179,267	156,313	194,788	236,349	19,491
Mexico	621,218	1,009,586	2,757,418	1,704,166	138,717
Caribbean	708,643	789,343	1,004,114	1,053,357	139,389
Central America	120,376	339,376	610,189	591,130	43,597
South America	273,529	399,803	570,596	856,508	85,783
Other America	603	83	37	19	4
Africa	71,405	141,987	346,410	759,734	98,246
Ethiopia	2,588	12,927	40,097	87,207	13,853
Oceania	39,983	41,432	56,800	65,793	5,946
Not specified	326	305,406	25,928	211,930	5,814

Source: Hoefer, Rytina, and Baker (2012).

Table 11.13.   Continued

Region and Country of Last Residence	2011	2012	2013	2014	2015	Total	Share (%)
Total	1,062,040	1,031,631	990,553	1,016,518	1,051,031	36,761,808	100.00
Europe	90,712	86,956	91,095	87,790	90,789	4,737,620	12.89
Asia	438,580	416,488	389,301	419,382	405,854	12,608,430	34.30
America	423,277	409,664	399,380	400,102	439,228	16,675,443	45.36
Canada and Newfoundland	19,506	20,138	20,489	17,670	19,309	883,320	2.40
Mexico	142,823	145,326	134,198	133,107	157,227	6,943,786	18.89
Caribbean	133,012	126,615	121,349	133,550	146,086	4,355,458	11.85
Central America	43,249	39,837	44,056	43,638	46,556	1,922,004	5.23
South America	84,687	77,748	79,287	72,135	70,049	2,570,125	6.99
Other America			1	2	1	750	0.00
Africa	97,429	103,685	94,589	94,834	98,677	1,906,996	5.19
Ethiopia	13,985	15,400	13,484	12,926	12,566	225,033	0.61
Oceania	5,825	5,573	6,061	5,980	6,227	239,620	0.65
Not specified	6,217	9,265	10,127	8,430	10,256	593,699	1.61

Source: Hoefer et al. (2012).

Table 11.14.   Immigrant Status Among Orthodox Christians

Survey Year	Immigrants	Second Generation	Third Generation or Higher
2014	40%	23%	36%
2007	38%	30%	32%

Source: Pew Research Center (n.d.).

See Table 11.14. With regard to immigrant's to the United States status among Orthodox Christianity, 40% of the followers are immigrants, 23% are second generation, and 36% are third generation or higher.

IMMIGRATION PATTERNS AND RELIGIOUS ADHERENCE

Degrees of religiosity for Orthodox Christians in America are determined by both private acts, beliefs, practices of prayer, and attendance of religious services. See Table 11.15 for changes within Orthodox Christians with the United States.

Orthodox Christians in the United States show little difference in practice from the years 2007 to 2014, with only private practices (prayer, religious study) showing a plus 5 percentage decline, indicating a fairly stable level of religiosity. See Table 11.16.

The suggestions from the data provided demonstrate a growing population of Orthodox Christians in the United States, with a high level of religiosity. For example, Ethiopians attend 42.7% more religious services than those from other religions surveyed in the United States. This may indicate that the EOTC who immigrate to the United States, carry with them personal existing commitments regarding days off requests. For example, research on Ethiopian Orthodox, EOTC, within the United States demonstrate that previous experiences in Ethiopia do determine expectations in the United States. Specifically, Kebede (2012), conducted research which indicated that those of the EOTC may expect a type of inclusivity which allows for accommodation of faith expression, including designated fasting (feast days) times.

CONCLUSION: IMPLICATIONS FOR THE AMERICAN WORKPLACE

The purpose of this chapter was to stress the importance of religious accommodation in the workplace by providing the EOTC as a counter narrative to the widely accepted perspective of an American workplace. The governing and accepted narrative describes an American where it has secularized Christianity and must accommodate other religious faith

**Table 11.15.   Pew Accounting Beliefs
of Orthodox Christians in the United States**

Frequency of Feeling Spiritual Peace and Well-Being Among Orthodox Christians

Survey Year	At Least Once a Week	Once or Twice a Month	Several Times a Year	Seldom/ Never	Don't Know	Sample Size
2014	53%	23%	10%	14%	< 1%	186
2007	45%	15%	17%	20%	3%	363

Belief in God Among Orthodox Christians

Survey Year	Believe in God: Absolutely Certain	Believe in God: Fairly Certain	Believe in God: Not too/Not at all Certain	Believe in God: Don't Know	Do not Believe in God	Other/Don't Know if They Believe in God
2014	61%	29%	7%	< 1%	3%	1%
2007	71%	19%	4%	1%	4%	1%

Importance of Religion in One's Life Among Orthodox Christians

Survey Year	Very Important	Somewhat Important	Not too Important	Not at All Important	Don't Know	Sample Size
2014	52%	33%	12%	3%	< 1%	186
2007	56%	31%	9%	4%	< 1%	363

Interpreting Scripture Among Orthodox Christians

Survey Year	Word of God: Should be Taken Literally	Word of God: Not Everything Taken Literally	Word of God: Other/ Don't Know	Not the Word of God	Other/Don't Know	Sample Size
2014	22%	39%	2%	27%	10%	186
2007	26%	29%	4%	29%	12%	363

Belief in Heaven Among Orthodox Christians

Survey Year	Believe	Don't Believe	Other/Don't Know	Sample Size
2014	81%	10%	9%	186
2007	74%	17%	10%	363

Belief in Hell Among Orthodox Christians

Survey Year	Believe	Don't Believe	Other/Don't Know	Sample Size
2014	59%	31%	11%	186
2007	56%	28%	15%	363

Source: Pew Research Center (n.d.).

**Table 11.16.   Pew Accounting Practices
of Orthodox Christians in The United States**

Attendance at Religious Services Among Orthodox Christians

Survey Year	At Least Once a Week	Once or Twice a Month/a Few Times a Year	Seldom/ Never	Don't Know	Sample Size
2014	31%	54%	15%	< 1%	186
2007	34%	49%	17%	1%	363

Frequency of Prayer Among Orthodox Christians

Survey Year	At Least Daily	Weekly	Monthly	Seldom/ Never	Don't Know	Sample Size
2014	57%	19%	8%	15%	2%	186
2007	60%	17%	5%	16%	2%	363

*Frequency of Participation in Prayer, Scripture Study,
or Religious Education Groups Among Orthodox Christians*

Survey Year	At Least Once a Week	Once or Twice a Month	Several Times a Year	Seldom/ Never	Don't Know	Sample Size
2014	18%	10%	17%	54%	< 1%	186
2007	10%	11%	10%	68%	1%	363

Frequency of Meditation Among Orthodox Christians

Survey Year	At Least Once a Week	Once or Twice a Month	Several Times a Year	Seldom/ Never	Don't Know	Sample Size
2014	35%	5%	5%	53%	1%	186
2007	32%	8%	7%	50%	4%	363

Frequency of Reading Scripture Among Orthodox Christians

Survey Year	At Least Once a Week	Once or Twice a Month	Several Times a Year	Seldom/ Never	Don't Know	Sample Size
2014	29%	13%	13%	44%	< 1%	186
2007	22%	11%	10%	56%	2%	363

Source: Pew Research Center (n.d.).

traditions (Alexis, 2015), and where Christians may tend to feel they deserve a special status (Hicks, 2003).

This chapter provided an introduction to the beliefs and practices of EOTC to aid in determining distinctions and similarities between Protestantism, Catholicism, and the EOTC. The chapter then discussed levels of religiosity in Ethiopian society as a means to better determine the respective impacts on the American workforce. The chapter also explored trends of the larger population of Orthodox Christians within the United States and compared them to immigration patterns of the EOTC in the United States. Finally, implications for the American workforce were explored.

The number of Americans who are born outside the United States has been and will continue to be on the increase within the American workforce. For example, in 1970 roughly 4.5% of Americans were born outside the United States, but by 2000 the number has increased to 12% (Grossman, 2008, p. 29). While the EOTC represent a minor percentage, it is none the less representative of this trend and challenges the governing narrative regarding the "Christian" American workplace, indicating the need for responsiveness from those who manage the American workplace.

For example, the significance of fasting for the EOTC can be underestimated by those outside the EOTC faith. As discussed, research demonstrates for the religiously faithful in the EOTC fasting is regarded as a moral obligation and one of the ways in which they gain perspective and meaning on living in a non-Orthodox society (Quinton & Ciccazzo, 2007). EOTC fasting practices, when coupled with an expectation of indigenous or country of origin cultural values of inclusivity with differing faiths (e.g., Islam) (Kebede, 2012) may lead to expectation directly pertaining to workplace accommodation. This especially relevant since research has demonstrated that EOTC Ethiopians when immigrating to the United States have experienced stress when asked to assimilate, and not being identified as "Ethiopian" thus resulting in the feeling of perceived cultural barriers (Alemu, 2012).

What is of note within this chapter is the EOTC is a longstanding Christian tradition, but those Orthodox who immigrate from Ethiopia still may face discrimination, despite the perception that Christianity has been secularized and institutionalized within American life, seen specifically in day off and dress codes (Greenwald, 2012). These issues are important where religious rights are considered as an international indelible part of what it means to be human as depicted by the Universal Declaration of Human Rights (Assembly, 1948), within the European Union presented as the Employment Equality Framework Directive of 2000 (Kramar & Syed, 2012) and within the United States under Title VII, Civil Rights Act of (1964) (Gregory, 2011).

The challenges unfamiliar and familiar religious traditions are raising should be noted, and the case of the EOTC makes the phenomena more patent for the American workforce, challenging the narrative to the widely accepted perspective of an American workplace by the EOTC which represents a Christian tradition that predates Protestantism. This case illustrates structural discrimination and should question the operating parameters that have been set for organizations seeking to be inclusive (Pincus, 1996).

If organizations and individuals do not acknowledge the governing discrimination built into structures, the result will be increased legal and social religious challenges (Atkinson, 2000; Gregory, 2011; Witte & Van Der Vyver 1996). If not acknowledged and addressed, the legal challenges will join existing increasing legal claims made to the Equal Employment Opportunity Commission in the United States (Atkinson, 2004). This is important considering the claims made to the Equal Employment Opportunity Commission (EEOC) have been steadily increasing and typically focus on accommodation requests for time off (for prayer and/or special holiday observances) and garb issues (Estreicher & Gray, 2006; Greenwald, 2012).

NOTE

1. Tewahedo means "being made one" or "one united in nature." The references is to the unified nature of Christ who was fully human and fully God.

REFERENCES

Abbink, J. (2011). Religion in public spaces: Emerging Muslim–Christian polemics in Ethiopia. *African Affairs.*

Ahmed, H. (2006). Coexistence and/or confrontation? Towards a reappraisal of Christian-Muslim encounter in contemporary Ethiopia. *Journal of religion in Africa, 36*(1), 4–22.

Alemu, L. A. (2012). *A study of socio-cultural identity and adjustment of Ethiopian immigrants in Atlanta* (Dissertation). Leulekal Akalu Alemu, Clark Atlanta University.

Alexis, G. Y. (2015). Not Christian, but nonetheless qualified: The secular workplace—Whose hardship? *Journal of Religion and Business Ethics, 3*(1). Retrieved from https://search.proquest.com/openview/3630cf344194555b7e9f66e5a8c52efb/1?pq-origsite=gscholar&cbl=2042285

Amundsen, D. W., & Mandahl, O. W., Jr. (1995). Ecumenical in spite of ourselves: A Protestant assessment of Roman Catholic, Eastern Orthodox, and Anglican Catholic approaches to bioethics. *Christian Bioethics, 1*(2), 213–245.

Assembly, U. G. (1948). Universal declaration of human rights. UN General Assembly. New York, NY: Author.

Atkinson, W. (2000). Divine accommodations: Religion in the workplace. *Risk Management, 47*, 12–17.

Atkinson, W. (2004) Religion in the workplace: Faith versus liability. *Risk Management, 15*(12), 18–23.

Basu-Zharku, I. O. (2011). The influence of religion on health. *Inquiries Journal*, *3*(1). Retrieved from http://www.inquiriesjournal.com/articles/367/2/the-influence-of-religion-on-health

Boylston, T. (2013). Food, life and material religion in Ethiopian Orthodox Christianity. New York, NY: Wiley-Blackwell.

Cash, K. C., & Gray, G. R. (2000). A framework for accommodating religion and spirituality in the workplace. *The Academy of Management Executive, 14*(3), 124–133.

Central Statistical Agency of Ethiopia. (n.d.). Retrieved from http://www.csa.gov.et/index.php/census-report/census-tables/category/301-census-tables

Desta, A. (2012). *Introduction to the Ethiopian Orthodox Tewahedo faith.* Bloomington, IN: Author House.

Engedayehu, W. (2014). The Ethiopian Orthodox Tewahedo Church in the diaspora: Expansion in the midst of division. *African Social Science Review, Volume 6*(1), 31–47.

Estreicher, S., & Gray, M. (2006). Religion and the U.S. workplace. *Human Rights: Journal of the Section of Individual Human Rights & Responsibilities, 33*(3), 17–21.

Greenwald, J. (2012). Religious discrimination claims rising. *Business Insurance. 46*(7), 3–18.

Gregory, R. (2011). *Encountering religion in the workplace: The legal right and responsibilities of workers and employers.* Ithaca, NY: Cornell University Press.

Grossman, R. J. (2008). Religion at work—Weaving religion or spirituality into company culture poses legal and managerial challenges galore. *HRMagazine, 53*(12), 26.

Hable Sellassie, S., & Tamerat, T. (1970). *The Church of Ethiopia a panorama of history and spiritual life.* Addis Ababa, Ethopia: EOTC.

Hassan, G., Rousseau, C., & Moreau, N. (2013). Ethnic and religious discrimination: The multifaceted role of religiosity and collective self-esteem. *Transcultural Psychiatry, 50*(4), 475–492.

Haustein, J., & Østebø, T. (2011). EPRDF's revolutionary democracy and religious plurality: Islam and Christianity in post-Derg Ethiopia. *Journal of Eastern African Studies, 5*(4), 755–772.

Hicks, D. A. (2003). *Religion and the workplace: Pluralism, spirituality, leadership.* Cambridge, England: Cambridge University Press.

Hoefer, M., Rytina, N. F., & Baker, B. (2012). Estimates of the unauthorized immigrant population residing in the United States: January 2011. Washington, DC: Department of Homeland Security, Office of Immigration Statistics.

Holdcroft, B. B. (2006). What is religiosity. *Catholic Education: A Journal of Inquiry and Practice, 10*(1), 89–103.

Immigration, U. S., Enforcement's, C., & Audit, F. S. (2011). Department of Homeland Security. Retrieved from https://www.dhs.gov/topic/data

Jenkins, P. (2011). *The next Christendom: The coming of global Christianity.* Oxford University Press.

Kebede, K. H. (2012). Double engagements: The transnational experiences of Ethiopian immigrants in the Washington, DC, metropolitan area (Doctoral dissertation). Syracuse University, New York.

Knutsson, K. E., & Selinus, R. (1970). Fasting in Ethiopia, an anthropological and nutritional study. *The American Journal of Clinical Nutrition, 23*(7), 956–969.

Kramar, R., & Syed, J. (2012). *Human resource management in a global context: A critical approach.* New York, NY: Palgrave Macmillan.

Larebo, H. M. (1988). The Ethiopian Orthodox Church and politics in the twentieth century: Part II. *Northeast African Studies,* 1–23.

Macro, O. R. C. (2008). Central Statistical Agency: Ethiopia demographic and health survey 2007. ORC Macro, Calverton, Maryland, USA.

Melaku, L. (2010). *History of the Ethiopian Orthodox Tewahedo Church: From the reign of Emperor Caleb to the end of Zagwe Dynasty and from the Classical (Golden) Age to the present.* Addis Ababa, Ethiopia: Elleni P. P. Plc.

Milik, J. T. (1976). The Books of Enoch: Aramaic fragments of Qumran Cave 4. Gloucestershire, England: Clarendon Press.

Molla, A. (2002). *The Ethiopic Calendar. An Ethiopian Journal.* Retrieved from https://tseday.wordpress.com/

Nonnemaker, J. M., McNeely, C. A., & Blum, R. W. (2003). Public and private domains of religiosity and adolescent health risk behaviors: Evidence from the National Longitudinal Study of Adolescent Health. *Social Science & Medicine, 57*(11), 2049–2054.

Persoon, J. (2010). The planting of the Tabot on European soil: The trajectory of Ethiopian Orthodox Involvement with the European Continent. *Studies in World Christianity, 16*(3), 320–340.

Pew Research Center. (n.d.) Retrieved from http://www.pewforum.org/religious-landscape-study/religious-tradition/orthodox-christian/

Pincus, F. L. (1996). Discrimination comes in many forms: Individual, institutional, and structural. *American Behavioral Scientist, 40*(2), 186–194.

Quinton, R. K., & Ciccazzo, M. (2007). Influences on Eastern Orthodox Christian fasting beliefs and practices. *Ecology of Food and Nutrition, 46*(5–6), 469–491.

Shenk, C. E. (1988). The Ethiopian Orthodox church: A study in indigenization. *Practical Anthropology, 16*(3), 259–278.

Strauss, P. L. (Ed.). (2009). *The Fetha Nagast.* Durham, NC: Carolina Academic Press.

Wainwright, G. (2006). *The Oxford history of Christian worship.* Oxford, England, Oxford University Press.

Weick, K. E. (1995). *Sensemaking in organizations.* Thousand Oaks, CA: SAGE.

Witte, J., Jr., & Van der Vyver, J. D. (Eds.). (1996). *Religious human rights in global perspective: religious perspectives* (Vol. 2). Grand Rapids, MI: Wm. B. Eerdmans.

World Values Survey Association. (2014). World Values Survey, Wave 5, 2005–2008, Official Aggregate v. 20140429. Madrid, Spain: Asep/JDS [producer].

Wuthnow, R. (2005). *American and the challenges of diversity.* Princeton, NJ: Princeton University Press.

CHAPTER 12

THE HOLISTIC MOTIVATION OF SOCIAL ENTREPRENEURS

Julia R. Marra and Kent W. Seibert
Gordon College, Boston, MA

For some, the motivation for a career is to confront problems with the hope of bringing about positive social change. Often this leads toward working for nonprofit organizations. Others are motivated by the challenge of creating economic gain and would prefer working in the for-profit sector. In the past these two options were seen as mutually exclusive. One was focused on service while the other was primarily about earnings. Frustrated by this binary choice as well as the inherent limits of both nonprofit and for-profit organizations, entrepreneurs have recently created a new standard for expected organizational output—the multiple bottom lines of the social enterprise (Bornstein & Davis, 2010). The social enterprise simultaneously pursues both problem attacking and profit making. For Christians, social entrepreneurship may provide a way to pursue a holistic calling, integrating skills in business with desire to confront social problems.

Social entrepreneurship is a relatively new, but quickly growing approach to business (Clark, 2012; Martin & Osberg, 2015). Additionally, it is conceptualized in a variety of ways (B Lab, 2012; Beugre, 2011; Dees, 1998; Helm, 2004; Lapowski, 2011; Nicholls, 2006). There is general agreement, however, that by "using market-based methods to solve social

Faith and Work: Christian Perspectives, Research, and Insights Into the Movement
pp. 211–225

problems," social entrepreneurs are challenging the conventional assumption that "creating social value and creating economic value" are competing goals by striving for both simultaneously (Miller, Grimes, McCullen, & Vogus, 2012, p. 616). Although the work of social enterprises is not universally seen as positive (e.g., Tracey & Phillips, 2016), the potential good these firms can contribute to society is substantial ("The Rise," 2006). And, their promise as a meaningful avenue for holistically integrating pursuits of faith and work is profound.

An important question that is only beginning to be addressed in the literature asks what motivates social entrepreneurs to choose this path (Miller et al., 2012). What drives an entrepreneur to pursue the calling of simultaneously pursuing business profit and societal problem solving, whether the focus be social problems or environmental ones? This chapter begins to answer that question by reporting the results of an exploratory study of what motivates people to become social entrepreneurs. After reviewing the existing literature, an inductive investigation will be described along with its findings. These results will be used to present a preliminary conceptual model of social entrepreneurial motivation. One of the specific motivational drivers we discovered is religious belief, indicating how social entrepreneurship offers a new avenue for integrating one's most important beliefs and one's work.

EXISTING KNOWLEDGE OF WHAT
MOTIVATES SOCIAL ENTREPRENEURS

There is a significant deficiency in research on social entrepreneurial motivation, made clear by the scarce literature currently available. Beugre (2011) provides a basic conceptual analysis of the connection between social entrepreneurial motivation and moral engagement. Social entrepreneurs use profit-making as a means to addressing social problems and creating social value. A concern for social problems is an identifying factor of the social entrepreneur. Beugre concludes that moral engagement is a potential indicator of motivation for an individual to start a social venture.

Miller et al. (2012) develop a conceptual model of the motivation of social entrepreneurs, positing compassion as the fundamental source of motivation. They suggest that "compassion may supplement traditional self-oriented motivations" of entrepreneurs to pursue social entrepreneurship (Miller et al., 2012, p. 616). Compassion, when aligned with humanitarian and philanthropic intentions, is a partial explanation for the risk taken on by social entrepreneurs to simultaneously attack problems and make profit.

Arend (2013) questions the legitimacy of compassion as the basis of a theory of social entrepreneurial motivation and suggests alternative approaches to building relevant theory. The concern is that the sources that drive compassion need to be identified and that variables other than compassion may be involved. Subsequently, Grimes, McMullen, Vogus, and Miller (2013) acknowledged that compassion is not the sole motivator for social entrepreneurs, although no connections are made to other potential motivations. These authors provide only conceptual arguments, offering no empirical evidence of social entrepreneurs' motivation nor do they examine actual social entrepreneurs.

Empirical work on what motivates social entrepreneurs is only recently appearing. Omorede (2014) used interviews and archival data to examine individuals' motivations for starting social enterprises in Nigeria. Entrepreneurs' passion for a social cause was fueled by local conditions and an intentional mindset of driving positive social change. Smith, Bell, and Watts (2014) explored whether traditional entrepreneurs and social entrepreneurs have different personalities. They found social entrepreneurs to have higher levels of creativity, risk-taking, and autonomy than traditional entrepreneurs.

Germak and Robinson (2014) found that a blended set of motivators, not one single motivator, moves someone to engage in social entrepreneurship by studying participants in a 6-month U.S. entrepreneurial training program. These nascent social entrepreneurs were motivated by personal fulfillment, a need for achievement, a desire to help society, a focus on things beyond money, and closeness to the social problem of concern. Germak and Robinson admit a weakness in that their study only covers trainees, who may or may not actually pursue their entrepreneurial aspirations.

In a study of social entrepreneurs in western England, Christopoulos and Vogl (2014) explored the multiple roles, agendas, and social relations of social entrepreneurs, whom they dubbed "altruistic economic actors." An ancillary finding of their research included potential motivators. One motivator was labeled "iconoclastic," indicating social entrepreneurs' dissatisfaction with the status quo and inclination to challenge perceived wisdom on what constitutes the best ways to conduct business. Other potential motives included the desire to address social issues such as sustainability and instances of social injustice to accomplish something worthwhile. An additional set of motives centered around personal fulfillment, having fun, personal achievement, ego, competing successfully, and leaving a legacy for one's children. While Christopoulos and Vogel's work nicely transcends proposing a simple univariate explanation of social entrepreneurial motivation like compassion, it ends up providing a laundry list of possible motivators with no particular unifying coherence.

Indeed, all the work to date on what motivates social entrepreneurs has limitations. None of the above studies considered the role of religious faith in motivating social entrepreneurs. Further conceptual and empirical work that builds on these initial studies of social entrepreneurial motivation is sorely needed. So, too, is discovering an initial understanding of what social entrepreneurs *themselves* see as motivating their call to social enterprise work. This was the basis of our exploratory research.

AN EXPLORATORY STUDY

The basic question our research attempted to answer is: What motivates an individual to pursue a career in social entrepreneurship?

To answer this question we invited 70 social entrepreneurs to be interviewed about their interest in social entrepreneurship (Find a B Corp, 2013). Eight individuals participated, with secondary data collected from a ninth. Seven social enterprises were represented. They are described in Table 12.1.

The results of these semistructured interviews were analyzed inductively (Easterby-Smith, Thorpe, & Lowe, 1991; Strauss & Corbin, 1990). That is, given the limited existing knowledge of social entrepreneurs' motivation, we did not seek to examine their responses in relation to any preexisting framework or hypotheses, but rather sought to let motivational factors emerge directly from participants' responses. By looking for patterns as well as similarities and differences within and across responses, we organized the findings into a structure from the interview data, rather than having a structure imposed a priori. Our findings follow, acknowledging their limited generalizability due to the small sample size.

FINDINGS

The results highlight several specific sources of motivation among the interviewees: religious belief, a feeling of compassion toward those who suffer social injustice, a life-long value of service, and the excitement of meeting financial and creative challenges. During the interviews, several interviewees also referenced dissatisfaction with their previous career in the for-profit business sector as well as with the nonprofit charitable approach to addressing social problems. Due to limited space, a representative selection of the findings is presented here.

Dissatisfaction With a For-Profit Career

Several of the interviewees expressed some level of dissatisfaction with previous for-profit work experiences. These individuals were driven to seek satisfaction and fulfillment in a different type of work environment.

Table 12.1.   Research Participants and Their Social Enterprises

World Stove (Gloucester, MA) Nathaniel Mulcahy, Founder & CEO Jesse Browning, Field Coordinator	Humanitarian engineering; Fuel-efficient, carbon negative, affordable household stoves for developing world poor with no other cooking option; Manufactured and managed by locals in 15 countries; Certified Benefit Corporation
Thirst Shoes (Boston, MA) Sam Winslow, Founder & CEO	Planned to market foot ware and partner with nonprofit organizations to fund water-well construction in rural Africa
Toms (Los Angeles, CA) Tracy Louis-Marie, Senior Account Manager, Blake Mycoskie, Founder & CEO	Markets shoes using one-for-one model of sales and giving; Partners with locals and nonprofit organizations to distribute shoes to children in need in 50+ countries; Health, eye-sight restoration and education programs in shoe distribution communities
Episcopal City Tutoring (Boston, MA) Alison Cook, Founder & CEO	Offers free tutoring and college application counseling to financially disadvantaged students in metro Boston
I Can Help the World (Indianapolis, IN) Lisa Masterson, Founder & CEO	Online game for children available in 33 countries; Children use superpowers to tackle social problems and learn the power of giving; 50% of income donated to nonprofit charitable organizations addressing the same problems presented in the game
Susty Party (New York, NY) Andrea Bonaiuto, Director of Online Sales	Renewable, recycled, compostable, and nontoxic party supplies; Partners with Clovernook Center for the Blind and Visually Impaired, a nonprofit empowering the visually impaired to manufacture products locally; Products made with green energy; Certified Benefit Corporation
Freeset Kolkata, India Kerry Hilton, Founder & Director	Trains and employs unskilled girls and women in the sex district of Kolkata, India; Provides economic freedom from prostitution; Offers education and health benefits to employees; small manufacturer

Lisa Masterson started her career as a traditional entrepreneur pursuing "the American dream" of success in business. Before starting I Can Help the World, Masterson had previously created a successful for-profit design business. However, she felt a "growing longing to give more, to help people more, to encourage people more." Financial success only meant so much. "There's this other side to life—there's this other side to humanity," Masterson says. "It's when I'm helping someone, that's when I feel fully alive." Masterson explains the fulfillment she found in a business that was focused on more than profit.

Nathaniel Mulcahy, founder of WorldStove, "lost track of the humanitarian aspect" of his interest in engineering—which is what drew him to engineering in the first place—after several years at a well-paying job in the single bottom-line focused appliance industry. After a personal medical crisis, he set off to start his own social enterprise designed to make household stoves available to people around the world with no other cooking options.

In all the cases, conventional for-profit work in business did not satisfy these individuals' strong desire in their careers to give to others.

Dissatisfaction With a Nonprofit Approach to Addressing Social Issues

Other interviewees came to see the limitations of nonprofits in solving social issues and thus described why they chose to pursue a business as the means to accomplish a social goal. Tracy Louis-Marie, senior account manager at *Toms*, shared: "I would probably have a hard time going back to work for an NGO [nongovernmental organization] because the business model aspect of philanthropic organizations like Toms liberates so many resources." A social enterprise presents a sustainable model for addressing social needs without the constant need for grant writing and fundraising.

Nathaniel Mulcahy believes the for-profit business model is the best option for his organization. He elaborates on the decision to create a for-profit company:

> We've always been a for-profit company. We've received a lot of flack for that, because they say, "Oh, you're not really a humanitarian. You're out to make money! You greedy bastard, making money off of poor people." Not a very nice thing to hear. But you have to actually take into [account] the business realities.

Mulcahy eagerly defends his choice of a for-profit company. "If we didn't have a profit, our business would collapse," he says. WorldStove has never received a grant or donation; it is "100% self-funded" and has been debt free for over 10 years. Mulcahy expounds on the decision against the nonprofit model, saying, "We found that a lot of nonprofits are spending 90% of their energy in capital drives. And if you're spending 90% of your time writing grants, that leaves you 10% to actually do any of the good." As a financially sustainable organization, Mulcahy finds WorldStove to be less distracted in its pursuit of humanitarian and business goals.

In the field of international humanitarian work, Mulcahy argues that a for-profit company is the better option. "Not every country will allow nonprofits in," and others will impose a higher cost and "years of paperwork" before an organization can begin working there. "It's cheaper to run a for-profit company," Mulcahy explains, because other countries tend to be more accepting of a company providing jobs and generating taxable income. "So it allows us to do more good with less money. We're still doing humanitarian things, but because we waste less in bureaucracy, we get more bang for the buck." Jesse Browning, Field Coordinator at World-Stove, explains that the freedom from third-party pressure is a benefit of WorldStove as a for-profit company. The "pressure to impress" foundations and attract donors can distract a humanitarian-driven company.

The interviewees chose a social enterprise over a nonprofit organization because they believe it is more efficient, flexible, sustainable, and ultimately more capable of achieving their humanitarian goals.

Five Motivational Drivers to Pursue Social Entrepreneurship

Dissatisfaction with the status quo—both conventional nonprofit and for-profit organizational models—served as a catalyst bonding *social change* motivation and *venture* motivation, thus producing social entrepreneurship (see Figure 12.1). Three drivers we discovered as motivating positive social change are religious belief, compassion toward those suffering social injustice, and a value for service. The drivers of venture motivation were desire to face and overcome financial and creative challenges.

BELIEF

An important motivational driver for the social entrepreneurs in this study was their belief that they could—and ought to—make a positive difference in the world. In our survey group, the source of this belief was Christian faith. Kerry Hilton, for example, specifically connects his religious beliefs to his decision to create a social enterprise. Prior to his current position, Hilton worked as a Baptist minister. According to Hilton, "God's heart for the poor is riddled throughout [the Bible]." He explains that "sadly, many Christians miss God's massive heart toward the poor," but through finding it, one can reach an awareness of the biblical call to help the poor and an understanding of "God's heart of justice for the poor and oppressed." Upon this realization, Hilton says that individuals should ask themselves: "How will I as a follower of Jesus respond?" Hilton responded through Freeset.

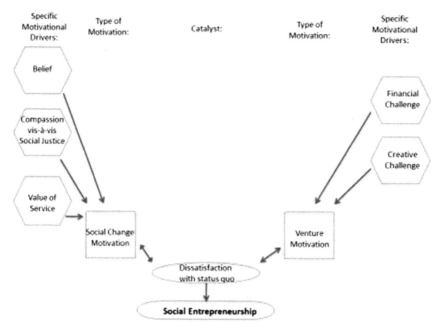

Figure 12.1.   Model of social entrepreneurship motivation.

The purpose of Freeset is to provide a practical solution to a major social problem in Kolkata, India. "Freeset was established to give girls and women an economic choice that they never had before entering prostitution." Employment options provide "an economic choice to be free" from poverty and prostitution. Hilton explains that initially he "didn't want to do business," but it was a solution to the problem faced by this group of women in India. "The purpose is freedom," Hilton says, "from sexual slavery and freedom to know Jesus Christ." Hilton is led by the need to find the best solution that brings the most physical and spiritual liberty to the community he serves. Hilton is "motivated by the fact that ultimate freedom" can be found in religion, but economic freedom provides the "opportunity of choice" for faith, lifestyle, and employment. To address this specific social problem, Hilton found that social entrepreneurship made the most sense. Upon this realization, Hilton asks, "Why would we want to do anything else?" Through the profitable business of Freeset, Hilton can offer economic freedom to those who are persecuted by the social problem that Freeset is attacking.

Alison Cook describes her religious faith as an influential factor in her path to social entrepreneurship. From the early stages of awareness of social issues, Cook explains, "Faith was a big part of it," referring to her belief in Christianity. It was through volunteering at Christian organiza-tions that Cook was first made "aware of [social] inequity" and "the differ-ences" of those on the margins of society. It was a "profound" moment and a "very formative" experience when this became apparent to Cook.

Additionally, Cook was influenced by her academic study of religion, which led to thinking deeply about the role of religion in social issues while earning a PhD in religion and psychology. This caused her to ask: "What's the responsibility of religion to social change?" From a biblical perspective, the answer may be found in the "clear directive" to treat "the least" of society in the way that Jesus said they should be treated. Cook has been inspired by the study of religion to take action. Overall, she says, "I think I've always been drawn to the idea of empowering the least of these in Jesus' name." Social entrepreneurship proved to be the best way she could act upon this idea and use her God-give talents.

Nathaniel Mulcahy "grew up with an incredibly strong faith." However, he struggled with aspects of institutionalized religion that he saw "as a bureaucracy." Mulcahy explains that this part of religion "often got in the way of some faith." This dilemma was solved, for Mulcahy, through humanitarian engineering and social entrepreneurship at WorldStove. He expounds on his belief as follows:

> By doing what I do, I thought that I could be respectful of what I saw every-body's job is on earth without having to struggle with the ins and outs of the ecclesiastical bureaucracies, which sometimes prevent some of the good from happening.

Through the work of WorldStove, Mulcahy is able to holistically combine his faith and his work.

Blake Mycoskie references his religious belief in Christianity while explaining how he was led to create *Toms*. Mycoskie mentions the biblical proverb calling one to give one's first fruit. This contradicts the popular idea of working first and giving second. Mycoskie recalls,

> I remember sitting in church my freshman year of college thinking, when I started my first entrepreneurial venture, that I would work really hard to be a very successful entrepreneur and make a ton of money so that later in my life, like my 60s and 70s, I could spend my time giving it away. And I knew that I would be really blessed by that. And I looked forward to that.

But he opted for a different career path. Mycoskie chose to pursue a career as a social entrepreneur, because it gave the option of being successful as an entrepreneur and helping others at the same time. If he had not chosen to create the social enterprise Toms, he would have had to wait several decades for "the blessings" he has today, referring to both the intrinsic and extrinsic benefits of giving. "It's never too early to start giving and start service," he says, "and you're going to be so blessed from it that it's better to start now than postpone it to something you do later in life."

FEELING COMPASSION TOWARD THOSE WHO SUFFER SOCIAL INJUSTICE

Interviewees were also moved to social entrepreneurship by compassion—an awareness of the suffering of others combined with a desire to relieve that suffering. Sources of the feeling of compassion included formal education and direct exposure to a particular social injustice.

Blake Mycoskie first imagined the concept of the Toms one-for-one giving model while in Argentina. There he saw the need for steady shoe donations for children. The compassion Mycoskie felt for Argentine children "really was life changing."

Tracy Louis-Marie, senior account manager at Toms, trained with the Peace Corps and earned a master's degree in international public health. "The nature of what I'm interested in, which is public health," Louis-Marie explains, inherently leads to an awareness of international social justice issues related to health. This background led to her interest in Toms and its goal of eradicating illnesses acquired by improper foot protection among poor children in developing countries. Louis-Marie is able to work to right this injustice through Toms' social entrepreneurial model.

During Andrea Bonaiuto's time living in Panama she met the founder and chief executive officer of Susty Party and became involved in the company. Throughout her education, Bonaiuto traveled through South Africa, Israel, Palestine, and several countries in South America. She found these experiences very enlightening. Bonaiuto explains that, "every trip wasn't completely focused on human rights and social justice, but it's an inevitable piece of your experience traveling abroad." She says these experiences inspired her lifestyle and career choices. [They] "taught me that life's too precious and too short not to do something meaningful and something you enjoy doing." Bonaiuto says, "so this has been my driving force in every job I've had." Working at Susty Party is Bonaiuto's compassionate response to the social justice issues she learned about through her prior life experiences.

A LIFE-LONG VALUE OF SERVICE

A central value of the interviewees was a commitment to service, manifested in providing assistance or benefit to others experiencing some type of deprivation. For most of the interviewees this value was sourced to their family.

Alison Cook mentions the effect of familial influence in her awareness of the needs of others. She grew up in a middle to upper-middle class family in an economically diverse community. She was exposed to a variety of social problems through volunteer experiences and familial influences. In her upbringing, "seeing people who struggle" and are limited in some abilities taught her that some disadvantages "genuinely make it harder for them to overcome obstacles." This realization from her youth affected Masterson's "awareness of inequities" and her desire to serve others through tutoring.

While providing free services to youth in underserved communities, Cook explains that the work of Episcopal City Tutoring extends beyond just tutoring. They are also able to address the need for college application counseling, which helps bring college into reality for these students. Helping them to reach this opportunity "excites all of us," says Cook.

As shown in Figure 12.1, belief, compassion in respect to social justice, and the value of service combine to drive social change motivation, which is the desire to ameliorate the suffering of others.

FINANCIAL AND CREATIVE CHALLENGES

The work of a social enterprise is unique and demanding. Founding any entrepreneurial venture is difficult, but adding a social agenda to the business model adds another layer to the challenge. For the interviewees, this challenge was another source of motivation. Meeting the demands of creating a new and financially sustainable business fuels a form of motivation similar in both conventional and social entrepreneurs, what we call *venture* motivation. Two drivers of this motivation are financial challenge and creative challenge, that is, making money and creating something new.

Kerry Hilton, founder of FreeSet, saw that for-profit business was the only way to offer his employees economic security through full-time employment. The nonprofit method would not provide his organization with the consistent financial resources needed to provide ongoing, full-time employment to girls and women in India.

Blake Mycoskie, founder of Toms, similarly holds a clear belief that the work of *Toms* requires a self-sustaining, profit-making business. In a nonprofit model, the money originally invested in Toms would have gone towards accomplishing the charitable intentions of the organization. But "resources would be depleted, and fundraising begins again." In the for-profit model of Toms, in contrast, the same amount of money invested into the company has been able to help "20 times" more people than the original cash input alone. As a profitable business, Toms is also able to continue to sustain its social mission.

The study participants were also energized by the creative challenge of building a brand new enterprise. Lisa Masterson sought to "fulfill a certain niche" with the work of I Can Help The World. No similar online children's game existed in the market prior to Masterson's company. She says, "I liked the challenge of being able to do something that wasn't currently being done." For Masterson, this achievement is meaningful especially in the context of the need for the unique services provided by I Can Help The World.

SOCIAL ENTREPRENEURS' MOTIVATION AND THE POTENTIAL FOR WORK-FAITH INTEGRATION

What motivates an individual to pursue a career in social entrepreneurship? The interview results here reveal two general types of motivation and five specific motivational drivers (see Figure 12.1). The combination of all these factors as well as dissatisfaction with conventional for-profit and nonprofit organizational structures is important to propel someone to create or work in a social enterprise. What we call venture motivation is common among traditional entrepreneurs and business people. They enjoy creating things of value and generating profit. Belief in a higher purpose (Christian or otherwise), compassion for the victims of social injustice, and a desire to serve are likely common among those who pursue work in the nonprofit arena. This is what we refer to as social change motivation. What is unique about social entrepreneurs is that they have *both* of these motivations. An environment that allows them to pursue only one of their motivations can be frustrating. In contrast, the model of social enterprise enables them to holistically achieve both motivations. This is eminently fulfilling for the social entrepreneur.

This suggests why social entrepreneurship can be so advantageous not just to help society tackle pressing problems in effective and sustainable ways, but also to provide a venue for more integrated, holistic work. Many workers today, especially those of the millennial generation, desire this type of life pursuit (Taylor, 2016). A life of integrity, as in an integrated life, should be the norm for Christians. Thus, social entrepreneurship provides a natural way to combine faith and work.

It is important to note that this research did not start out looking for religious belief in social entrepreneurs, but it emerged as a motivational driver nonetheless, proving its significance. While it was not a surprise, it is evidence that the social entrepreneurial model of business can prove to be a significant means to holistically pursue God's call on one's life.

Social entrepreneurship provides a new avenue to pursue "good" at work that is inherently built into a company and recognizes the ability and power to address needs beyond traditional business or nonprofit models. Blake Mycoskie was moved by the many problems caused by simply not having an adequate pair of shoes. Whether it led to disease or prevented a child from attending school, it was a serious problem. He also felt he had been gifted with business skills that ought to serve a greater purpose. Starting a social enterprise was the ideal way to live out his faith and combine his social change motivation and venture motivation. Other interviewees in our study found similar satisfaction through social enterprise opportunities. These opportunities provide a way to make tangible the theological expositions others have provided of how Christianity can be incorporated into the marketplace (e.g., Van Duzer, 2010; Wong & Rae, 2011).

Next Steps

There are obvious limitations to the exploratory study reported here. Most obvious is the small and nonrepresentative sample of social entrepreneurs interviewed. Further research with a larger and more diverse sample is called for. In addition, the interview data are self-reported. While self-reporting has limitations, it is appropriate here since the purpose of this research was to learn what social entrepreneurs believe about their own motivations.

Surely additional research of the motivations of social entrepreneurs is needed, as this model of business continues to increase in popularity and take shape in many ways. In terms of motivation, many questions remain. Should other specific drivers be added to the five discovered here? Are there motivations beyond social change and venture? Do motivations vary based on the type of social enterprise? Do they vary based on the demographic characteristics of the entrepreneurs? Are the motivations of Christian social entrepreneurs unique? Is social enterprise new for Christian business people? Might historical examples exist of Christians and others simultaneously attacking social problems and pursuing profit? Today's social entrepreneurs, and past examples, are only beginning to be understood. Opportunities for further research leading to increased understanding of social entrepreneurship are plentiful.

This chapter has described social entrepreneurship and its great potential for faith-work integration. More specifically it has considered what motivates an individual to pursue a career within a social enterprise. Based on the results of this research, five motivational drivers and two types of motivation are proposed. These factors along with dissatisfaction with the status quo are integrated to form a conceptual model of social entrepreneurial motivation. This is one of the first research studies to focus specifically on how social entrepreneurs *themselves* describe their motivation. It is also one of the first to identify the importance of social entrepreneurs' religious belief. Further, the study helps clarify why someone might be motivated to work for a social enterprise versus a conventional for-profit business or a nonprofit organization. Social entrepreneurs are motivated to pursue a new type of calling, one that holistically integrates problem attacking and profit making in innovative, productive, and exciting ways and that affords an inspiring approach to integrating faith and work. Since social problems will not be disappearing any time soon, this opportunity is available to anyone with a heart for helping others and a mind for business.

REFERENCES

Arend, R. J. (2013). A heart-mind-opportunity nexus: Distinguishing social entrepreneurship for entrepreneurs. *Academy of Management Review, 38,* 313–315.

B Lab. (2012). Passing Legislation: B Corporation. Retrieved from http://www.bcorporation.net.

Beugre, C. D. (2011). Motivation to create social ventures: A theory of moral engagement. *United States Association for Small Business and Entrepreneurship,* 61.

Bornstein, D., & Davis, S. (2010). *Social entrepreneurship: What everyone needs to know.* New York, NY: Oxford University Press.

Christopoulos, D., & Vogl, S. (2014). The motivation of social entrepreneurs: The roles, agendas, and relations of altruistic economic actors. *Journal of Social Entrepreneurship, 10,* 1–30.

Clark, B. (2012, December). Presentation given at Gordon College, Wenham, Massachusetts.

Dees, J. G. (1998). *The meaning of social entrepreneurship.* Kansas City, MO: Kauffman Foundation.

Easterby-Smith, M., Thorpe, R., & Lowe, A. (1991). *Management research: An introduction.* London, England: SAGE.

Find a B Corp | B Corporation. (2013). B Corporation. Retrieved February 1, 2013, from http://www.bcorporation.net/community/find-a-b-corp

Germak, A. J., & Robinson, J. A. (2014). Exploring the motivation of nascent social entrepreneurs. *Journal of Social Entrepreneurship, 5*(1), 5–21.

Grimes, M. G., McMullen, J. S., Vogus, T. J., & Miller, T. L. (2013). Studying the origins of social entrepreneurship: Compassion and the role of embedded agency. *Academy of Management Review, 38*(3), 460–463.

Helm, S. (2004, July, 2004). *Motivation for social entrepreneurship: Building an analytical framework.* Paper presented at The International Society for Third-Sector Research Sixth International Conference, Toronto, Canada.

Lapowski, I. (2011). B Corporations. *Inc*, *33*(4), 78.

Martin, R. L., & Osberg, S. (2015). *Getting beyond better: How social entrepreneurship works*. Boston, MA: Harvard Business Review Press.

Miller, T. L., Grimes, M. G., McCullen, J. S., & Vogus, T. J. (2012). Venturing for others with heart and head: How compassion encourages social entrepreneurship. *Academy of Management Review, 37*(4), 616–640.

Nicholls, A. (2006). *Social entrepreneurship: New models of sustainable social change*. New York, NY: Oxford University Press.

Omorede, A. (2014). Exploration of motivational drivers towards social entrepreneurship. *Social Enterprise Journal, 10*(3), 239–267.

The rise of the social entrepreneur. (2006, February 25). *The Economist*, pp. 11–13.

Smith, R., Bell, R., & Watts, H. (2014). Personality trait differences between traditional and social entrepreneurs. *Social Enterprise Journal, 10*(3), 200–221.

Strauss, A., & Corbin, J. (1990). *Basics of qualitative research: Grounded theory procedures and techniques*. Newbury Park, CA: SAGE.

Taylor, P. (2016) *The next America: Boomers, millennials, and the looming generational showdown*. New York, NY: Public Affairs.

Tracey, P., & Phillips, N. (2016) Managing the consequences of organizational stigmatization: Identity work in a social enterprise. *Academy of Management Journal, 59*(3), 740–765.

Van Duzer, J. (2010). *Why business matters to God, and what still needs to be fixed*. Downers Grove, IL: InterVarsity Press.

Wong, K. L., & Rae, S. B. (2011). *Business for the common good: A Christian vision for the marketplace*. Downers Grove, IL: IVP Academic.

CHAPTER 13

HEADING FOR THE
MULTIFAITH WORKPLACE

Stuart Allen
Robert Morris University

Peter Williams
Abilene Christian University

Religious expression in the workplace has generally become muted in modern American culture (Ewest, 2015), and the Christian-dominated education system that once existed has largely transitioned to a secular model (Mixon, Lyon, & Beaty, 2004; Thielen, 2011). Most university graduates will encounter religious diversity in the workplace, except in the most religiously homogeneous areas of America. These workplaces may have pluralistic or even secular cultures, including people who believe differently (Christians from other denominations, cultures, and religious traditions) or not at all (Miller & Ewest, 2015). While faith provides meaning and inner nourishment for Christians in the workplace, few receive specific preparation for living their faith in a religiously diverse or secular workplace, whether they have attended a Christian or nonsectarian university or college. How can Christians express their beliefs in appropriate ways to be a positive influence within these workplaces? How do Christians prepare for a spiritually and religiously diverse American workplace when many of the avenues through which Christians

Faith and Work: Christian Perspectives, Research, and Insights Into the Movement
pp. 227–243
Copyright © 2018 by Information Age Publishing
227

are educated or socialized do not equip them for secular or multifaith work environments?

This chapter explores how the Christian community can play a role in the largely secularized chain of preparation from higher education to the workplace in support of the common Christian mission. We discuss the context, changes, and challenges Christian workers face, and emphasize the opportunities inherent in the adjustment to a more pluralistic society and workplace. We then propose ways the Christian community can support current and future workers, adding to the flow of conversation on faith in the workplace.

CHANGING CONTEXTS

Religious America is changing. Jacobsen and Jacobsen (2012) suggest that America is shifting away from a monoreligious culture. While Christians remain the majority, non-Christian religions increased from 2% to 5% and nonreligious affiliates grew from 1% to 16% between 1900 and 2010. The 2014 Pew Survey (Pew Research Center, 2015) found that "in the past 7 years, the percentage of adults who describe themselves as Christians has dropped from 78.4% to 70.6%" (p. 20). In addition, "all major religion surveys find that the unaffiliated share of the U.S. population (the percentage of religious 'nones') is growing rapidly" (Pew Research Center, 2015, p. 112). Chaves (2011) argues that some Christians remain Christian in their faith, but do not identify as Christians because of its social stigma or their desire to separate themselves from other Christian groups they do not identify with (e.g., conservative beliefs and politics).

Along with these broader demographic changes there has been a shift away from Christian and religious influence and expression in higher education (Jacobsen & Jacobsen, 2012). Similar trends can also be seen in the workplace (Ewest, 2015; Miller & Ewest, 2015). In 1992, Dallas Willard noted, "Only a few decades ago, well past the Second World War and into the early Sixties, American culture was almost universally regarded as based upon Christianity" (para. 1). Many private colleges and universities supported the connection between learning and faith (Thielen, 2011). Students would also enter a workplace in which most colleagues were Christian and Christian faith expression was the norm (e.g., Christian holiday calendars). Many previously Christian religious colleges and universities have since become nonsectarian (not affiliated to any religion or expressly multifaith) (Thielen, 2011). Despite these changes, Seifert (2007) suggests that Christian privilege persists on American higher education campuses in the form of a dominant norm and ethos.

Higher education has shifted from an earlier era of stronger alignment with (Christian) religious education (Jacobsen & Jacobsen, 2012; Shahjahan, 2009; Waggoner, 2011). In Fall 2014, only 9.3% of total postsecondary enrollment was at one of the 882 religiously affiliated postsecondary institutions, which account for 19.1% of the total of 4,614 postsecondary institutions in the United States (U.S. Department of Education, National Center for Education Statistics, 2016). Since 1980, over 90% of all postsecondary students have been educated at religiously unaffiliated universities. Many professors support the separation of religion, spirituality, and education (Astin, Lindholm, & Astin, 2011; Jacobsen & Jacobsen, 2012). Some professors are even aggressively opposed to religion having a role in higher education (Shahjahan, 2009; Williams & Allen, 2014). Astin et al. (2011) note that "most students (62%) report that their professors 'never' encourage discussion of religious/spiritual matters" (p. 37), even though four out of five faculty in the United States consider themselves spiritual, and three out of five (64%) consider themselves religious (Lindholm & Astin, 2006). A further third (37%) consider themselves nonreligious. The shift in educators' attitudes to religion has inevitably influenced the tone of higher education.

The workplace has reflected similar changes in the post-Fordist industrial era (Ewest, 2015), with challenges to the role of organized religion (Franz & Wong, 2005; Mitroff & Denton, 1999) further embedding the tradition of American workplace secularism. Ewest (2015) states, "Early Americans saw religious values as instrumental and motivational to their behaviors in the marketplace" (p. 1), contrasting with the perceived divorce between religion and economic life in later generations. Mitroff and Denton (1999) note the distaste that developed in the American workplace for (Christian) religious expression and for proselytizing. Miller (2006) suggests that in the 1980s and 1990s many Americans came to believe that religious expression in the workplace was not legal. Employees may shy away from expressing faith in the workplace out of fear of alienation or attack, as religious expression in the workplace can be interpreted by members of other religions as a religious identity threat (Lund Dean, Safranski, & Lee, 2014). Religious identity can also play a role in the formation of in-groups and out-groups, impacting a worker's sense of belonging (Hogg, Adelman, & Blagg, 2010). Despite Christian privilege, some Christians argue that discrimination against Christians in the workplace has become as severe as discrimination against other religious groups (Bennett-Alexander & Hartman, 2015).

The negative shift in attitudes to religious expression in the workplace has been followed by a steady growth in positive attitudes to, and interest in, workplace spirituality since the late 1990s (Benefiel, Fry, & Geigle, 2014). In addition to the workplace spirituality movement, Miller (2006) points to the faith at work movement, which incorporates interest in religion and religiously based spirituality. Some authors (Hicks, 2003; Lund Dean et al., 2014) also note an increasing unwillingness of employees to have work-selves that exclude religious identity. Workplace spirituality encourages attitudes and practices such as seeking or following a calling, altruistic love, and sharing in community which are clearly conducive to the Christian mission (Benefiel et al., 2014; Tanyi, 2002). However, as stressed by Andre Delbecq, despite religions' history of divisiveness, workplace spirituality as a movement should avoid "closing the door on the centuries of wisdom that is possessed in a religious tradition" (Allen & Williams, 2017, p. 220).

In higher education, authors such as Vogel (2000), Lentz (2005), and Jacobsen and Jacobsen (2012) point to a growing interest in renegotiating the role of faith and spirituality in higher education through a focus on the whole person of students and faculty (Vogel, 2000). As Jacobsen and Jacobsen (2012) note:

> Religion has "returned" to higher education in the last 2 decades ... but we add the qualification that the religion that has returned to universities in recent years is not the same kind of religion that dominated higher learning in America during the eighteenth and nineteenth centuries ... [it] is more pluriform than it was in past and much less easily distinguished from other lifestances that formerly have been called secular. (p. 153)

Theodore (2010) emphasizes the need for a balanced understanding of the First Amendment's emphasis on "neither promoting any religious belief nor inhibiting the religious beliefs of students" (p. 157) in education.

Given the percentage of Americans who are religious, it can be argued that religion itself is not the problem; rather it is religious expression that needs to be redefined and renegotiated given the demographic shifts and changes in attitudes toward religion in the public space. The role of Christianity in America seems unlikely to return to what it was and a new orientation to other religions and spiritualities may be required. Lotz (2003) suggests that Christian higher education must avoid "wholesale adaptation and disengaged preservation" in response to the "wider culture" (p. 172). While the faith at work and workplace spirituality movements both suggest a reawakening to spiritual and religious expression in the workplace presenting an opportunity for Christian voices in organizations, this transformation is inevitably slow for many organizations and results in the Christian voice being one among many rather than the dominant voice.

THE CHRISTIAN RESPONSE

Before presenting our proposals on a Christian response to a secular or religiously and spiritually diverse workplace, we discuss the essential challenges Christians face, as well as tendencies in the Christian response to religiously diverse others.

Continued Trend Toward Diversity

The religiously diverse workplace raises challenges for the Christian, and there are no signs that religious diversity in the workplace will lessen. Eck (2003) points out that U.S. immigration reform in 1965 was a watershed event resulting in increased immigration from Asian countries, introducing further religious diversity. More recently, the global refugee crises have led to groups of immigrants from Africa, the Middle East, and Asia relocating to American communities. American Christians' attitudes toward this continued trend of cultural and religious diversification ranges from muted excitement for encountering other cultures to xenophobic fear (Amos, 2016; Kelly, 2016). Merino (2010) found that while over 90% of American respondents had a positive attitude toward religious diversity in the general sense, far fewer responded positively to having a Buddhist temple or Muslim mosque in their community, suggesting that many Americans' idea of religious diversity includes only the range of Judeo-Christian denominations.

Some Americans lament the United States no longer being an exclusively Christian nation and would like to see that status restored (Miller, 2006). Such Christian triumphalism, or the desire to see Christians win or dominate (Pope Francis, 2013), would suggest that educational reform must return a *presiding Jesus* to the classroom, bring prayer back into education, or reassert Christian dominance over other faiths in learning institutions. Pope Francis and Christians of many other denominations (Eck, 2003) refer to its nonalignment with the calling, example, and words of Christ in questioning the ideal of forced Christian dominion, as well as the importance of human choice in deciding whether to believe in God or follow Christ. The conflation of U.S. cultural values and Christianity in American Christianity has resulted in an inability among many American Christians to differentiate between faith expression and the exertion of ethnocentric cultural hegemony (Eck, 2003). Christian theology asserts that non-Christians should be attracted or persuaded, not forced, to become Christ's followers.

Intergroup relationships are difficult when cultures and values differ, and some conflict between faith and cultural groups seems inevitable. But this challenge may be greater for Christians who wish to restore a Christian nation, are less welcoming of difference (Merino, 2010), and hesitant to accept other faiths as a permanent or valued part of the community and workplace. However, there is an opportunity within these demographic changes for Christians to revisit what it means to live their faith in the workplace and to renew commitment to the essentials of faith in Christ.

Religious and Spiritual Literacy

The ability to converse with, learn from, and work productively with people of other faith traditions may be hindered by Christians' lack of knowledge of other religions and even of their own faith (Jacobsen & Jacobsen, 2012). For example, some overlook how Christianity calls for respect for other faiths (Eck, 2003; Peace, Rose, & Mobley, 2012). Authors such as Foster (1998) have encouraged Christians to remember their spiritual heritage, while Eck (2003) reminds Christians of the invented nature of many spiritual practices, suggesting that Christians be open to discovering new or unfamiliar spiritual practices that allow them to draw near to God. While the need for religious and spiritual education is ever-present for Christians, we specifically focus on the need for religious and spiritual literary as foundation for participation in the multifaith workplace.

This highlighted lack of awareness includes overlooking the many ways the Christian community through the centuries has understood God's mission in the world, and the various avenues for serving God. One such view of God's mission entails Christians only expressing their faith through evangelizing (Bosch, 1991). Christians may experience a conflict between the exclusivist values taught in their church and the prevailing relativist values in society and the workplace. Exclusivist values, as described by Eck (2003), lead to interfaith dialogue being evangelical or apologetic in nature. Within Christian history the emphasis on an evangelical response to non-Christians is recent (Bosch, 1991). Individual proselytizing is only one form of faith expression (Miller & Ewest, 2011), while others include service, ethical conduct, promoting social justice, and (silently) modeling and experiencing Christian virtues. Eck (2003) further highlights in her "yearning for a new theological thinking that moves beyond the patrolling of Christian borders" (p. xii), that simply guarding the Christian space without addressing questions of religious freedom, respect and hospitality, social justice, and dignity, does not align with the example of Christ. A more in-depth understanding of historical Christian teaching about participating in God's work in the world through service might empower Christians in the workplace to interact with peers from other faith traditions with attitudes of appreciation, receptivity to learning, and mutuality (Bosch, 1991, Eck, 2003).

Christian scripture supports positive interaction with people of other faiths (Eck, 2003; Hicks, 2003), but these scriptures are rarely emphasized. One such example from the Christian Bible is, "But in your hearts revere Christ as Lord. Always be prepared to give an answer to everyone who asks you to give the reason for the hope that you have. But do this with gentleness and respect" (1 Peter 3:15). The earlier part of this verse is frequently quoted in support of having ready testimonies of one's Christian faith, but the last stanza regarding gentleness and respect is sometimes overlooked. Joshua 24:15 ("But as for me and my household, we will serve the LORD") echoes a similar respect (differentiated from agreement) for faith choices. Arriving in higher education or the workplace with this respect for others' choice of faith and dignity as human beings as well as some skill in interfaith dialogue is essential to a renewed role for Christians in the pluralistic workplace.

Skill at Interfaith Dialogue

The skills of interfaith dialogue need to be fostered from all sides to reduce perceived hostility and incompatibility, which amplify the perceptions of conflict implicit in a distributive or win-lose approach to differences (Folger, Poole, & Stutmam, 2013). For example, Merino (2010) found that interreligious contact was associated with religious tolerance. The ability to dialogue with others who have different beliefs has been underdeveloped and possibly was unnecessary to previous generations of Christian workers, given past religious homogeneity (Allen & Williams, 2017). With the gradual change toward religious diversity in the U.S. workplace, Christians have had few role models for interacting with people of other faiths (or nonfaiths) for purposes other than proselytizing. Few opportunities exist outside of trial and error for learning how to engage in interfaith dialogue, so the skills for such dialogue may not be well developed among many Christians except for those living in regions that have been religiously diverse for generations.

Christians are commanded to love their neighbors (Luke 10:27). This love can be expressed in the workplace by acknowledging humanity of others and their equality before God as well as working toward overcoming human-invented divisions (Eck, 2003). Without some exposure to other religions and the resulting understanding of the commonalities of the human experience that enable people of different faiths to interact, Christians risk silence or awkward overresponse during interactions. Religious tolerance or agreements to exclude faith from the workplace, as an alternative, only foster or extend existing hostility (Eck, 2003), excluding the collaboration and compromise needed for peace (Folger et al., 2013).

Eck (2003) provides a more complete discussion of Christian conceptualizations of pluralism, emphasizing that the term must not be confused with relativism (all beliefs are subjective and therefore equal) or syncretism (all religions ultimately believe in the same god and can or will be merged). Her notion of pluralism, rather, emanates from the proposal that:

> we not limit God to the God we know or the particular language and image through which we know God ... [and that] it is our confidence in Jesus, the Christ, who was open to all people regardless of religion or status, that pushes Christians into the wider world of faith. (p. 185)

Willard (1992) reinforces that "pluralism is not a bad arrangement," noting that God expected and designed a world in which there is choice, and that Christians should not be seeking to suppress the freedom of the human mind, but rather to inspire it.

Christian Stereotypes and Tensions

Jesus and his early followers did not live in an exclusively Christian society and neither were they intimidated by or hostile to other faiths (Eck, 2003). Jesus's followers were seen a Jewish sect within the existing Jewish culture (Gonzalez, 2010). The social milieu of the times was not constructed around Christian values, norms, or dominance, and yet Jesus's followers grew in numbers and lived with joy (often in spite of persecution common to minority religions). The current U.S. context creates its own challenges. While there are universities and workplaces that are hospitable and welcoming of faith expression (Jacobsen & Jacobsen, 2012; Miller & Ewest, 2015), Christians encounter resistance to sharing or expressing their faith in higher education and the workplace (Bradley & Kauanui, 2003; Bryant, 2005). Whether their intentions are to proselytize, share deeply held values, be of service, seek social justice, enrich their spiritual journey, or express personal experience (Miller & Ewest, 2013), many students and faculty are reticent to reveal their faith (Bradley & Kauanui, 2003; Bryant, 2005; Williams & Allen, 2014). The media portrayal of conservative Christian faith in American society supports stereotypes of Christians (Bryant, 2005), including noninclusive attitudes toward other faiths (Eck, 2003). It seems increasingly acceptable to reject Christians in return, with their *outdated* values and exclusive beliefs

(Willard, 1992), and many Christians do not do enough to counter either the stereotype or the rejection of stereotypical Christians.

The Bible provides more guidance on interacting with people of other faiths than many Christians are aware (Willard, 1992), as these are not the first times in which Christians find themselves amongst a plurality of beliefs. Internal defenses and stereotypical beliefs about Christian roles and social identities provide considerable challenges to Christians engaging those with differing views. One danger is Christians creating an oppositional identity (Eck, 2003), in which they define themselves in terms of what they are against or do not believe, more than in the strength of what they believe. This identity becomes a barrier to meaningful Christian presence in the workplace and reinforces stereotypes about Christians and religious people in general.

Folger et al. (2013) stated, "The roots of intergroup conflict lie in the basic human need for identity" (p. 96). The social categorization used by religious groups to define their identity becomes the basis for who is right and wrong, and identifying who is a threat to Christians' beliefs and way of life. The fear of contaminating one's religious or spiritual beliefs by exposure to or engagement with religious others suggests a lack of knowledge of Biblical Christianity and confidence in the Christian biblical promise of salvation, especially when Christian teaching reinforces that Christians need only fear God. In addition, a fragile religious identity can exaggerate the perception that other religions are a (social or religious identity) threat in the workplace (Lund Dean et al., 2014). Having a secure self-identity, on the other hand, would allow an employee to encounter the *other* without feeling threatened. Seul (1999) wrote "because religion provides such powerful support to individuals and groups as they endeavor to establish and maintain secure identities, it is not surprising that much intergroup identity competition occurs between religious groups" (p. 567). In practice, many Christians report that their religious beliefs and spiritual practices are actually enriched and strengthened by engaging others with different beliefs (Bryant, 2005; Eck, 2003).

MOVING FORWARD

The role of religion in both higher education and the workplace cannot be ignored (Hicks, 2009). Business schools and other disciplines within higher education are often focused on professional preparation and aligning with state and independent accreditation authorities (Grubb & Lazerson, 2005; Waggoner, 2011). Thielen (2011) discusses how American higher education's need for federal and private funding led to a steady separation from alignment with the Christian church. In modern universities, issues of faith and spirituality are frequently overlooked, leaving Christians ill-prepared for higher education or the workplace (Hicks, 2009). However, religion and spirituality has found its way into the Academy of Management (as an important work-related academic association) in the last two decades in the form of the growing Management, Spirituality, and Religion Interest Group. The impact of this greater interest in the role of religion and spirituality in the workplace is yet to be fully acknowledged as substantial or impactful on most business school curricula (Grzeda & Assogbavi, 2011; Williams & Allen, 2014). The transition from the privatized age of religion and spirituality to an openly plural society is not complete.

Marx, Neal, Manz, and Manz (2008) emphasize the need for higher education to include religious literacy preparation for future organizational leaders, but there is scant literature addressing this problem from a Christian perspective. Miller (2006) points out that many Christians struggle with the Sunday–Monday gap, where their learning in the church is not easily applied to their jobs. Miller also points to a lack of interest and skill amongst clergy regarding the workplace as a unique context. In addition, not all young Christians completing their higher education will add religion or theology as electives to their program of study, even if these courses specifically addressed faith issues in the workplace. Collectively these points highlight an unfulfilled need to address Christian conduct in the religiously and spiritually diverse workplace, particularly if Christians choose to be a positive influence, to convey the Biblical notion of love for one's neighbors, and to integrate with society. Alternatively, Christians lose the opportunity to teach their own adherents to be a positive, acknowledged, respected, competent, and hospitable influence in the workplace.

Spiritual and religious beliefs are an essential aspect of people's identities (Ewest, 2015; Seul, 1999) and opportunities for religious expression and inclusion in the workplace are not only possible but necessary (Hicks, 2003). Religious diversity in society and the workplace are largely a *fact* of 21st century America. Eck (2003) and Willard (1992) even suggest that this diversity may be divinely intended. Together these assumptions draw attention to the need for new insights on the Christian role in the workplace and preparation for that role. While Christian higher education and the faith at work movement (e.g., Christian peer mentoring or support groups) might encourage and educate a percentage of Christians entering the workplace (Miller, 2006), the lack of preparation seems considerable. This need is underscored by the continuous unfolding of globalization and its impacts, resulting in exposure to and influence from other religions and systems of thought, as well as the burgeoning influence of the media powered by continuous advances in technology. With the Christian gospel mandate to be a light in the world (a beacon of hope and positive influence), *learning to* work in a culturally and religiously diverse America, and world, is a poignant challenge.

PROPOSALS

The new American landscape is distinctly pluralistic, but that does not automatically prevent Christians from expressing their faith in higher education or the workplace. It does, however, require that this be done in new and relevant ways. As Eck (2003) notes, many aspects of Christian culture were created for the needs of the time, allowing opportunity for new practices and traditions to be invented (Rolheiser, 2014). Early Christians were not a majority within their communities (Eck, 2003), yet Jesus and his followers began an entire movement in a pluralistic context without the weight of Christian traditions and doctrines that exist today. Ways of being Christian in the workplace must be discovered (or rediscovered), contemplated, and shared. Such adaptation to a more plural and global context need not be a hostile venture (Hicks, 2003) to clearly demarcate the boundaries of Christianity from others groups (Eck, 2003), but could rather be characterized and united by the faith, hope, and love exemplified by Jesus as the center of Christian faith rather than the wall between faiths.

Christians, as a diverse group differentiated by their various denominations, practices, and doctrines, are unlikely to present a united perspective on how to prepare Christians for the pluralistic workplace. The proposals below are not an attempt to promote a unified vision for the Christian response, but rather to highlight the need for Christians to think about their particular response.

Awareness.   Christians are called to continually renew their minds (Romans 12:2) with greater awareness of God's will. Greater Christian awareness of Biblically based principles for interfaith engagement and appropriate attitudes (e.g., hospitality) toward foreigners, nonbelievers, and those who believe differently is essential. Such awareness includes knowledge of the Christian religion and of other religions, avoiding furthering triumphalism and giving in to the "patterns of this world" such as divisiveness and ethno-centrism. In this context, Christians center their identity more on Jesus Christ than on Christianity, taking on his openhearted and loving attitudes and behaviors in response to nonbelievers. Awareness includes knowledge and skill in Christian spiritual practices for drawing close to God, as well as real understanding of other religions, knowledge of the Constitutional right to freedom of religion, and an understanding of changing demographics of the country.

Jesus, in the gospels, did not limit or alter his behavior for those nominally classified as being of other religions, but "freely and boldly crossed the barriers than might separate one group from another" (Eck, 2003, p. 93). Jesus's words (John 14:6) "I am the way" are frequently used to set Christianity apart from other religions, to emphasize its exclusivity, but as Eck argues, Jesus's words in the context were intended to comfort his anxious followers, letting them know the way to heaven, rather than to condemn other people. Overcoming the identity threats implicit in living and working with non-Christians is not possible without a deeper understanding of the character of Christ. From this perspective, awareness does not further fear, but rather focuses upon understanding the context American Christians are in and the opportunities for faith expression within this context. Eck (2003) highlights this notion in proposing a new disposition to pluralism:

> What is new is our sharply heightened awareness of religious diversity in every part of our world and the fact that today everyone ... encounters and needs to understand people and faiths other than their own ... our religious ghettos are gone or almost gone, and the question of how we respond to religious difference is unavoidable.... Diversity, of course, is not pluralism. Diversity is simply a fact, but what will we make of that fact, individually or as a culture? Will it arouse new forms of ethnic and religious chauvinism and isolation? Or might it lead to a genuine pluralism, a positive and interactive interpretation of plurality? (pp. 42–43)

As Eck rightly notes, Christians can either chose to shape pluralism or wage war with it. However, waging war with the unfamiliar makes little sense when the Christian faith is grounded in love, attitudes, and behaviors based on the Biblical teachings of Jesus Christ.

Interfaith Dialogue.   Humans have both voices and ears. In a new age of pluralism, there is an opportunity to represent Christ through hospitality (Rine, 2013) and mutuality, but this is not a one-way relationship with nonbelievers. "Today the language of dialogue has come to express the kind of two-way discourse that is essential to relationship, not domination" (Eck, 2003, p. 19). Hence, there is an argument to be made for training and educating Christian workers in interfaith dialogue and ethics from a foundation of Christian values and traditions. Hicks's (2003) *respectful pluralism* is especially relevant here, highlighting that in a multifaith workplace there must be a presumption of inclusion (people's right to dignity, respect, and expression of their identity), and the supporting norms of nondegradation (avoidance of acts or speech that disrespect others), noncoercion (avoidance of persuasion via threat or force, both implicit and explicit), and nonestablishment (immorality of institutionally imposed spiritual or religious position, even if a generic or common spirituality).

As already suggested, the skills of interfaith dialogue were less relevant in a homogenous Christian society, limiting the extent to which previous generations passed these skills to younger generations. We propose that these skills can be taught and learned in secular *and* faith-based learning contexts, when grounded in respectful pluralism. When so many Christians are educated through nonsectarian and secular institutions, it seems desirable to find a form of negotiated religious and spiritual education that Christians can live with. Furthermore there are many opportunities for students and workers to learn these interfaith skills through community projects, working with other faith groups toward shared goals such as helping community members and groups in need. Student clubs and societies can also play a role in this preparation through interfaith outreach and collaboration.

Understanding Faith Expression. Together with Hick's (2010) respectful pluralism, Miller and Ewest's (2011) *Integration Box* provides a powerful guide for Christian behavior in the workplace. The Integration Box, similar to Thomas's (1996) concept of *sacred pathways*, emphasizes that religion and spirituality can be expressed in many ways in work and the community. Some Christians are burdened with the perception that the only (or primary) faith expression they are duty-bound to is proselytizing. However, this view sometimes excludes a host of other forms of Christian faith expression key to collaborating in service projects with other faith groups, advocating for ethical behavior in organizations (and by organizations) in the cause of social justice, and living lives enriched by deep faith and prayer through excellence in one's work. Knowledge of the multifaceted nature of the Christian faith expression empowers Christians to use their talents in the workplace. Further study is also needed of Christian workplace leaders who have found constructive ways to express their faith in the workplace, providing models for current and future generations, beyond the negative cases which make their way into the news (Hicks in Allen, Williams, & DiLauro, 2015).

Advocacy. Christians can also participate in advocacy in organizations, higher education, and society that seeks to create equal and positive relations among religious groups, while preserving the right to express faith and religious identity in constructive ways. For example, in higher education Rine (2013) proposes that Christian higher education institutions take a fallibilist stance (an understanding that knowledge of ultimate reality is always incomplete, provisional, and uncertain) that is theologically anchored in Christianity, but inclusivist and humble. This exemplifies a form of Christian advocacy that is firm in its core beliefs, but aware of the limits of knowledge and hospitable to others. As Waggoner (2011) argues, both religious and nonreligious voices must be heard. One practical way in which this can be encouraged is that Christians, like all Americans, can benefit from a greater understanding of the First Amendment and how the Constitution protects and enables freedom of religion and religious expression, beyond the simplistic understanding that seems to pervade and polarize society. Purposeful dialogue on the legal and social enactment of this amendment is necessary to maintain a peaceful and productive society. Christian advocacy for freedom of religious and spiritual choice and expression would create a society that all religions can live in and would include the creation of faith-safe and faith-friendly organizations (Miller & Ewest, 2015) and higher education institutions.

CONCLUSION

Higher education and the collective church have a role to play in developing positive intergroup relationships and respectful, productive workplaces and communities. These roles include Christian faculty in both Christian and secular higher education, Christian students in secular higher education (including Christian student associations), Christian managers and leaders (including those participating in the faith at work movement), Christian authors and researchers, Christian higher education institutions, and the church. Each has a role to play in a multi-pronged approach to the delineated challenges.,

Drawing upon the literature in management, religion and spirituality, social psychology, religion in higher education, and Christian religious literature, we have explored the need for a Christian response to the diverse religious and cultural workplace in America. Preparation for religiously and spiritually diverse colleges, universities, and workplaces should not be taken for granted or overlooked. We have also proposed ways to move forward in addressing these issues. However, faith is also needed in response to the challenges presented in this chapter, faith that Christians, as has happened many times in history, will hear the voice of God when change is needed, and believe that these challenges can be overcome.

REFERENCES

Allen, S., & Williams, P. (2017). Navigating the study of executive leaders' spirituality: André Delbecq's journey. *Journal of Management Inquiry, 26*(2), 216–224.
Allen, S., Williams, P., & DiLauro, M. (2015). *Leadership, religion, and spirituality* [Video file]. Retrieved from https://youtu.be/v7Aio3jl0Z8

Amos, D. (2016, September 14). N.J. church group to resettle Syrian refugee family with special needs. Retrieved from: http://www.npr.org/2016/09/14/493881290/n-j-church-group-to-resettle-syrian-refugee-family-with-special-needs

Astin, A. W., Astin, H. S., & Lindholm, J. A. (2010). *Cultivating the spirit: How college can enhance students' inner lives.* San Francisco, CA: Jossey-Bass.

Bennett-Alexander, D. D., & Hartman, L. P. (2015). *Employment law for business* (8th ed.). New York, NY: McGraw Hill.

Benefiel, M., Fry, L. W., & Geigle, D. (2014). Spirituality and religion in the workplace: History, theory, and research. *Psychology of Religion and Spirituality, 6*(3), 175.

Bosch, D. J. (1991). *Transforming mission: Paradigm shifts in theology of mission.* Maryknoll, NY: Orbis Books.

Bradley, J., & Kauanui, S. (2003). Comparing spirituality on three Southern California college campuses. *Journal of Organizational Change Management, 16*(4), 448–462.

Bryant, A. N. (2005). Evangelicals on campus: An exploration of culture, faith, and college life. *Religion & Education,* 30, 1–25. http://dx.doi.org/10.1080/15507394.2005.10012355

Chaves, M. (2011). *American religion: Contemporary trends.* Princeton, NJ: Princeton University Press.

Eck, D. L. (2003). *Encountering God: A spiritual journey from Bozeman to Banaras* (2nd ed.). Boston, MA: Beacon Press.

Ewest, T. G. (2015). Sociological, psychological and historical perspectives on the reemergence of religion and spirituality within organizational life. *Journal of Religion and Business Ethics, 3*(2), 1–14.

Folger, J. P., Poole, M. S., & Stutman, R. K. (2013). *Working through conflict: Strategies for relationships, groups, and organizations* (7th ed.). Boston, MA: Pearson.

Foster, R. (1998). Celebration of discipline: The path to spiritual growth (3rd ed.). New York NY: HarperCollins.

Franz, R. S., & Wong, K. L. (2005). Spirituality and management: A wider lens (A comment on D. Steingard's "Spiritually informed management"). *Journal of Management Inquiry, 14*(3), 247–250.

Gonzalez, J. L. (2010). *The story of Christianity: The early church to the dawn of the reformation* (Vol. 1, 2nd ed.). New York, NY: HarperCollins.

Grzeda, M., & Assogbavi, T. (2011). Spirituality in management education and development: Toward an authentic transformation. *Journal of American Academy of Business, 16*(2), 238–244.

Grubb, W. N., & Lazerson, M. (2005). Vocationalism in higher education: The triumph of the education gospel. *Journal of Higher Education, 76*(1), 1–25.

Hicks, D. A. (2003). Religion in the workplace: Pluralism, spirituality, leadership. Cambridge, England: Cambridge University Press.

Hicks, D. A. (2009). *With God on all sides: Leadership in a devout and diverse America.* New York, NY: Oxford University Press.

Hogg, M. A., Adelman, J. R., & Blagg, R. D. (2010). Religion in the face of uncertainty: An uncertainty-identity theory account of religiousness. *Personality and Social Psychology Review, 14*(1), 72–83.

Jacobsen, R. H., & Jacobsen, D. (2012). *No longer invisible: Religion in university education.* New York, NY: Oxford University Press.

Kelly, M. L. (2016, October 16). What you need to know about the Somali refugee community in Kansas. Retrieved from: http://www.npr.org/2016/10/16/498135766/what-you-need-to-know-about-the-somali-refugee-community-in-kansas

Lentz, R. E. (2005). Jesus, the Enlightenment, and teaching world history: The struggles of an evangelical scholar. *Religion and Education, 32*(2), 46–64.

Lindholm, J. A., & Astin, H. S. (2006). Understanding the "interior" life of faculty: How important is spirituality? *Religion and Education, 33*(2), 64–90.

Lotz, D. (2003). Christian higher education in the twenty-first century and the clash of civilizations. In D. V. Henry & B. R. Agee (Eds.), *Faithful learning and the Christian scholarly vocation* (pp. 158–175). Grand Rapids, MI: Eerdmans.

Lund Dean, K., Safranski, S. R., & Lee, E. S. (2014). Religious accommodation in the workplace: Understanding religious identity threat and workplace behaviors in legal disputes. *Employee Responsibilities and Rights Journal, 26*(2), 75–94.

Marx, R., Neal, J., Manz, K., & Manz, C. (2008). Teaching about spirituality and work: Experiential exercises for management educators. In J. Biberman & L. Tischler (Eds.), *Spirituality in business: Theory, practice, and future directions* (pp. 203–215). New York, NY: Palgrave Macmillan.

Merino, S. (2010). Religious diversity in a "Christian nation": The effects of theological exclusivity and interreligious contact on the acceptance of religious diversity. *Journal for the Scientific Study of Religion, 49*(2), 231–246.

Miller, D. W. (2006). *God at work: The history and promise of the faith at work movement.* New York, NY: Oxford.

Miller, D. W., & Ewest, T. (2011, August). *The present state of workplace spirituality: A literature review considering context, theory, and measurement assessment.* Paper presented at the Academy of Management annual meeting, San Antonio, TX.

Miller, D. W., & Ewest, T. (2013). The integration box (TIB): An individual and institutional faith, religion, and spirituality at work assessment tool. In J. Neal (Ed.), *Handbook of faith and spirituality in the workplace: Emerging research and practice* (pp. 403–418). New York, NY: Springer.

Miller, D. W., & Ewest, T. (2015). A new framework for analyzing organizational workplace religion and spirituality. *Journal of Management, Spirituality & Religion, 12*(4), 305–328.

Mitroff, I. I., & Denton, E. A. (1999). *A spiritual audit of corporate America.* San Francisco, CA: Jossey-Bass.

Mixon, S. L., Lyon, L., & Beaty, M. D. (2004). Secularization and national universities: The effect of religious identity on academic reputation. *The Journal of Higher Education, 75*(4), 400–419.

Peace, J. H., Rose, O. N., & Mobley, G. (2012). *My neighbor's faith.* Maryknoll, NY: Orbis Books.

Pew Research Center. (2015). *America's changing religious landscape.* Washington, DC: Author.

Pope Francis. (2013, September 10). Pope: Proclaim Jesus without fear, shame or triumphalism. Retrieved from: http://www.romereports.com/2013/09/10/pope-proclaim-jesus-without-fear-shame-or-triumphalism

Rine, P. J. (2013). Christian college persistence in the postmodern turn. In A. Bryant Rockenbach & M. J. Mayhew (Eds.), *Spirituality in college students' lives: Translating research into practice* (pp. 69–87). New York, NY: Routledge.

Rolheiser, R. (2014). *The holy longing: The search for a Christian spirituality.* New York, NY: Image Books.

Seifert, T. (2007). Understanding Christian privilege: Managing the tensions of spiritual plurality. *About Campus 12*(2), 10–18.

Seul, J. R. (1999). 'Ours is the way of god': Religion, identity, and intergroup conflict. *Journal of Peace Research, 36*(5), 553–569.

Shahjahan, R. (2005). Spirituality in the academy: Reclaiming from the margins and evoking a transformative way of knowing the world. *International Journal of Qualitative Studies in Education, 18*(6), 685–711.

Tanyi, R. A. (2002). Towards clarification of the meaning of spirituality. *Journal of Advanced Nursing, 39*(5), 500–509.

Theodore, P. A. (2010). Neither establishing nor prohibiting: Exploring some of the complexities of taking a neutral stance toward religion in public schools. *Journal of Philosophy and History of Education, 60*, 157–160.

Thielen, J. R. (2011). *A history of American higher education* (2nd ed.). Baltimore, MD: The Johns Hopkins University Press.

U.S. Department of Education, National Center for Education Statistics. (2016). Table 303.90. Fall enrollment and number of degree-granting postsecondary institutions, by control and religious affiliation of institution: Selected years, 1980 through 2014. *Digest of Education Statistics* (2016 ed.). Retrieved from https://nces.ed.gov/pubs2016/2016014.pdf

Vogel, L. J. (2000). Reckoning with the spiritual lives of adult educators. *New Directions for Adult & Continuing Education, 85*, 17–27.

Waggoner, M. D. (Ed.). (2011). *Sacred and secular tensions in higher education: Connecting parallel universities.* New York, NY: Routledge.

Willard, D. A. (1992). *Being a Christian in a pluralistic society.* Nashville, TN: Southern Baptist Convention.

Williams, P., & Allen, S. (2014). Faculty perspectives on the inclusion of spirituality topics in nonsectarian leadership and management education programs. *International Journal of Management Education, 12*(3) 293–303.

PART IV

CONCLUSION

CHAPTER 14

SECULAR AND THE SACRED

Tracing Their Dimensionality and Tension

Timothy Ewest
Houston Baptist University
Visiting Research Collaborator Princeton University

Jean Vanier is best known as the founder of the L'Arche, an international network of communities for people with intellectual disabilities. The vision for L'Arche was born while spending time with Father Thomas, the chaplain of the Val Fleuri in Trosly-Breuil. Father Thomas brought Vanier along to a small institution, the Val Fleuri, that welcomed about 30 men with intellectual disabilities. From this experience Vanier was awakened to his compassion for these men. Later he was prompted to return to France and begin a journey of compassion and friendship with two men with similar disabilities, whom he lived with and cared for. Today, there are 151 communities spread over five continents, with more than 5,000 members, known as L'Arche International Communities. When pressed for what motivates him, Vanier responded, "The point of inclusion is the belief that each of us is important, unique, sacred, in fact" (Vanier, 2008, p. 95). Vanier, is one example of how the reality of the sacred works as a motivator in the lives of Christians, directing their individual actions, their organizational actions, and ultimately creates a social force.

Faith and Work: Christian Perspectives, Research, and Insights Into the Movement
pp. 247–263
Copyright © 2018 by Information Age Publishing
247

This chapter considers the two forces of the secular and the sacred, which have been recognized by numerous scholars (e.g., Berger, 1969; Talyor, 2008). Specific attention is given to the sacred/secular tension described by Inglehart and Norris (2004). The chapter then considers the multiple dimensions of the secular force and alternatively the dimensions of the sacred force. The chapter also examines the sacred themes in this book using a simple content analysis and these themes are then compared to the secular force themes presented within. The chapter resolves by providing a brief suggestion on future research to be explored by scholars.

SOCIAL FORCES OF THE SECULAR AND SACRED

The research by management and organizational scholars typically emphasizes analysis of individuals and organizations. But, what is often overlooked is the importance of larger societal movements and forces which are facts in their own right. Sociological methods elicit an alternative perspective within the social sciences by generally avoiding proscriptions and is generally typified by being descriptive in nature (Steensland et al., 2000). Sociological methods can be used to capture broad phenomena within society. Forces within society are created from the interaction of individuals, organizations and social structures which have effects on society and are effected by society (Giddens, 1986). The need for the inculcation of social sciences in management research is suggested by Grant (2005) who states that researchers should build "on sociological understandings of the sacred, culture, and organizations that are more attuned to the cultural aspect of meaning-making" (p. 2).

Social forces are driven by large-scale social events, values, and processes that convey deep meaning which are pursued by organizations, individuals, and societies, yet may be undetected by participants (Rosenberg, 2015, p.145). The larger meaning found within societal forces are the motivational impetus for individuals and organizations, even if these organizations and individuals are geographically and ideologically alienated. Researchers like Durkheim (1994) argued that society was a vast organism which cultivates a group mind. These social forces are seen most distinctly, after the fact in historical movements, and even though history is open to hermeneutical illusions, and is salient, as history it is none the less factual (Eliade, 2013).

For example, Norris and Inglehart (2011) used data from the World Values Survey (WVS) and from it identified two social forces in greater society: the sacred and the secular. The World Values Survey was conducted between the years 1981–2015 and represented values from over 100 countries, with over 400,000 respondents considering 14 thematic

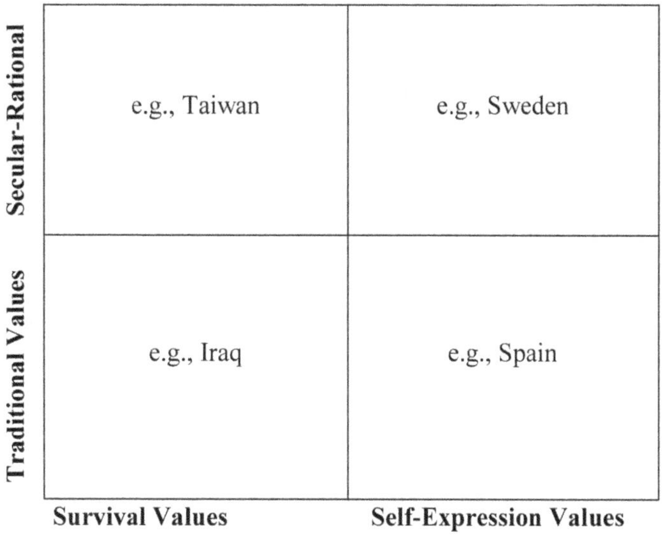

	Survival Values	Self-Expression Values
Secular-Rational	e.g., Taiwan	e.g., Sweden
Traditional Values	e.g., Iraq	e.g., Spain

Source: Adapted from Inglehart and Welzel (2010).

Figure 14.1.   Inglehart-Welzel cultural map.

categories (World Values Survey Association, 2015). Inglehart and Welzel (2010) analyzed the data from the World Values Survey and created a cultural map of the world as a means to codify and describe these expressed values. Their analysis depicted tensions between two cultural value dimensions, (1) traditional values verses secular-rational values and (2) survival values verses self-expression values. Graphically, sacred and secular values run along the "Y" axis and survival verses self-expression values run along the "X" axis, indicating that nations have core sets of values that drive their behavior, even if organizations and individuals are largely alienated from each other. See Figure 14.1.

Norris and Inglehart (2011) believe that religious individuals without conferring, collectivity take corresponding stances on social issues that align with their religious beliefs such as rejecting abortion, euthanasia, divorce and suicide. The sacred consists of those individuals who self-identify as adhering to a world faith tradition, and the secular are regarded as those who display no such adherence. Most importantly, this descriptive analysis is an attestation to the social forces of sacred and secular, these social forces also set the context for belief.

Table 14.1.   Values in Tension

	Traditional Values	*Secular-Rational*
Religious orientation	Emphasis is placed on the importance of religious belief, on parent child-child ties, respect for authority, the importance of religion, parent-child ties, deference to authority and traditional family values.	Values have the opposite preferences to the traditional values. These societies place less emphasis on religion, traditional family values and authority.
Social issues	People who embrace these values also reject divorce, abortion, euthanasia and suicide.	Divorce, abortion, euthanasia. and suicide are seen as relatively acceptable.

Source: Inglehart and Welzel (2010).

THE SECULAR

The word secular is derived from the Latin word *saeculum*, intending to indicate "the world" as opposed to "the church." The original use of the word is ascribed to Roman Catholic priests during the middle ages that would serve outside the church (Kosmin & Keysar, 2007).

There is an ongoing debate among sociologists concerning to what degree global cultures are secularizing (Nandy, 2007). The debate considers secularization to be determined by the amount of individuals within a society who self-identify with one of the world's major religions. The issue is compounded by areas of the world which have experienced a decline in religious adherence (e.g., Europe) over and against regions of the world where religion is flourishing (e.g., Middle East). Moreover, there are regions where religion is stable but individuals are less willing to continue to self-identify with what they consider(ed) to be their faith, because their judgment regarding social issues has changed and are now different than the traditionally accepted view held by their faith tradition (e.g., evolution). But ultimately this discussion generally pertains to religious adherence. The "level of self-identified adherence" which demonstrates the presence of the sacred, determines either the abatement or growth of religion in a national region. And, while this measure is important, it only recognizes one dimension of secularization.

Kosmin and Keysar (2007) outline the aspects of the secular force in society. Secularity is a binary typology, referring to "Individual actors' personal behavior and identification with secular ideas and traditions as modes of consciousness" (Kosmin & Keysar, 2007, p. 1). Secularism, involves "organizations and legal constructs that reflect the institutional expression of the secular in a nation's political realm and public life" (p. 1). Being able to understand these larger expressions is difficult to qualify and its global perspectives are even more challenging. Kosmin and Keysar also provide a further distinction within secularism and secularity suggesting an individual or organization can either be more committed to secularism, and thus referred to as *hard* or alternatively less committed and be *soft*.

Charles Taylor (2008), in his work *A Secular Age*, suggests some of the same ideas regarding the presence of secularization within individual, organizational, and societal life, but adds an additional category. Taylor suggests the idea of the concept secular has changed based on its evolution semantically within its historical context, but each usage and corresponding definition can still be operative today.

The first usage of secular, in classic or medieval era pertained to choices individuals made regarding service to the sacred or other worldly realm, or service to the temporal or earthly realm. During this epoch, the thought of not believing in God was not in the realm of possibility, for the world was enchanted, where mental illness was seen as demon possession (Smith, 2014). Here, the reference or context individuals had for defining and framing the secular was the natural world. They regarded the natural world as a realm that traced the spiritual or the other world, the heavenly realm. To deny the presence of the heavenly realm within the context of the natural world, would be tantamount to heresy, or paganism. Paganism, was not the absence of God in the world, instead it was the inscription of world to a false god.

This is captured by the medieval theologian Saint Augustine (2010) in his work, *The City of God*, which outlined two possible societies for humanity, one being the "city of man" and the other being the "city of god." The book was written as an apology to defend Roman Christians who were blamed for the fall of Rome, believing Christianity aided in the weakening of Rome. Augustine argues that the city of man was comprised of individuals who are damned, who worshiped false gods which cannot come to aid or protect their followers (e.g., Rome), and were contrasted by the city of god, wherein individuals believe in God's providential control of history in the world, and ever present engagement and care for the world (Conybeare, 2014).

Taylor's (2008) second tracing of the semantical use of the concept depicted by the word secular begins with the enlightenment era. Here secular refers to a neutral space or an areligious space or point of view. Likened to the work of Inglehart and Norris's (2004) definition of secularity, the secular, or secular space, is rationally oriented, and therefore the rational perspective disenchants the world of the religious. This is necessary since religious beliefs, have enchanted notions of the world which interfere with modernization; so the tendency for modern people is to avoid or marginalize anything which interferes with modern advancement (Berger, 1969). The secular space is where all or some of religious expression is subdued, because religion contains its own unique sense making (Weick, 1995) which to be useful, must be in line with the modern understanding, presented in enlightenment perspective. This is a challenge since religion is a part of a person's core identity (Emmons, 2003) and is a vital component for personal sense making. And, for the most part the central claims of the church could not stand against empirical claims (e.g. Death is to be welcomed). Therefore, the rational disenchanted person and correspondingly the organization both desire a decline in, or moderation of religion, understanding religion as not necessary in organizational and societal life (Berger, 1969; King 2012; Wilson, 1982); known as secularization theory (e.g. Swatos & Christiano, 1999).

Today, secularization theory is largely unsupported, with the majority of sociologists now understanding that there is no tendency in greater society to repress religion, and religion within society continues to grow and is an influence in society as it continues to modernize (Casanova, 2011; Nandy, 2007). One well known example, is the often cited work of Casanova (2011) who refuted the idea that religion had retreated to a private sphere, because the public secular sphere had caused it to retreat. Miller (2008) also suggested that faith was present in the workplace, being present in institutional life.

Yet, while it is widely accepted that religion is still influential in modern life, organizations appear to be slow to embrace this reality, believing that religion is still to be excluded from the modern workplace (Ashforth & Vaidyanath, 2002; King 2012; Wilson, 1982). Kelly (2008) states,

> The prevailing assumption in business, as in most contemporary activities in America, is that there must be a wall of separation between a person's beliefs and the workplace. It is assumed that this wall is required because we do not all share the same faith-based worldview. (p. 51)

It is this understanding of the secular from Taylor's second semantic use of secularization that is utilized by most Academy of Management researchers; whereby the worker has been asked to keep the religious part of themselves at home, because it could potentially interfere with work. Moreover, it may also be the grounds for the investment by researchers into the language and concepts of spirituality, wherein much spirituality focuses on finding the higher self, without reference to the transcendent God (Capra & Luisi, 2014) and thus can more readily frame itself within enlightenment reasoning (Sutcliffe & Bowman, 2000; Wedemeyer & Jue, 2002).

The final semantic use of the word secular traced by Taylor (2008) is where religious belief becomes one option among others and thus belief in God becomes contestable—which indicates that the conditions of a person believing in God has changed. Today, there is a move away from a society where a person's belief in God is unchallenged or not problematic, to a time when belief in God is only one option, and not the easiest one to embrace. These shifts in usage and corresponding understandings have also allowed for the emergence of the individual to exclusively embrace humanism, which allow for a person to have no transcendent goals beyond human flourishing, removing all together the "enchantment" of the other world (Smith, 2014).

The freedom to choose if one believes or not may be alluded to in a recent survey conducted by the Pew Foundation (Gallup, 1999) concerning America's religious landscape. The survey found a new category emerged which they regarded as the "nones—those who choose not to affiliate with any religions tradition, even though they profess a belief in God, presently represent one fifth of the U.S. public" (Funk & Smith, 2012, p. 14).

This survey of the concept of the secular in this chapter intends to provide an overview of one of the social forces within society, the secular force. While Inglehart and Welzel's (2010) (see Figure 14.1) conceptual model is helpful to understand the relative position of individuals and corresponding their aggregate placement regarding adherence to secular or sacred, it only addresses one aspect or dimension of the secular. Moreover, none of these theories of secular are comprehensive, identifying individual, organizational and societal impacts. See Table 14.2.

Researchers have been observing the phenomena of secularism, identifying its dynamics and also calling attention to its force in marginalizing religion, with the intention of engaging, identifying, and speaking against this force, thus creating space for the sacred. But, research may be better served by not simply identifying and addressing what is a counter to people of faith, but also to consider the facts of a sacred existence found in people of faith. These considerations may call attention to the reality of the formative and motivational contribution religion has in the lives of individuals, organizations and society—the force of the sacred.

THE SACRED

Recognized by Inglehart and Welzel (2010) among others, a vital component of Christian belief, as depicted in theology, scriptures and tradition, is the concept of the sacred. Sacred, from the Latin word *sacer*, means something which has a dedicated purpose or something that is set apart.

Table 14.2.   Concepts of Secular

Concept	Author	Definition	Individual	Organizational	Societal
Secular-rational	Inglehart & Welzel, 2010	Secular are regarded as those who display no such adherence religion	Yes	No	No
Secularism	Kosmin & Keysar, 2007	Organizations and legal constructs that reflect the institutional expression of the secular in a nation's political realm and public life	No	Yes	Yes
Secularity	Kosmin & Keysar, 2007	A binary typology, referring to individual actors' personal behavior and identification with secular ideas	Yes	No	No
Secularism 1	Taylor, 2008	Service to the sacred or other worldly realm or service to the temporal or earthly realm	Yes	No	No
Secularism 2	Taylor, 2008	A neutral space or an areligious space or point of view, is rationally oriented, and therefore the perspective disenchants the world of the religious.	No	Yes	Yes
Secularism 3	Taylor, 2008	Societal context that a belief in God as one option among many and not the easiest choice to make	Yes	No	Yes
Secularization theory	Numerous (e.g., Swatos and Christiano, 1999)	Organizations desire a decline in or moderation of religion, understanding religion as not necessary in organizational and societal life	No	Yes	No

This term is similar to another commonly used word, *holiness*, which is derived from the Greek word, *hagios* (ἅγιος), meaning different, separate or other (Johnson, 1882; McCann, 2008). While there may be some subtle nuances in usage, generally both of these terms are used interchangeably (McCann, 2008). The idea of sacredness as being a central component for the religiously devoted is recognized by scholarship (Durkheim, 1994). Applied to the life of the religious, it connotes an object, activity, belief or person strongly associated with divinity and thus being worthy of respect, since the object identifies the transcendent or God.

The usage of sacred in theology and Christian belief directly refers to God's otherness, but is also applied to Christian practice and personal development. Christians are intended to be "holy as God is holy" (1 Peter 1:16), to store up treasures in heaven (Matthew 6:20) and to be cognoscente of their heavenly citizenship (Philippians 3:20). Finally there is an application of items and activities as being set apart in their design and to be used in worship for God alone (e.g., Sabbath, Communion Wine). God, Christian behavior, and practices that are set apart as different from what is typical of natural existence, or the immanent, are regarded as sacred, or part of the transcendent.

Ironically, many academics define sacred using apophatic techniques; sacred is not secular. Durkheim (1994) defines sacred as those things which are unusual and they are set apart from the normal routines of life as special events. Berger (1969) defines sacred as

> a quality of mysterious and awesome power, other than man and yet related to him, which is believed to reside in certain objects of experience. The quality may be attributed to natural or art icicle objects, to animals or to men or the obectivations of human culture.... The quality may finally be embodied in sacred beings. (p. 57)

What is of importance, is to understand how faith can be a motivator for behavior (Graafland, Kaptein, & Mazereeuw-van der Duijn Schouten, 2007), can be used as a sense making apparatus to make sense of the world (Weick, 1995) and also as to a means to form personal identity (Emmons, 2003; Ewest, 2017). The person's identity, including their religious identity, is formed within a community, the interactions within an organization, and society which reciprocates and impresses values back on the individual. This was seen early by Weber (Swedberg, 2009) and later by Lambert (2009) and Giddens (1986). And, if Christian faith is used as a motivator, it is sacred in that it addresses and conveys an interest and belief in the transcendent or God and thus is unlike other forms of reasoning. For example, Gert (1998) defines multiple ways in which Christian sense-making is contestable with the world around it, such as welcoming death as a desirable end state.

There is existing tension between the sacred and the secular forces, as depicted by research which traces individual, organizational, and societal movements. The tension has also been addressed in theology, which typically frames the conversation using the transcendence of God, verses his imminence within God's created order. Christian theology has endeavored to seek ways to reconcile the sacred God and the created human (Barth, 1960), or culture and the Christian faith (Niebuhr, 1956) or the citizenship of humans to a secular realm, or the heavenly realm (Saint Augustine).

THEMES IN THE BOOK

Following the depiction of the social forces, the sacred and the secular, by Inglehart and Norris (2004), a simple exploratory content analysis was done on the chapters submitted in this volume to determine what aspects of the sacred or uniquely Christian dimensions are commonly found within the book, and then align those sacred dimensions to the secular dimensions presented earlier. Rather than codifying themes based on editorial perspective, the summary is guided by qualitative research techniques.

While primarily exploratory, word frequency was conducted on the chapters in this submitted volume to guide in determining the themes and general trends within this work. Word frequency is largely an inaccurate measure of trends, since it does not account for exact denotations within word groups as they are contextualized within the sentence (Rosenberg, Schnurr, & Oxman, 1990). Here, some margin of error exists since theologies determine semantic use. For example, communion for Catholic and Orthodox is regarded as a transcendent sacramental act (Cluster 8), but regarded as a symbolic religious act by Protestants (Cluster 3). There are also issues regarding a lack of synonyms increasing word usage. For example, the word "chaplin," may not have an appropriate synonym since it is contracted in its meaning or in some cases given a specified meaning. Also, the simple analysis is limited to the findings within this book and not directly transferable to another context.

However, word frequency should not be readily dismissed, since it is recognized to be valid research method of content analysis as a means to initially detect the "greatest concerns" (Stemler, 2001, p.2) and has found applications in linguistic research which suggests that words frequently used within communities establish demand patterns (Popescu, 2009). When these ideas are applied to this book, it would suggest that this work could create demand for future similar research, or these scholars may have been responding to demands and thus indicative of larger social forces. For example, research by Vasconcellos-Silva, Carvalho, and Lucena (2013) used word frequency to determine which communities were developing awareness about Hepatitis C treatment within Brazilian communities, as a way to understand present and future demand.

METHOD

All documents were loaded into AtlasTi, with the reference sections removed from the documents. The word frequency tool in AtlasTi was used which determined a total world count ($N = 73,192$), and the frequencies of all words in the book displayed in both occurrence and percentage. To conduct the simple content analysis, words were selected based on (1) their frequency of occurrence within the book, (2) the association they had with the Christian faith, (3) additional terms associated or synonymous within the forming cluster theme that were included to provide dimensionality, (4) words were placed within a cluster based on their use within the context of their linguistic intent and finally, (5) definitions were applied to clusters based on contextual usage.

RESULTS

Based on the research method, words clustered around eight concepts, from which eight themes were determined to be central to the book, or being of greatest concern. Table 14.3 depicts the most frequent word used, the word which initiated forming the cluster is denoted with an asterisk, the associated terms in the cluster and within the parenthesis the frequency of occurrence.

The result is that the clusters provide a general orientation, or a tracing of the understandings of the sacred as a social force within this book. Eight orientations emerged pertaining to the concept of "the sacred" from the word frequently study, and were presented as general themes, and then definitions were applied which suited both the context of usage within the book and Berger's (1969) definition of sacred. See Table 14.4. These eight clusters are regarded as the various dimensional aspects of the sacred depicted in the research contained in this book.

Finally, the themes of sacred explored in this book, were mapped onto the various dimensions of secularity described earlier within this chapter. Each of the seven secular dimensions described in this book are further

**Table 14.3.   Word Frequency
From Chapters Denoting the Sacred (N = 73,192)**

Cluster 1 Belief (n = 960)	Cluster 2 Meaning (n = 520)	Cluster 3 Religious Acts (n = 485)	Cluster 4 Religious Persons (n = 328)
Ethics, (109); belief, beliefs, believe, believed, believes, believing (183); eschatological (10); faith (547*); forgiveness, (7); grace (10); salvation (15); theology, theological, theologically (81); redeemed (8)	Meaning, meaningful, meaningfulness, meaningless, meaninglessness, meanings (375); important, importance (70); significance, significant, significantly (75)	Baptism, baptized (7); believing (7); communion (15); confession; (6); ethical, ethically, (66); forgiving (6); prophetic (5); preach, preaching (21); Pray, prayer, prayers, praying, prays (29); religiosity (270*); wise, wisdom (11), worship, worshiping, worshiped (34); Sabbath (7)	Chaplain, chaplaincy, chaplains (183*); Christ (62); Hebrew (2); priest, priesthood, priestly (49); prophet, prophets (9); theologians (1); pastor, pastoral, pastors (8); pope (14)

Cluster 5 Religious Identity (n =1,796)	Cluster 6 Religious Objects, Day, Place (n = 213)	Cluster 7 Purpose (n = 155)	Cluster 8 Religious Transcendence (n =193)
Believer, believers (12); Catholic, Catholicism, Catholics (71); Christian, Christianity (502); Evangelical (15); identities, identification, identifies, identify identifying (110); Orthodox (81); Protestant, Protestantism, (74); religion, religions, religious (579*); spiritual, spirituality (352).	Bible, biblical, biblically (73*); scripture, scriptures (33); holy days, holiday, holidays (41); congregation, congregations, congregational (59); Nazareth (7)	Call, calling, callings (89*); Purpose, purposeful, purposely, purposes (66)	Bless, blessed, blessing, blessings (14); eternal (3); glory, glorified (18); heaven, heavenly, heavens (13); redeemer (9); holy (40*); redeem (6); sacred, sacredness, sacredity (31); worship (34); king, kingdom (31)

described with countering sacred definitions alongside. Then, the various eight clusters, or themes that emerged from this book are mapped against the secular themes to determine if the sacred theme or cluster is an opposing ideal, being present for Christians as a source of sense-making, identity or motivation. See Table 14.5.

Table 14.4.   Cluster Definitions

C1 Belief:	Sense-making which creates a perspective and for interpretation of events for the religious person, motivating action
C2 Meaning:	Significance attached to events, people or objects because of their ability to enhance, portray, or reflect the sacred
C3 Religious Acts:	Behaviors, practices, either communal or individual, which are required or advised by the adherent's religion
C4 Religious Persons:	Individuals who exemplify religious ideals, or serve on behalf of and/or are connected to the transcendent
C5 Religious Identity:	An interpersonal contracted way to ossify actions, belief, persons, place, and transcendence under a nomenclature
C6 Religious Objects:	Religious which include objects, specific days, or places that represent or embody the transcendent.
C7 Purpose:	An activity, place, or people that fits the designed intention of the person
C8 Transcendence:	Actions, character, or values attributed to Deity (Christ, God, Holy Spirit) alone

DISCUSSION

First it should be noted that both the sacred and the secular have multiple dimensions regarding their use and construct. Researchers are encouraged to think in less Newtonian deterministic ways and embrace multi-causal, multi-dimensional constructs and attend to descriptive research. Research like this chapter is more descriptive and less proscriptive, in that it does allow for an essential understanding of deeper individual, organizational and structural meaning to be formed, which is imperative in understanding implications. Yet, social sciences have been less invested in multivariate techniques, and thus it has lost an understanding of what is ultimately meaningful and understandable (Rosenberg, 2015).

Second, the indication from the exploratory research in this chapter, is that unwittingly research being conducted by researchers herein surrounding the issues of faith and work, contributed to forming, addressing or broadening the social dimension of the sacred. This in turn supports that the suggestion that researchers are creating or meeting preexisting demand with their research (Popescu, 2009; Stemler, 2001) and suggests the role research plays in directing or supporting these social forces.

Finally, the congruence within this chapter regarding definitions of the sacred as represented in the formation of the clusters derived from the chapters in this text is suggestive of what Durkheim (1994) referred to as a group mind, wherein these authors may be part of a movement, even

Table 14.5. Sacred/Secular Matrix

Concept	Secular Definition	Sacred Definition	C1	C2	C3	C4	C5	C6	C7
Secular-rational	Secular are regarded as those who display no such adherence religion	Sacred requires belief and action	Yes	Yes	Yes		Yes	Yes	
Secularism	Organizations and legal constructs that reflect the institutional expression of the secular in a nation's political realm and public life	Sacred can be aligned or misaligned with organizational and legal constructs	Yes	Yes	Yes		Yes	Yes	Yes
Secularity	A binary typology referring to individual actors' personal behavior and identification with secular ideas	Sacred requires belief and action which can identify them with the sacred	Yes	Yes	Yes	Yes		Yes	
Secularism 1	Service to the sacred or other worldly realm or service to the temporal or earthly realm	Sacred can require sole allegiance to heavenly realm	Yes	Yes	Yes				Yes
Secularism 2	A neutral space or an areligious space or point of view, is rationally oriented, and therefore the perspective disenchants the world of the religious	Sacred can find transcendent within the world	Yes	Yes			Yes		Yes
Secularism 3	Societal context that a belief in God as one option among many and not the easiest choice to make	Sacred belief can find nonbelief in God equivalent to losing the personal identity or meaning	Yes				Yes		Yes
Secularization theory	Organizations desire a decline in or moderation of religion, understanding religion as not necessary in organizational and societal life	Sacred can find religious belief and practice as necessary to all aspects of life	Yes	Yes			Yes		Yes

with various hermeneutical illusions, and levels of saliency, are supporting or moving forward one historically based and factual faith and work movement (Eliade, 2013).

CONCLUSION

The intention of this chapter is to trace the two social forces of the sacred and the secular, including their dimensionality. This chapter considered the two forces of the secular and the sacred which are recognized by numerous scholars (e.g., Berger, 1969; Talyor, 2008). Specific attention was given to the sacred/secular tension described by Inglehart and Norris (2004). The chapter then considered the multiple dimensions of secularity and alternatively the dimensions of the sacred force. The chapter then considered the sacred themes in this book using a simple content analysis and these themes are compared to the secular force. The chapter then resolved by providing a brief suggestion on future research to be explored by scholars.

This book was dedicated to Christians who rise each day to join with the rest of humanity in the common rhythm of work. These individuals engage in work because it enables them to express and form their Christian identity, and thus provides a deep meaning and purpose for their lives. It is the hope that this work ultimately enables these woman and men to bring their whole selves to work, and like Jean Vanier, let the sacred motivate their individual and organizational actions as a means to support the sacreds' movement in society—this is their right as Christians, this it is their right as humans.

REFERENCES

Ashforth, B., & Vaidyanath, D. (2002). Work organizations as secular religions. *Journal of Management Inquiry, 11*(4), 359–370.

Augustine, S. (2010). *The city of God, Books XVII–XXII* (The Fathers of the Church, Volume 24). Washington, DC: CUA Press.

Barth, K. (1960). *The humanity of God.* Louisville, KY: Westminster John Knox Press.

Berger, P. L. (1969). *The sacred canopy: Elements of a sociological theory of religion.* Garden City, NY: Doubleday.

Capra, F., & Luisi, P. L. (2014). *The systems view of life: A unifying vision.* Cambridge, England: Cambridge University Press.

Casanova, J. (2011). *Public religions in the modern world.* Chicago, IL: University of Chicago Press.

Conybeare, C. (2014). The City of Augustine: On the interpretation of Civitas. In C. Harrison, C. Humfress, & I. Sandwell (Eds.), *Being Christian in Late Antiq-*

uity: A Festschrift for Gillian Clark (pp. 138–155). Cambridge, England: Oxford University Press.

Durkheim, É. (1994). Durkheim on religion (W. S. F. Pickering, Ed.). Atlanta, GA: Scholars Press.

Eliade, M. (2013). *The quest: History and meaning in religion.* Chicago, IL: University of Chicago Press.

Emmons, R. (2003). *The psychology of ultimate concerns: Motivation and spirituality in personality.* New York, NY: Guilford Press.

Ewest, T. (2015). Christian identity as primary foundation to workplace ethics. *Religions, 12,* 22–30.

Funk, C., & Smith, G. (2012). *"Nones" on the rise: One-in-five adults have no religious affiliation.* Washington, DC: Pew Research Center.

Gallup, G. (1999). *Surveying the religious landscape: Trends in US beliefs.* New York, NY: Morehouse.

Giddens, A. (1986). *The constitution of society: Outline of the theory of structuration.* Berkley, CA: University of California Press.

Graafland, J., Kaptein, M., & Mazereeuw-van der Duijn Schouten, C. (2007). Conceptions of God, normative convictions, and socially responsible business conduct: An explorative study among executives. *Business & Society, 46*(3), 331–368.

Grant, D. (2005, August). *What should a science of workplace spirituality study?* Paper presented at the annual meeting of the Academy of Management, Honolulu, HI.

Inglehart, R., & Welzel, C. (2010). The WVS cultural map of the world. World Values Survey. Retrieved from http://www.worldvaluessurvey.org/wvs/articles/folder_published/article_base_54

Johnson, S. (1882). *A dictionary of the English language* (Vol. 2, No. 1). London, England: Longmans, Green.

Jue, R. W., & Wedemeyer, R. A. (2002). *The inner edge: Effective spirituality in your life and work.* New York, NY: The McGraw-Hill Companies.

Kelly, E. P. (2008). Accommodating religious expression in the workplace. *Employee Responsibilities and Rights Journal, 20*(1), 45–56.

King, J. (2012). (Dis)Missing the obvious: Will mainstream research ever take religion seriously? *Journal of Management Inquiry, 17*(3), 214–224.

Kosmin, B. A., & Keysar, A. (2007). *Secularism & secularity: Contemporary international perspectives.* Hartford, CT: ISSSC.

Lambert, L. (2009). *Spirituality, Inc: Religion in the American workplace.* New York, NY: NYU Press.

McCann, C. (2008). *New paths toward the sacred: Awakening the awe experience in everyday living.* Mahwah, NJ: Paulist Press.

Nandy, A. (2007). Closing the debate on secularism. The crisis of secularism in India. Durham, NC: Duke University Press.

Niebuhr, H. R. (1956). *Christ and culture.* New York, NY: Harper & Row.

Norris, P., & Inglehart, R. (2011). *Sacred and secular: Religion and politics worldwide.* Cambridge, England: Cambridge University Press.

Popescu, I. I. (2009). *Word frequency studies* (Vol. 64). Berlin, Germany: Walter de Gruyter.

Rosenberg, A. (2015). *Philosophy of social science.* Chicago, IL: Westview Press.

Rosenberg, S. D., Schnurr, P. P., & Oxman, T. E. (1990). Content analysis: A comparison of manual and computerized systems. *Journal of Personality Assessment, 54*(1 & 2), 298–310.

Smith, J. K. (2014). *How (not) to be secular: Reading Charles Taylor.* Grand Rapids, MI: Wm. B. Eerdmans.

Steensland, B., Park, J. Z., Regnerus, M. D., Robinson, L. D., Wilcox, W. B., & Woodberry, R. D. (2000). The measure of American Religion: Toward improving the state of the art. *Social Forces, 79*(1), 291–318.

Stemler, S. (2001). An overview of content analysis. *Practical Assessment, Research & Evaluation, 7*(17), 137–146.

Sutcliffe, S., & Bowman, M. (2000). *Beyond new age: Exploring alternative spirituality.* Edinburgh, Scotland: Edinburgh University Press.

Swatos, W. H., & Christiano, K. J. (1999). Introduction—Secularization theory: The course of a concept. *Sociology of Religion, 60*(3), 209–228.

Swedberg, R. (2009). *The Protestant ethic and the spirit of capitalism.* London, England: Penguin Random House.

Taylor, C. (2008). *A secular age.* Cambridge, MA: Belknap Press of Harvard University Press.

Vanier, J. (2008). *Becoming human.* Toronto, Canada: House of Anansi.

Vasconcellos-Silva, P. R., Carvalho, D., & Lucena, C. (2013). Word frequency and content analysis approach to identify demand patterns in a virtual community of carriers of hepatitis C. *Interactive Journal of Medical Research, 2*(2), e12.

Weick, K. E. (1995). *Sensemaking in organizations* (Vol. 3). Thousand Oaks, CA: SAGE.

Wilson, B. R. (1982). *Religion in sociological perspective.* Oxford, England: Oxford University Press.

World Values Survey Association. (2015). World Values Survey 1981–2014 Longitudinal Aggregate v. 20150418. Retrieved from www.worldvaluessurvey.org

ABOUT THE CONTRIBUTORS

ABOUT THE EDITOR

Timothy Ewest has worked in higher education since 2002 teaching management, leadership, ethics, corporate social responsibility, and stewardship. Dr. Ewest's research interests include issues surrounding the integration of faith at work and prosocial leadership. He has published journal articles and books on leadership and faith at work. He also consults with organizations focusing on strategy, ethics, and leadership development. Besides his duties at Houston Baptist University, as an associate professor of management, he is also a visiting research collaborator with David Miller at Princeton University's Faith & Work Initiative. His prior work experience includes 11 years in ministry, 15 years in higher education, and 5 years in corporate America. Dr. Ewest holds a master's degree in theology from Wheaton College, a master's degree in theology from Regent University, an MBA from George Fox University, is an ordained minister in the Christian and Missionary Alliance, and holds a DMgnt from George Fox University.

ABOUT THE AUTHORS

Stuart Allen is an associate professor in the Department of Organizational Leadership at Robert Morris University. He has a PhD in organizational leadership from Regent University in Virginia. Stuart spent the earlier part of his career working as an industrial-organizational psychologist and nonprofit chief executive officer in South Africa, before becoming a full-time academic in the United States. Stuart has worked with organizational leaders from various industries and has consulted to organizations in the education, for profit, healthcare, nonprofit, and public sectors. His consulting experience includes areas such as psycho-

265

logical testing, change management, organizational development, leadership development, leadership coaching, and team development. Stuart is an active researcher with interests in adult teaching and learning, leadership and workplace spirituality, doctoral pedagogy, and leadership theory.

Sharlene Buszka is an associate professor of business administration at Daemen College in Amherst, New York. She is also chair of the Accounting, Business Administration, and Paralegal degree programs. Dr. Buszka maintains Senior Professional in Human Resources certification, is a member of SHRM (Society for Human Resource Management) and Buffalo Niagara Human Resource Association. She is the faculty advisor for the Daemen student SHRM Chapter which has received recognition for its contributions to the campus and local community. In addition, she serves as the secretary for the board of directors of the Buffalo City Mission in Buffalo, New York. Besides her current interests in faith and work integration, she is currently involved in research on refugee workforce development and employer attitudes towards employees with disabilities. Past research and publications have focused on topics related to work and family balance.

Allan Discua Cruz, PhD, is lecturer (assistant professor) in entrepreneurship at the Lancaster University Management School, United Kingdom. He has published in entrepreneurship journals such as *Entrepreneurship Theory and Practice*, *Entrepreneurship & Regional Development*, *Journal of Family Business Strategy*, and *Business History*. He has recently contributed a chapter on family entrepreneurial teams to an edited book on entrepreneurship teams. His current research focuses on entrepreneurial dynamics by families in business, cooperative forms of entrepreneurship, and the influence of religion on families in business.

Kevin D. Dougherty is an associate professor of sociology at Baylor University and the executive officer of the Religious Research Association. Religion and religious organizations are his research expertise. His has written on religious affiliation, religious participation, racial diversity in congregations, congregational growth and decline, and the impact of religion on other realms of social life including work, family, and civic engagement. From 2009–2014, he was a coinvestigator on the National Study of Entrepreneurial Behavior and Religion funded by the National Science Foundation. His published research appears in leading academic journals and has been featured in popular media such as CNN, National Public Radio, and *USA Today*.

Cathy Driscoll (PhD, Queen's University) is professor of management, Sobey School of Business at Saint Mary's University in Halifax, Nova Scotia, Canada. Her primary research interests include ethical leadership, management education, stakeholder management, and spiritual and religious values in ethical decision making. She has published articles in *The Journal of Business Ethics, Organization, Journal of Management Inquiry, Business and Society, Journal of Religion and Business Ethics,* and *The Journal of Management, Spirituality, and Religion.* Cathy currently serves on the regional council for Development and Peace—Caritas Canada and the Halifax-Yarmouth Diocesan Ecological-Justice Committee.

Tamrat W. Gashaw was born in Addis Ababa, Ethiopia in 1977. He attended his education both in Ethiopia and in the United States. He is the follower of the EOTC teachings and Orthodox Christianity since birth. Professionally, he has an extensive teaching experience in Ethiopia (at Addis Ababa University and other private colleges) and in the United States (at Western Michigan University and Wartburg College). Additionally, he has worked as a researcher with the Ethiopian Economics Association/Ethiopian Economic Policy Research Institute, as international trade expert with the Ethiopian Export Promotion Agency and as a loan officer with the Development Bank of Ethiopia. Tamrat is married and father of three children. At present, he is working as assistant professor of economics and finance at Wartburg College.

Myk Habets is a senior academic at Carey Baptist College and lectures in systematic theology and ethics, and has lectured in theology and ethics at the University of Otago, Bible College of New Zealand (now Laidlaw College), Living Stones, and Pathways College. Dr. Habets is the head of Carey Graduate School and is editor of *Pacific Journal of Baptist Research,* associate editor of *Participatio: The Journal of the Thomas Torrance Theological Fellowship,* vice-president of the Thomas F. Torrance Theological Fellowship, and is on the editorial board of *Journal for Theological Interpretation.* Myk is also on the steering committee of the Theological Interpretation of Scripture Seminar at SBL. Myk has earned his bachelor of ministries (BCNZ, 1998); master of theology research (Merit) (BCNZ, 2001); graduate diploma in tertiary teaching [Grad Dip Tert Tchg] (AUT, 2002); PhD [theology] (Otago University, 2006).

Julia R. Marra is the Events & Individual Giving Officer at Equality Now, an international organization using legal advocacy to protect and promote the human rights of women and girls. Her professional and research interests include nonprofit social entrepreneurial causes.

Peter McGhee, is a senior lecturer in sustainability and ethics in the Department of Management, Faculty of Business Economics and Law, Auckland University of Technology, New Zealand. Dr. McGhee has published several articles in a variety of journals on spirituality and ethics in the workplace. His current research focuses on ethical leadership and virtue ethics.

Domènec Melé is the holder of the chair of business ethics at IESE Business School, University of Navarra, Spain. Over the last 30 years, he has been teaching and publishing extensively on the areas of business ethics, humanistic management, and Christian thought on economic and business. He has been coguest editor of five special issues of the *Journal of Business Ethics* and authored, coauthored, or edited 14 books, including *Business Ethics in Action* (Palgrave, 2009), *Management Ethics* (Palgrave, 2012), *Human Foundations of Management* (Palgrave, 2014, coauthored with C. González Canton), *Human Development in Business* (Palgrave, 2012, coedited with Claus Dierksmeier) and *Humanism in Economics and Business. Perspectives of the Catholic Social Tradition* (Springer, 2015, coedited with Martin Schlag). In addition, he has published over 60 scientific chapters and articles in referred journals and some 20 case studies on business ethics. Professor Melé serves as associate editor of the *Humanistic Management Journal*, as section editor of *Journal of Business Ethics* and in several editorial boards. He has also been the chairperson in 18 editions of the IESE International Symposia on Ethics, Business, and Society and co-organizer of four editions of the International Colloquia on Christian Humanism in Economic and Business.

Simone Meskelis, MBA, is a DBA student and an adjunct professor of management in the Satish & Yasmin Gupta College of Business at the University of Dallas. She is also an adjunct professor at Fundacao Dom Cabral, in Brazil. Her research has been presented in several conferences. Her research interests are related to engagement, work meaningfulness, personality traits, and leadership. In addition to the academic experience, she has worked as a business consultant for 15 years serving organizations in Brazil and in the United States.

Mitchell J. Neubert is a professor of management and the Chavanne Chair of Christian Ethics in Business at Baylor University. Dr. Neubert's teaching and research focus on equipping leaders to lead individuals, teams, and organizations in a virtuous manner that results in positive change. He is a coauthor of textbooks in organizational behavior (Wiley) and management (Cengage). He also was coinvestigator of a National Science Foundation (Grant #0925907), the National Study of Entrepreneurial Behavior and Religion, from which this study originated. Dr. Neubert is a leading scholar in research on servant leadership, ethics, and faith-work integration. He has published in numerous academic journals including *Business Ethics Quarterly, Christian Scholars Review, Entrepreneurship Theory and Practice, Journal of Applied Psychology, Journal of Business Venturing, Journal of Business Ethics, Leadership Quarterly,* and *Personnel Psychology.* His faith-work integration research has been the focus of an interview with *Harvard Business Review.*

Faith Ngunjiri is the director of the Lorentzsen Center for Faith and Work, and a tenured associate professor of ethics and leadership at the Offutt School of Business at Concordia College. Faith's research focuses on leadership at the intersections of gender, race/ethnicity, spirituality, nationality, and the various roles that women play, as well as on the integration of spirituality in the workplace. Her work has been published in various journals including *Journal of Management, Spirituality and Religion; International Journal of Qualitative Studies in Education; Journal of Business Communication,* and *Journal of Educational Administration,* among others. She is author of *Women's Spiritual Leadership in Africa* (SUNY, 2010) and coauthor of *Collaborative Autoethnography* (Left Coast Press, 2013). She is coeditor of two books: *Women as Global Leaders* and *Women and Leadership Around the World* both published by Information Age Publishing. Faith is coeditor of two book series: *Woman and Leadership: Theory, Research and Practice* (Information Age Publishing) and *Palgrave Studies in African Leadership* (Palgrave McMillan). She earned a doctorate in leadership studies from Bowling Green State University.

Peter Seele is professor of corporate social responsibility and business ethics at the Università della Svizzera italiana in Lugano, Switzerland. Previously he was assistant professor at the University of Basel at the department of theology (Center for Religion, Politics and Economy). He holds a PhD in economics from Witten/Herdecke (Germany) and a PhD in philosophy from Düsseldorf (Germany) and worked 2 years as business consultant.

Kent W. Seibert, DBA, is professor and chair of the department of economics and business at Gordon College (Massachusetts). A member of the advisory board of Gordon's Center for Entrepreneurial Leadership, his research interests include social entrepreneurship, multistream management, and the intersection of Christianity and business. He has coauthored a book on management development and published in *Organizational Dynamics, Human Resource Management Journal,* and other peer-reviewed journals.

J. Lee Whittington, PhD, is a professor of management in the Satish & Yasmin Gupta College of Business at the University of Dallas. His research has been published in *The Leadership Quarterly, Journal of Management, Academy of Management Review,* and the *Journal of Organizational Behavior.* He is the author of *Biblical Perspectives on Leadership and Organizations* (Palgrave Macmillan, 2015) and *Leading the Sustainable Organization* (with Tim Galpin and Greg Bell, Routledge, 2012). He was selected by students and alumni to receive the Haggerty Teaching Excellence Award at the University of Dallas. As dean of the College of Business, J. Lee led the effort for initial accreditation of the College of Business by AACSB International. His consulting experience includes engagements with Life.Church, Nokia, FedEx-Kinko's, and Siemens.

Elden Wiebe (PhD, University of Alberta) is dean and associate professor of management, Leder School of Business at The King's University, Edmonton, Alberta, Canada. He also has a master of arts (biblical theology) from Regent College, Vancouver, Canada. Elden's primary research interests include spirituality in the workplace, and time/temporality in relation to organizations, organizational change, and strategic management. He has published in *Perspectives in Process Organization Studies, Organization, Journal of Business Ethics, Journal of Management Inquiry, Management and Organizational History, Journal of Religion and Business Ethics,* and *Healthcare Quarterly.* He is coeditor (with Albert J. Mills and Gabrielle Durepos) of the *Sage Encyclopedia of Case Study Research*.

Peter Williams is an assistant dean for the School of Educational Leadership and program director of the EdD in organizational leadership at Abilene Christian University in Dallas. He has taught adults for over 30 years in various contexts including English as a second language at a seminary in Honduras (where he became fluent in Spanish), literacy education in state prisons, and research in blended and online doctoral leadership programs. With the PhD in human resource development from Texas A&M, and several years in leadership roles under his belt, he does applied research on how adults learn, lead, and work in online, blended, and multicultural (including multifaith) environments. Peter has consulted and trained internationally on leader development, designing online learning, and program planning. He enjoys coaching and mentoring leaders, collaborating with colleagues, learning languages, and running.

Chr. Lucas Zapf works as post-doc at the University of Basel. He holds a PhD in the economics of religion and served as a researcher at the University of Lugano and the University of Munich. His research focuses on connections of market economy to religion and ethical risk management.

CPSIA information can be obtained
at www.ICGtesting.com
Printed in the USA
LVHW040207130420
653218LV00006B/791